NOT UNDER OATH

NOT
UNDER
OATH

Recollections and Reflections by

JOHN
KIERAN

ILLUSTRATED WITH PHOTOGRAPHS

HOUGHTON MIFFLIN COMPANY BOSTON

The Riverside Press Cambridge

TO MY WIFE,
MARGARET FORD KIERAN,
WHO HAS GIVEN ME THE BEST YEARS
OF HER LIFE — AND MINE

GRATEFUL acknowledgment is made of the courtesy of the *New York Times* in permitting the reprinting of material from the column "Sports of the Times" written by the author years ago.

TABLE OF CONTENTS

ILLUSTRATIONS

(following page 174)

AVANT-PROPOS

or

(in this age of super-sonic missiles)

DISTANT EARLY WARNING LINES

IN DEFENSE of the honored custom of carving flattering
phrases on cemetery headstones and memorial shafts, Dr. Samuel Johnson made the monumental remark: "In lapidary inscriptions a man is not under oath."

Be advised that a man setting down his recollections is not
under oath, either. He is not required to tell the truth, the
whole truth and nothing but the truth. If everybody told the
whole truth about himself we should all be in jail and, by official report, the jails are overcrowded as it is. Timid by nature
and modest by force of circumstances, I am one who believes
that the naked truth should be decently clad before being exposed to public view. A man should be allowed a conveniently faulty memory about ghastly gaffes or trifling errors in
his past. He must be permitted to mask the bare facts with a
touch of harmless embroidery here and there.

On the other hand, this opus is not offered as current fiction.
Au contraire! It will be truthful enough — just about enough.
My wife, who spent a score of years writing for the *Boston
Herald*, says that her favorite newspaper headline was the one
she saw over a front-page story of a local bribery inquiry:
"Facts Are Revealed." It lingers in loving memory, the acme

of the inane. Indeed, she cherishes it so much that she uses it as a stock phrase around the house when the truth emerges from the unknown or the merely suspected.

Well, facts will be revealed here, too, but not necessarily in the raw. They will be garnished with pertinent or impertinent observations and seasoned with the proper amount of personal prejudice. In speech or writing, I run to quotations and digressions. Quotations are honest admissions that somebody else put the point with greater clarity or wit. Digressions often are the plums in the pudding. Consider this fair warning of what will turn up if you persist in turning the following pages.

While mulling over the plan and scope of this offering of recollections and revelations there came to mind a huge painting by Gauguin that hangs in the Museum of Fine Arts on Huntington Avenue in Boston, the last big canvas the artist did before he died on one of the Marquesas Islands in the South Pacific. It's a striking picture of tropical greenery filled with brooding brown-skinned natives and, in dark letters on a yellow background in the upper left-hand corner, these words inscribed by the artist:

> D'où Venons Nous
> Que Sommes Nous
> Où Allons Nous

These were questions that bothered Paul Gauguin all through the last half of his troubled and lonely life. Where do we come from? What are we? Where are we going? To the three lines of the artist I irreverently added a fourth of World War II vintage:

> Is This Trip Necessary

The whole idea came and went in a flash but in that instant of consideration and rejection it brought two other mental images into focus. One was the proposal of a salesman in Yonkers who, in a burst of enthusiasm for my patronage, offered to get me anything I wanted if it wasn't "too hot to handle or too heavy to lift." The expression may have been old in the selling game but it was new to me and it certainly was relevant to the problem I was facing. As guide lines for anything that I could write, the Gauguin questions were too hot for me to handle and too heavy for me to lift.

The other thought dredged up from the past was more helpful. Some years ago there was a rehearsal of a community chorus in a certain New England town not far from Boston and the composition the choristers were working on was Gabriel Fauré's *Requiem*. The words were in Latin and all went well until the singers reached the passage "et incarnatus est." At that point a brisk and bright-eyed young lady interrupted with a firm complaint.

"Wait a minute," she said in vigorous protest. " 'Et incarnatus est'! Some of us are Unitarians. We can't sing that. You know we don't believe it."

"Don't worry," said the leader soothingly, "we'll take that allegretto."

With this happy recollection, the right tempo for this report is no longer a problem. We'll take the whole thing allegretto.

NOT UNDER OATH

I

MYSELF WHEN YOUNG

THOUGH I was born in a great city and grew up there, I was really a country boy all the time. In 1892, the year that saw me added to the roster of native-born New Yorkers, the street in front of our Kingsbridge home was not yet paved. Single-family houses were scattered about the area but the greater part of the region was open ground that included a few small farms and a fair number of apple orchards. There was no electricity in the district. The streets were lighted with gas lamps. Telephones were still to come. Autos were unknown. Horses were necessary. Cows were common. There were chickens in many back yards and it was a poor house that didn't have a little vegetable garden on the premises.

To the left rear of our house we had a neat two-story stable with a carriage room and two stalls on the ground floor and a hayloft and grain bins above. In the carriage room we had a surrey, a buggy, and a two-seater sleigh upholstered in red plush. As a small child I remember a team, a coachman, a cook and an upstairs girl but as the number of Kierans increased, the number of horses and helpers decreased. When the children numbered seven, there were no horses and just one hard-working maid. My father must have been a financial wizard on a small scale to make a college professor's salary go as far as it did. We never had luxuries but we had all the comforts of life.

When I was a toddler and we still had horses my mother usually drove down to "the village" in the morning in the buggy to do the day's marketing. The surrey was for family excursions on Sunday to Riverdale, Van Cortlandt Park, Yonkers or even Pelham Bay — a distant Aidenn in those days — where my father took me out in a rowboat, my first venture on navigable waters. I remember little else of our horse-drawn adventures except that one day when my father was alone in the surrey in the driveway the team took fright, dashed out into the street, swerved into a lamppost and went down in a welter of tangled harness. The surrey was upended in the crash and my father was carried into the house with a broken leg.

Our house was on the east side of Boston Avenue (now Kingsbridge Terrace) close to its northern terminus where it merges with Sedgwick Avenue. Indeed, the back door of the stable was practically on Sedgwick Avenue, to the eastward of which was the wide green expanse of what had been the famous Jerome Park racetrack where the thoroughbreds began running under the eager patronage of New York "high society" in 1866. Learning a few years before I was foaled that the city was going to take the property for a much needed new city reservoir, the Jockey Club built another track a little farther out at Morris Park and moved the racing there in 1890. However, there was still some independent or wildcat racing at Jerome Park as late as 1894. Part of the folklore of our family is that I went to the races there as a two-year-old under the escort of my mother's Uncle John Moran and that before the afternoon was over I had learned to yelp

"They're off!" with the grownups around me when the barrier was sprung.

It may be so, but my only clear recollection concerned with the historic track is of the big old wooden clubhouse on the hill where so many turf celebrations and society dinners and dances had been held. I can still see myself going up the rise to the back door to ask for a drink of water one summer day when I was hot and thirsty from playing tag with my sisters in the meadow below. It sticks in mind that the caretaker's name was McCormick and it was Mrs. McCormick who very kindly gave the glass of water to the stubby, freckle-faced little boy. (To Mrs. McCormick in Heaven: Thank you again, ma'am.) Shortly thereafter the old clubhouse was torn down, the rail fences of the famous racing strip broken up and construction of the new reservoir started.

Work on the Jerome Reservoir lasted well into my school years and we youngsters of the neighborhood took great interest in it. We watched the noisy steam shovels scooping up muck and dropping it into rows of "dump cars" that were pulled along rickety narrow-gauge tracks by huffing and puffing "dinkey engines." The blasting foremen must have been an enthusiastic lot because their detonations regularly broke windows and cracked walls in the houses on our street and Sedgwick Avenue. Every so often an inspector would come around to appraise the damage and arrange to pay for needed repairs. The lengthy digging operations provided temporary swimming holes in summer and skating ponds in winter.

At some point during this period I made the acquaintance of a famous prizefighter. He was "Terrible Terry" McGovern and he held the world's featherweight championship at the beginning of the century. His training quarters were at Johnson's Roadhouse at 167th Street and Jerome Avenue and his daily roadwork consisted of a morning trot from there to the southern edge of Van Cortlandt Park and back again. Close to the boundary of the park there was a fine spring in a shady spot. Terry and many lesser fighters who trained at Johnson's Roadhouse used to make the spring the turn-around point in their roadwork.

Clad in gray pants, gray sweater and gray cap, Terry would come jogging up Sedgwick Avenue on his morning trip to the spring. It was vacation time and I usually was play-ing ball in the street with other boys of my age, watching for Terry to appear from the southward. We had fallen into the habit of tossing the ball to him a few times as he jogged by. He would catch it and toss it back without breaking stride. On his return journey a half hour later we would do the same thing. We felt important. We were part of the champion's training program. Terry was our man. But, alas, when the fight came off that autumn our hero was knocked out by Young Corbett, an upstart of whom we had never even heard up to that dark moment. Even so, my passing acquaint-ance with a ring champion was impressive. It was my first brush with greatness.

Thus passed my schoolboy years. We kept rabbits and pigeons. We picked flowers in the woods in spring. We played baseball and went swimming in summer. We played pick-up football in the autumn fields. Skating and bobsled-ding filled our winters.

> *By sports like these are all their cares beguiled,*
> *The sports of children satisfy the child.*

Then came high school and college days with long sum-mers on the old farm in Dutchess County that my father had bought and turned into a family vacation playground. There I developed an ever-increasing love of nature. I dreaded the return to the city in autumn. I roamed the fields and woods all day and at night I slept in a tent on a knoll just above the farmhouse. On clear nights I would move my cot outside the tent and sleep under the stars. During the school year I slipped away to the farm whenever I could — over Thanksgiving, during Christmas holidays or the Easter vacation. There were winter days when the snow was deep, the wind high and the temperature low — 16° below zero — and I still thought it was wonderful.

In short, I wanted to live there if possible. When I was graduated from Fordham University in 1912 and "went out into the world," my world was the farm. I went there to set myself up in the poultry business as quickly as possible. Build coops, buy breeding stock, sell eggs and broilers, that was my program. If my father was disappointed that I didn't take to the law, study medicine or go in for a teaching career, he gave no sign of it. Indeed, he backed me with ready cash in my poultry venture.

Not all our acquaintances approved it. There was an old Irishwoman who kept a little general store near our Kingsbridge home. We children used to buy candy there with regularity and she saw all of us grow up in turn. About the time of my graduation my mother happened to go into the store and the old lady asked her what I was going to do now that I had finished college. My mother told her the truth, to the undisguised disgust of the old lady.

"Raisin' chickens, is it?" she said in a rich brogue and a tone of deep disgust. "After all his damn schoolin'!"

I did raise chickens by the hundred, all of them Barred Plymouth Rocks, a favorite all-purpose breed in New England at the time. Good layers, good size for broilers and roasters. I also engaged in other activities. The little one-room district schoolhouse down the road in the woods lacked a teacher that year and I was asked to fill the gap, which I did. I had six farm children for scholars ranging from five to eleven years in age and my salary was $40 a month, which helped out with the bills for chicken feed. In the early autumn I picked, packed and sent to market from our own orchard and that of a neighbor about two hundred barrels of fine Dutchess County apples than which, said he, whipping out a Colt automatic and looking the reader right in the eye, there are no better apples grown anywhere in the world.

The picking and the packing of the apples led to a little argument that was settled quietly in the orchard but the result almost floored a complete stranger about thirty years later in Rochester, New York. When shipping to market we were required to stencil on the head of the barrel the name of the variety contained therein. As in most orchards of the region, Baldwins and Rhode Island Greenings predominated, but we also had a few trees of Fall Pippins, Newtown Pippins, Northern Spies, Russets and Spitzenburgs. All these apples had been identified for me years earlier by our nearest neighbor whose family had originally owned the farm and whose great-grandfather had planted the trees. Until I was big enough to pick and pack, my father used to sell the apple crops on the trees to buyers who came through the valley for that purpose each year. A good price was a dollar a barrel for what the buyer picked and carried off. When I grew up, I took over and handled the apple crop myself. I enjoyed doing it.

One September day I was stenciling "Spitzenburg" on a barrel head when I was challenged by a farmer from a few miles away who used to come over and help us with our bees occasionally. He was a bee expert and as we had fourteen hives at one time, we needed help now and then. The bee man scoffed at the idea that there were Spitzenburgs in our orchard. I showed him two Spitzenburg trees with piles of fruit still under them. He said the trees were Baldwins, just like all the other trees in the row. He vowed he couldn't tell the fruit apart and neither could I. Red, firm, juicy apples, good keepers. But Baldwins all. So he said. I offered to turn my back while he picked out apples from the Spitzenburg piles and the Baldwin piles and I would say which was which. We went through the test. I correctly identified two of his choice as Spitzenburgs and two as Baldwins. He said I must have peeked. I explained that the Spitzenburg had a little different shape, not quite so round as a Baldwin. He was unconvinced.

"Blindfold me," I said.

When I was thoroughly blindfolded with a handkerchief, I asked the Doubting Thomas to put what I called a Spitzenburg in one hand and what I called a Baldwin in the other, which he did. If he thought I was going to finger the apples and test the shape of each, he must have been astonished when I merely took a bite out of each. For me it was easier to tell them apart by taste than by sight. As a confirmed apple eater I doted on both varieties but I preferred the flavor of the Spitzenburg and knew it well from eating them so often.

Thirty years later I made a speech at a luncheon of the local advertising club in Rochester, New York. That's a real apple district. I was there at the urging of the Advertising Department of the *New York Times* and my mission was to entertain my listeners and gain readers for the *New York Times*. My speeches on such occasions were of the dirigible or lighter-than-air type and I have no recollection of anything I said at the luncheon. What I can't forget is that as we were filing off the dais at the end of the talk somebody came up from the center of the dining room with a red apple in his hand, gave it to the man just ahead of me in line and said in a challenging tone: "There! Tell me what that is!"

The accused turned the apple over in his hand, looked at it

doubtfully and popped a question of his own, to wit: "You mean it isn't a Baldwin?"

"No siree!"

At that point I leaned over and asked politely whether or not I might have a look at the apple. One look was enough. It was my old cherished acquaintance. With assumed modesty — I was really puffed up with pride — I said as I handed the apple back to the owner: "My guess is Spitzenburg."

The man stood stunned for a moment. He stared at me for perhaps ten seconds, took a deep breath, gulped "Well, by God!" and was still staring after me as I walked out of the room. If he hasn't died since, he is probably still trying to figure out how I knew.

If I learned something about apples in my days on the farm, I learned a good deal more about the poultry business in the only full year I spent there. At the very start of the venture my trust in humanity was betrayed. Lured by a resplendent advertisement in a poultry journal of magnificent Plymouth Rock breeding stock for sale at bargain rates, I sent off for a pen of the beauties and in return received a shipment of scrawny, undersized, poorly marked, half-naked hens fairly swarming with lice. I wrote a letter of complaint of which I remember only the opening lines:

> Dear Sirs: Received your consignment of lice. There were also some chickens in the box . . .

Nothing came of it. Perhaps I should have been more direct. I had better luck with breeding stock I bought nearer home but weasels and raccoons raised hob in the coops at night and diseases of various kinds fell upon my flock, so that I did not prosper. I had a hound and a horse and a gun and I loved the life on the farm, but I couldn't make a living there and I was determined not to sponge on my father any longer.

In the autumn of 1913 I went back to the city to look for a paying job. My dream of living in the country was over.

Even so, the year on the farm had left a deep mark on me. It had quickened my youthful love of the outdoors into a growing interest in natural history. From the neighboring farmer folk with whom I walked, talked, fished and hunted, I picked up some knowledge of the trees, flowers and four-footed wildlife of the region. On the road to the school where I taught I saw handsome sparrows I never before had noticed. In late May I investigated some chipping in the underbrush and found four eggs in the nest of a pair of tiny birds with little gold crowns and reddish-brown patches along their sides. One hot summer day I was pushing my way through a thick growth of young white pines when suddenly there popped up just ahead of me a little yellow bird wearing the black mask of a bank robber. I had to find out about these matters.

The first thing I did when I returned to the city was to buy a copy of Chapman's *Handbook of Birds of Northeastern North America.* This was the bird watcher's bible of that time. With the aid of the Chapman text and the color plates in the book, I had no trouble tracking down the strange birds I had seen in Dutchess County. The handsome roadside sparrows were whitethroats. The golden-crowned owners of the neat little nest in the underbrush were chestnut-sided warblers. The little yellow bird with the black mask of a bandit was another warbler, the yellowthroat. Along with the bird book I acquired a good pair of field glasses which, of course, helped immeasurably in the identification of birds in the fields. Within a year I had taken notice of and identified most of the common residents as well as a good many migrants and seasonal visitors in our section of the city.

This was, of course, a side issue. The main purpose of my

return to the city was to find a job and I found one through a family friend who lived nearby on Sedgwick Avenue. His name was James Pilkington and undoubtedly he was one of the greatest all-around amateur athletes that this country ever produced. He won the national amateur heavyweight boxing championship and the national amateur heavyweight wrestling championship in the old Madison Square Garden in the same ring on the same night! He was one of the leading amateur oarsmen of his day. When he was thirty-nine years old, he and a nineteen-year-old partner won the national double sculls championship in time that stood as a record for many years. He was a great broad jumper, a fine bowler, an expert trapshooter. When I went to work for him he was in his middle sixties, tall, white-haired, broad-shouldered, rather lean and just a bit slow of foot because his sight was beginning to fail, but he was still as strong as an ox.

He was the active head of his own construction firm and at the time I signed aboard he was engaged in what was trifling work for him, the construction of a reinforced concrete sewer that ran from 230th Street and Riverdale Avenue to the Harlem Ship Canal. I was taken on as office boy, timekeeper and general handy man at a starting salary of $8 per week. I could walk from my home to the job in fifteen minutes. We worked an eight-hour day five days a week. Saturday was a half-day, eight o'clock to noon. Other days work began at eight o'clock and, with an hour out for lunch, ended at five o'clock. How the common laborers, mostly Italians, managed to live on their pay of 25 cents an hour — $11 for a 44-hour week — I never could understand but they raised families on it and seemed contented enough. I know how I managed to get along royally on my own salary of $8 per week. I had free lodging at home and contributed only $2.50 a week to the household exchequer for my meals, "wine included" as my mother used to remind me when the claret bottle was passed at dinner.

I liked construction work. It was outdoors and it was healthful and interesting. It was all new to me and I was learning something every day. This was a sewer that was seven feet wide and six feet high and, since steel rods for reinforcing concrete were just coming into fashion, we had to devise our own technique for setting the rods in place before pouring the concrete. That became one of my assignments and with the aid of a genial little rotund Italian nicknamed "Baby" because of his angelic countenance, I turned out networks of steel rods that were a delight to my eye at least before they were buried in concrete.

The superintendant was a huge former professional oarsman who had come out of the woods without much schooling. He looked upon me skeptically at first as a "college boy" but he changed quickly when he found that I would buckle down and work hard at any task he gave me. I even cheerfully trotted over to Broadway to buy him a package of chewing tobacco. I think that convinced him that I was all right. When he decided that he could trust me he confessed that blueprints baffled him and, furthermore, he didn't know how to use the surveyor's rod and level we had in the office for running grades along the line of construction. To his expressed relief, I took over the reading of the blueprints and the running of the grades and he was most appreciative. He was a lumberman at heart and when he headed back to the woods after we completed this sewer he tried to persuade me to go with him. He even promised to pay me "some real money, boy, not the chicken feed you're getting here," but I stuck with Mr. Pilkington who shifted me to a much bigger job in Manhattan.

This was a sewer that was being built in conjunction with

the construction of the Seventh Avenue Subway and it ran
from Seventh Avenue westward on 30th Street all the way
to the outer end of the long pier jutting into the Hudson
River at that point. For all except the last nine hundred feet
of this journey, where it was merely a wooden "barrel
sewer" suspended on steel cables from the overhead beams of
the pier, it was a monster. In addition to its regular duties it
was to serve as a "storm sewer" to carry off the surface drain-
age of a considerable area on the south side of the Pennsylvania Station, wherefor the modest regular oval sewer had a
spillway all along the south side opening into the "overflow
chamber" that was 11 feet six inches wide and seven feet high.
When it was finished you could have driven a motor truck
down it all the way to the Hudson River. But when I arrived on the scene only the digging was in process.

The shanty we used as a field office was set up in a vacant
lot just south of the corner of 30th Street and Tenth Avenue and I had to be out on the job in my working clothes by
8 A.M. each morning. To do this I had to get up at 5 A.M.,
make my own breakfast, put up my lunch of sandwiches,
walk down the hill to the 231st Street subway station and
catch the 6:20 southbound express that carried me to the
Grand Central Station where I switched to a local and debarked at 28th Street and Fourth Avenue. From there I
walked across town to the office, a distance of a little over a
mile. We stopped work at five o'clock and, on foot and by
subway, I retraced the journey to Kingsbridge, arriving home
just in time to scrub up and sit down to the family dinner at
seven o'clock.

Once again I was a general handy man with all sorts of odd
duties. One was to go down "the hole" at Tenth Avenue
every morning just before eight o'clock and start the electric
fans to clear the air in a tunnel that we were "drifting"

through sand beneath all the street traffic above. The top of
our tunnel was about eight feet below the street surface and
the traffic at that point included puffing locomotives and
loaded freight cars rolling in and out of the West 30th Street
freight station of the New York Central Railroad just across
the street from our office shanty.

Beneath the pavement of any city street there is a network
of pipes and conduits of all sizes and kinds. These are for
water, gas, electric power and light, telephone lines and various other utilities. In the network between the top of our
tunnel and the street surface at Tenth Avenue there were
three gas mains, a 4-incher, a 6-incher and a whopper of 18
inches. With us hollowing out the ground underneath and
great freight locomotives and loaded cars rolling overhead, it
was natural that the gas mains would give a little under the
strain. They did, and in the process they began to leak at the
joints and the escaping gas seeped down into our tunnel. We
had some water seepage, too, but that wasn't dangerous. The
gas was.

Before I appeared on the job the man who went down into
the tunnel to start the electric fans each morning was our
staff engineer, a delightful gentleman named Mr. Thompson.
I didn't meet him immediately because when I arrived he
was in the French Hospital on West 34th Street suffering
from horrible burns caused by a gas explosion in the tunnel
when he turned on the fans a few days earlier. Apparently
there was a broken wire or a loose connection that caused a
spark and the resultant explosion. I don't know who served
in the short interregnum before I took over the task, but each
morning when I went down the ladder and disappeared in the
tunnel I was watched by the tunnel gang gathered at the top
of the shaft. They didn't inspire me with confidence. They
looked as though they thought there might be another explo-

sion, of which I would get the first news. Nothing untoward happened, but I was always a little relieved when I came up safely from the dripping depths and, with the fans whirring merrily, the men climbed down the ladder to push the tunnel front a little further eastward each day.

Once I was sent on an errand that didn't bother me at all but might have disturbed those around me if they had known all the circumstances. The only rock we had to tackle along the line was a high ridge in the Ninth Avenue area and through it we had to bore a tunnel far below the elevated railroad that ran down Ninth Avenue in those days. That, of course, was a drilling and blasting operation. One winter day we ran short of dynamite and I was sent up to 59th Street to borrow a dozen sticks from the "powder monkey" — man in charge of explosives — on another job in that area. I filled my jacket and overcoat pockets with the half-pound sticks and boarded a Seventh Avenue trolley for the return journey to 30th Street. I bulged a bit at the middle but otherwise offered no external evidence of my unusual and actually illegal cargo.

I was brought up to yield my seat to any lady in a crowded public conveyance and by the time the trolley reached 42nd Street I was among the swaying standees. There was the usual amount of rough jostling by incoming or outgoing passengers at each stop and more than once I was roughly shoved aside by impatient hands. I couldn't help thinking that the shovers would have been much more gentle in my case if they had known that the shovee's pockets were stuffed with dynamite. To be sure, dynamite ordinarily is as safe to carry about as salt or potatoes but extraordinary things do happen from time to time and I do not advise putting all your trust in dynamite.

One of my regular chores on the job was to go to a bank in the Wall Street area with the paymaster each Saturday and

bring back the payroll money that was doled out to the workers in little envelopes when they quit at noon. The paymaster
carried a pistol. I carried a satchel. We went down to the
bank together but on the return journey we acted as strangers.
I carried the bulk of the money in small bills and silver in the
satchel. He kept a little distance behind me apparently carrying no money at all, but he had the tens and twenties and the
pistol in his pocket. On the elevated train he sat opposite me.
The theory behind this practice was that if a man was stupid
enough to be a robber, he would naturally go for the man
who was carrying the satchel. In short, I was the bait. But
nobody even as much as snapped at me.

Another chore I had was to check on what the workers
for the Consolidated Gas Company were doing all along West
30th Street. The company kept billing us for the repairing of
leaky joints in house gas connections, claiming that we didn't
hold up the street mains at the level we found them and the
sagging opened the joints and caused leaking in the service
pipes, too. We admitted that this was true to a certain extent
but we found that they were billing us for further repairs to
house services that could not have been caused by our activities. I walked the length of the job each day, writing down in
a little book how many Consolidated Gas workers were there
and what each one or each gang was doing. After some weeks
of that, we were pretty well acquainted. They were all Irish,
every last man of them, and many of them recent imports with
rich brogues. Since the bottom of the cuts and tunnels along
the job often had pools of water in them and I was climbing
up and down ladders a good part of the day, I worked in overalls and rubber boots. I was taken aback when one of the Consolidated Gas workers looked up out of the hole at me one day
and said with a serious air and a thick brogue: "You ought to
be ashamed of yourself."

I thought he meant that I was acting the part of a spy on him and his co-workers but before I had a chance to say anything his next volley undeceived me.

"You with your education goin' around in overalls an' boots and doin' a poor bye out of a job!"

I never thought of it that way, and it wasn't any such matter that led me to abandon the overalls, boots and construction business. I quit for other reasons. The first and foremost was that we finished the job and Mr. Pilkington, whose sight was failing fast, went out of business. The second reason was that I found the subway crush on the way home each night intolerable. Getting on the train at the 28th Street station was like taking part in a wrestling match with no holds barred. Changing to the express at Grand Central Station was a double dose of the same. The subway guards pushed, shouldered and even kneed the final strugglers into the cars so that the doors could be closed. Everyone who got on a train north of Brooklyn Bridge was a standee and we were packed in so tightly that it was impossible to fall down. You were pressed into a fixed position either breathing down some woman's neck or looking over some man's shoulder. It was indecent and disgusting. One night in such a crush I said to myself: I will not go through life traveling in this horrible way; I will find a better.

And I did.

II

THE NEWSPAPER GAME

AFTER giving the matter little thought, I decided to become a newspaperman. Like everybody else, I believed that I could write if I had the chance but, unlike most other young fellows looking for jobs as reporters, I knew a man who could turn the trick for me. He was the late Frederick T. Birchall, the bustling, bald and red-whiskered Assistant Managing Editor of the *New York Times*. He had been a family friend for years and I felt he couldn't refuse my simple request for a job as a reporter. I was right. When I saw him at the *Times* office he gave in more or less gracefully and welcomed me into the newspaper world with these encouraging words: "Very well. Come back in three weeks and I'll put you on as a district man. But I'll tell you two things. First, you won't like the work. Second, you'll never be any good at it."

I thanked him profusely for his kindness and his confidence in me and I left. But I didn't stay away three weeks. I was back a few days later with a suggestion. It was summer and perhaps some of the *Times* sports writers were on vacation. If the Sports Department was short-handed, perhaps I could fill in for one or more of the missing men until I was needed as a district man in the News Department. I had played five different sports in college and knew the field fairly well.

"Good idea," snapped Mr. Birchall, and took me around to the Sports Department where he introduced me to the head man whose name was pronounced like his own but was spelled Burchell. As Sports Editor, this chap was in no position to argue with the Assistant Managing Editor and I became a member of the Sports Staff on the spot. I then discovered that it was at no fixed salary. In those days all the sports writers and most of the regular reporters were paid "space rates," the going rate at the time being $7 per column. The well-known slogan of the *New York Times* is that it publishes "all the news that's fit to print." For the first three weeks that I was on the job I didn't make a cent. I was sent out on a roving commission to dig up sports news and I wrote daily stories that were tossed into the wastebasket. Apparently nothing that I wrote was fit to print.

Before I starved to death, however, a rainstorm came to my rescue. What had ruined Napoleon at Waterloo saved my life as a sports writer on West 43rd Street. I was a rather good golfer and a day earlier I had played the links of the Ardsley Country Club with the local professional, Val Flood, who had been there for years and was full of good stories about the course, the club members and famous golfers who had played there. I wrote it all down and turned in a column-long story on the Ardsley links, thinking that it would end up in the wastebasket where all the others had been interred, but this time it was different. It had rained buckets all over the eastern half of the United States that day. No baseball. No tennis. No yachting. There were empty columns to fill in the sports section that night. In desperation, my long story on the Ardsley links was tossed into the breach and came out in print the next morning.

The City Editor, Ralph Graves, was an ardent golfer. For several years he had been insisting at editorial conferences that the *Times* needed a special golf writer to lure the golfers into reading the sports section of the *Times*. Golf was a fast-growing game and those who played it had money to spend. Advertisers dote on newspapers whose readers have money to spend. Ergo, get golfers to read your newspaper. The *Times* had been buying its golf news from a chap named Percy Pulver who was a one-man syndicate in a small way and supplied golf news to seven or eight of the city's newspapers. When my Ardsley story appeared in the paper, the City Editor stalked around to the Sports Department and asked who had written it.

"A young fellow I put on recently," said Sports Editor Burchell.

"Don't let him get away," said Ralph Graves. "Make him your golf writer."

Thus I became the golf writer for the *New York Times* and a most pleasant assignment it was. In the first place, I was a golf enthusiast myself and it was wonderful to walk in the wake of good golfers in tournaments and see how they made their shots. Secondly, covering golf I met so many nice people in beautiful settings — lovely rolling fairways, incredibly manicured putting greens, spacious clubhouses with loud and cheerful locker rooms echoing to the clump of spiked shoes on the floor and the tinkle of ice in drinking glasses. One of my fellow golf writers was Grantland Rice, who became a lifelong friend. Another was the drama critic Burns Mantle who covered golf during the summer as an extracurricular activity simply because he liked the game and the players.

Of course, I covered other sports when golf was out of season in the New York area. On winter nights I was sent to report on track meets, basketball games, ice hockey at the old St. Nicholas Rink, amateur boxing, fencing, billiards and even dog and cat shows. I had to be at the office at 1 P.M. for assignment each day and often I was in the office still pounding my typewriter at midnight. I didn't mind it. The more assignments I had the more money I made. Also, traveling the subway at the hours I kept was a luxury. The rush hour jam was a thing of the past for me.

All this happened in 1915 and for the next quarter of a century I spent most of my waking hours watching games and players and writing about them. There were only two interruptions of note. World War I was going into its second dreadful winter when Germany announced that its submarine commanders were being ordered to sink merchant vessels without warning. The United States countered with notice that our merchant ships were to be armed to resist any attack. Word went around our office that a *Times* reporter would be sent along on the first armed merchant ship to leave New York. The man who would hand out the assignment was the City Editor, Ralph Graves. Because I wrote golf and he had a hand in setting me at it, he took a particular interest in me. As soon as I heard of the armed ship assignment, I scurried around to his desk and asked for the job. But Carl Dickey, whose desk was closer to the command post, had been there ahead of me and already had gone home to pack.

"Never mind," said Editor Graves by way of consolation. "If the ship is sunk, I'll send you on the next one."

Nothing happened to the ship — the *St. Paul* unless memory is at fault — and Carl Dickey could report only a routine transatlantic trip. No more *Times* reporters were to enjoy quiet ocean travel on office expense accounts. However, a few months later we were having trouble with Pancho Villa on the Mexican Border and the National Guard was mobilized

to meet the situation. The *Times* was going to send a man
with each New York unit that went to the Border. Again I
dashed around to put in my application at the city desk and
again Carl Dickey was ahead of me. So were four or five
others. But they couldn't strip the city room of all of its
reporters and I was finally assigned to go with the 22nd
Engineers, N.G.N.Y., the last of the seven New York outfits
to leave for their assigned position at McAllen, Texas.

I was at home at noon and just about to start for the office
when Ralph Graves phoned that I was to go to Camp Whitman near Hopewell Junction in Dutchess County that very
afternoon, write a front page story about the switch of commanding officers of the famous 69th Infantry as the regiment
was taking off for the Border that day and then join the 22nd
Engineers who were leaving for Texas the next morning. I
had to pack, find a uniform somewhere and dig up transportation to Camp Whitman. There was no way of getting there
on time by train. I borrowed a uniform from a friend who
had been at the Plattsburgh training camp for civilians. He
was three inches taller than I was and the fit was ghastly. My
brother-in-law had a rickety old car in which he drove me
over bad roads to Dutchess County and I stepped out at the
entrance to Camp Whitman as twilight was falling. I hadn't
the faintest idea what to do or where to go. The guard at
the gate waved me through without question and I didn't dare
to question him. I walked straight ahead with my portable
typewriter in one hand and my suitcase in the other.

In the dusk ahead I saw a light and I headed for it. I was in
luck. It was the Western Union office. I walked in and saw
two men in uniform at the counter writing in longhand and
passing the sheets to a man behind the counter. Only newspapermen do that sort of thing so I introduced myself and
asked for help. The stouter of the two identified himself as

George Boothby of the *Evening World* and I stepped back in awe. He was one of the newspaper notables of Park Row. He asked what he could do for me and I told him I had to file the front page story on the change of command in the 69th and then join the 22nd Engineers. He filled me in nobly on the sudden and unexpected change of command as the 69th took off for the Border and he stood by as I wrote and filed the story for the *Times*. Then he said: "Where next? Had your dinner? No? Follow me."

He took me to some eating place in the camp and had a cup of coffee as I wolfed down a hasty dinner. All this time he was giving me information and helpful hints on how to cover my assignment with the troops. Then he marched me off in the darkness to the tent of the commanding officer of the 22nd Engineers and, after a proper salute, said to that worthy gentleman: "Colonel, this is Kieran of the *Times* who has been assigned to go to the Border with you. He needs a place to sleep tonight — and a blanket."

The colonel bedded me down in an empty tent next to his own and I stuttered my thanks to George Boothby as best I could. He brushed it all aside as little or nothing and was around the next morning to make sure that I was properly fed and watered and all set for the trip with the troops to the Rio Grande. He couldn't have done more for me if I had been his favorite nephew. He was a newspaper notable and I was a raw newcomer. I was a complete stranger to him when he held out that helping hand. The man, I felt as the troop train carrying the 22nd Engineers rolled out of camp, was utterly and irretrievably a great gentleman.

Stand by now for a slight digression and a brief account of one of the most pleasant episodes of my life. Some twenty-five years later Hollywood was preparing to do a feature film on the life of George M. Cohan with Jimmy Cagney in the role of the famous song and dance man. There was a job open for somebody who had an intimate knowledge of "little old New York" when Cohan was dancing his way up those golden stairs. Hollywood needed such an expert to prevent geographical, historical or theatrical errors in the filmed background of the Cohan story.

Frank A. Munsey had devastated the newspaper field in New York and many a star reporter of the old days was looking for work, George Boothby among them. You might say that when Munsey started firing, George's "World" had been shot out from under him. He learned of the job open in Hollywood on the Cohan story and he put in his application. Nobody was better fitted for the task than a veteran reporter whose regular beat had been Broadway, City Hall, Police Headquarters, old Madison Square Garden, the Hippodrome, Jack's, Mouquin's, Shanley's, Rector's and selected little nooks like the place that Ben de Casseres ran largely for the newspaper trade on 41st Street just west of Seventh Avenue, one flight up.

Boothby received word that his application was on file and would receive consideration. One day he came to see me. Somebody had told him that I knew George M. Cohan rather well. It was true enough. I had known the famed actor and playwright for twenty years, had visited with him backstage on different occasions and had sat through many ball games at the Polo Grounds and the Yankee Stadium with him and his theatrical crony, Sam Forrest.

"Would you give me a letter of introduction to him?" asked Boothby, "I think that would clinch the job for me."

I was delighted to give him the letter and I didn't hold back in telling Cohan how much I admired Boothby. Within a week Boothby was back to see me with a broad grin on his careworn face. It looked good to me there.

"John," he said, holding out his hand, "that did it! I got the job. I'm leaving for the West Coast tomorrow. Thanks a million."

What a wonderful stroke of luck, after a lapse of a quarter of a century, to be able to pay back in some part the kindness of a great gentleman to a cub reporter in a tough spot. The film, under the title *Yankee Doodle Dandy*, was a smash hit with Cagney playing the Cohan role to perfection. But we're on a side track. We have to get back on the main line and the troop train carrying the 22nd Engineers, N.G.N.Y. and a *New York Times* reporter to Texas in July, 1916. It took us four days to reach the Mexican Border town of McAllen, which was small, hot, dusty, surrounded by mesquite and overrun with soldiery. Furthermore, the outsize uniform I had hurriedly borrowed for the trip was a heavy woolen one and did not wear well in the heat that was 105° in the shade.

Carl Dickey was the chief of staff of the seven *Times* reporters in and around McAllen. One day he was standing at the entrance to the headquarters tent of the dandy Seventh Regiment listening to a complaint by the regimental adjutant that unkempt soldiers from "the dirty Twelfth" lodged behind them in the mesquite came rambling through the Seventh's company streets on the way to the public road that led to town.

"Look!" said the adjutant. "Here comes one of the scarecrows now. That man is a disgrace to the American army!"

Yes, it was I, and it wasn't until I met Carl in town at dinner that I learned of the distinction conferred upon me. In all modesty, I think I deserved the nomination.

Since there was no immediate prospect of military action along the Border, the *Times* home office decided to cut its expeditionary force from seven men to three. Carl Dickey called me aside and whispered: "You and Bruce Rae and I are staying."

I whispered back: "You and Bruce Rae and somebody else are staying. Too hot here."

I took the train to New Orleans, a boat from there to New York, and reached home nourishing a flock of fleas I had picked up en route. I strongly suspected the bunk on the ship. The day after I arrived home I was back on the job covering golf. Six weeks later I was at the Merion Cricket Club near Philadelphia watching the play in the National Amateur Golf Championship of 1916 and enjoying every minute of it. This was the tournament in which Bob Jones made his debut in national championship competition as a chunky fourteen-year-old "boy wonder" from Atlanta, Georgia. The youngster did well but was finally put out by the reigning champion, Bob Gardner, in a close match in the quarter-final round. Everybody predicted a brilliant future on the links for the boy and for once at least, everybody was right.

On January 1, 1917, I became admiral of the Central Park Navy. It came about through the fact that I was a good hard worker on that sewer job several years earlier. One of the young city engineers who checked up on the work we were doing admired my energy and earnestness and we became good friends. His name was Joseph Vincent Hogue. I invited him to our Kingsbridge home to meet my family and he must have been taken by something he saw because about a year later he married my sister Kitty, my immediate junior in the family. He also had switched from engineering to operating the boating, skating and golfing concessions in Van Cortlandt Park.

He found the change profitable. He heard that the boating concession on the three lakes in Central Park was coming up for sealed bids late in 1916, the operation to start at the beginning of 1917. He suggested that I put in a bid. Even if I got it, I wouldn't have to interrupt my newspaper work. He knew a good man who could manage it for me. I put in the

bid at the figure he advised. To my astonishment, when the
sealed envelopes were opened and the bids called off, mine
was low. I put up a stock certificate — borrowed from a
cousin — to cover a $7500 bond required by the city to
guarantee payment of the rent and I was further financed by
a family friend to the extent of $2500. All my own savings
went into the hopper and my brother-in-law backed me with
cash as well as much needed advice.

He also produced the able manager he had promised and
we had extraordinary luck in the weather. We had skating on
New Year's Day and many days thereafter, which brought in
a flow of cash immediately through the checkrooms at the
three lakes — 59th Street, 72nd Street and 110th Street —
and the lunch counter at 72nd Street. Eventually, when our
boatbuilding program was completed, I was First Sea Lord
of 475 rowboats, 4 swan boats and two 40-passenger electric launches. This cost us about $40,000, but in our five-
year tenancy we got it back and had something to spare.

All this didn't interfere with my newspaper work in the
least. I made the rounds of the three lakes in the morning
"just to show my authority" but the capable manager really
ran the show and I went about my newspaper chores in the
afternoons and at nights as usual. What did interrupt my
career as a sports reporter was the United States declaration
of war against Germany and its associates on April 6, 1917.
One month later I enlisted in a volunteer outfit whose re-
cruiting slogan was: "Join The Engineers. First To France."
This was the New York unit of a group of nine such engineer regiments being hastily recruited in nine different large
cities scattered across the country from Boston to San Francisco. After some delay at the baptismal font, our outfit was
named the Eleventh Engineers (Railway) and as such we
were loaded aboard the old *Carpathia* on July 14 (Bastille
Day) and steamed off to the war zone. The recruiters had

made good on their promise; we were among the first 20,000 Americans to land in France in World War I.

We went by way of England and in a brief stay at a camp near Aldershot we had the distinction of being the first American regiment ever to be reviewed by a British monarch. George V, now more familiar to Americans as the name of a hotel in Paris than as that of a former occupant of Buckingham Palace in London, came down to our little camp with his staff and we swept past him in a column of companies. I was in A Company, which led the parade, and I could see skylarks rising out of the grass ahead of us. Since we had no band playing for us, I could hear them, too, as they went singing aloft. I was much more interested in the skylarks than in the review by royalty. It was my first acquaintance with the famous songsters. After a week of gas training and bayonet drill at this camp, we made a swift crossing of the Channel on an overcast afternoon with other troopships ahead of us and behind us and British destroyers guarding on both sides. We left from Folkstone and landed in Boulogne on August 7. In camp on a hill that night we could see the flash of the big guns firing along the Western Front. I suppose we were all duly impressed by the distant spectacle. I know I was.

Unless restrained, any old soldier will babble along interminably on the subject of his experiences while in uniform but there is no need for the reader to reach around in search of a club. I restrain myself. All I say is that we had a good outfit, we did good work, we had grandstand seats at the war and we got off lightly. For almost a year we spent most of our time working in the support area behind the British lines. The first battle casualty report issued by the A.E.F. was a modest one. Two men wounded, September 5, 1917. The men were Sergeant Matt Calderwood and Private Bill Brannigan. The report naturally did not further state that both men were in F Company, Eleventh Engineers, and

were wounded by shell fragments while working behind the
British front on the Somme. It was our outfit that unloaded
the 438 big British tanks for the celebrated Cambrai attack
on November 20 during which a big hole was opened through
the German line.

The Germans were really surprised by this first assault of
tanks en masse. Ten days later, however, they had recovered
enough from their surprise to pinch off the salient made by
the tank attack and in the process they trapped two and a half
companies of our regiment that had been laying a broad-gauge
track behind the British advance. Most of our men made it
back to safety in the general confusion but six were killed,
thirteen were wounded and eleven were captured, including
the best piano player in the regiment, Charley Geoghegan of
B Company.

Personally I never experienced anything worse than a good
shaking up now and then when a bomb or a shell landed too
close for comfort. These were easily turned into laughing
matters but it wasn't all beer and skittles for some of the boys.
We left a few dead behind us in every sector through which
we passed — the Somme, Arras, the Lys, St. Mihiel and the
Argonne. We landed back in New York late in April, 1919,
and I was discharged on May 5. Thus I had been in the army
two years, of which I spent less than three months in this
country. Lucky!

The really lucky part was that I had kept up my French
after I left college without any idea that it would ever be use-
ful to me. I just liked the language and I read all the French
books in our local public library several times over. I bought
Hugo, Dumas the Elder, Daudet, Anatole France, Balzac
and others in the reasonable Nelson editions. I knew Ros-
tand's rhymed romances almost by heart. I reached the point
where I could read French about as easily as I could English,
but I had few opportunities to speak it. The war changed that

in a big way. As soon as we landed in France I began to officiate as interpreter for my enlisted cronies and later I had regimental assignments as a go-between when we had dealings with French military or civilian personnel. I became fluent enough — j'ai la langue bien pendue — but the less said about my accent the better. Come to think of it, I have never received any compliments on my accent in English, either.

I did some sporadic birding while I was in France. I remember that the marsh in the Somme River under the walls of Peronne was filled with "coot and hern" and some smaller marsh birds that I could not identify since I had neither field glasses nor European bird book to help me out. Later I did acquire a pair of field glasses and with these I could at least identify certain birds as sparrows, warblers, woodpeckers, titmice, nuthatches and such even if I had no idea what the species might be. In July, 1918, when we were building an ammunition dump halfway between Paris and Château-Thierry, our office tent was in a lovely patch of woods through which ran a seven-foot wire fence enclosing the game preserve of one of the Rothschild clan. The preserve was a wonderful place for birds and I often scaled the fence to go in search of them. One day as I started to climb the fence I heard one of my fellow staff sergeants say to the office force:

"There goes John with his field glasses. Now the birds will catch hell!"

It's a long way back to those old days in France and some of them have faded into oblivion. I still remember months of mud and misery, moments of stark terror, and hopeless hours when there seemed to be no way out and we were all wandering —

as on a darkling plain
Swept with confused alarms of struggle and flight
Where ignorant armies clash by night.

More pleasant are three other memories that never fail me; red poppies in the wheat, flashing black-and-white magpies flitting over the fields, and long lines of tall Lombardy poplars marking the roads and canals on the distant landscape. "*Adieu, plaisant pays de France.*" Back to Newspaper Row in New York.

III

HOBNOBBING WITH CHAMPIONS

As soon as I was turned loose by the army I married the girl I left behind me — Alma Boldtmann, slim, dark, beautiful and very gentle, a native New Yorker of French and German descent — and we went off on a honeymoon that took in California and the Canadian Rockies before I returned to my job as golf writer for the *New York Times*. In a little over four years we had three children — two boys and a girl in that order — and a rambling old wooden house in Riverdale with oaks trees around it and a wide lawn on which the children could play.

In the interim my lease on the rowboat concession had terminated and I had lost my title of First Sea Lord of the Central Park Navy. I had sold my rowboats and auxiliary vessels to the Greek merchant who had outbid me for the concession at the auction block and I was free to concentrate on my newspaper career. In 1922 I had shifted from the *Times* to the *New York Tribune*, when Grantland Rice offered me a job there as a baseball writer with a "by line." It was the "by line," the chance to have my name over the stories I wrote, that was the big inducement. On the *Times* all the sports writers were anonymous and in the news columns only a few star staff men were allowed to sign stories on special occasions.

I was sorry to part company with the *Times* but the chance to make a name for myself was too good to miss. The fact that I was to write baseball was important, too. When he first spoke to me, Grant offered me the golf job at the *Tribune*. This I turned down. In those days baseball was the big attraction for those newspaper readers who turned to the sports section with regularity. Other sports had their seasons and big days but big league baseball was the year-round staple article to feed the sports fans. It was a circulation builder and the newspaper publishers knew it.

I interpolate an item to stress the point. Early in his career as a drama critic for the *New York Times*, the rotund and dapper Alexander Woollcott approached the publisher, Adolph S. Ochs, with a polite request for an increase in salary. Mr. Ochs replied that he thought his drama critic's salary was adequate, but if Alec would switch to writing baseball he would raise his pay. The outraged Woollcott rejected the offer as an affront to his dignity and went back to his customary two seats on the aisle. Eventually Alec obtained a measure of revenge for the insult. He became a radio star as "The Town Crier" and reveled richly in the new medium that was cutting heavily into the advertising harvest that newspaper and magazine publishers once had pretty well to themselves.

When I became a baseball writer for the *Tribune* in 1922 radio had penetrated comparatively few homes and even in those it was mostly a series of squeals and squawks. The writers of signed stories in the newspapers were still the important links between games and their followers. When my first signed baseball story appeared in the paper, I felt as though I had made a varsity team. Beyond that, baseball was my favorite game at the time and I was thrilled at the prospect of meeting and mixing with the great diamond stars of those days. I would go on a southern training trip. Weather permitting, I would watch a big league ball game every day during the regular season. I would cover the world series. And I would be paid well — $75 a week — for having all that fun. Some are born lucky.

What I anticipated turned out to be true. I had a wonderful time watching the games and getting to know the players. I met Babe Ruth at Hot Springs, Arkansas, where he was "boiling out" before reporting to the Yankee training camp at New Orleans. The first time I saw him he was in a "sweat box" at one of the baths with only his head visible. A week later at New Orleans I met all the Yankee veterans and rookies of the year and — to my delight — was allowed to put on a uniform and play shortstop during batting practice. I was only thirty years old at the time and still agile enough to get away with it. In college I had been the type of ball player so aptly described by a famous old catcher and coach, Mike Gonzales, as "good field, no hit."

Before the 1922 season was over I knew every regular on all sixteen major league teams and, in most cases, was delighted to make their acquaintance. There were a few grumpy ones but I soon learned how to work my way past them on the field or in the dugout before the game. I played golf with some of them, including Babe Ruth, and in later years I went duck hunting with the Babe and his great friend, Frank Stevens, on Chesapeake Bay and Pamlico Sound. That is, I was there with them but I wasn't armed as they were. They had shotguns while my weapon was a pair of field glasses. I was only interested in watching the assorted waterfowl streaming by.

There turned out to be "fringe benefits" in baseball writing that I knew nothing about until I began to travel with the teams. Road trips with the Yankees and Giants carried me to the nine other cities outside New York that constituted the major league circuits of those days. A baseball writer had his mornings to himself on the road and I made use of them for such extracurricular activities as the inspection of art museums, zoos, public libraries, municipal parks and other local attractions open to the public in Philadelphia, Washington, Boston, Cleveland, Detroit, Pittsburgh, Cincinnati, Chicago and St. Louis. I enjoyed this immensely and also learned a lot at no cost except a trifling expenditure in shoe leather. I generally went afoot on such excursions.

It was quite educational in a mild way. I remember reading Proust in French in the big downtown library in St. Louis before that author's works were allowed on the shelves of the public libraries in New York. My first glimpse of the stars indoors came when I entered the Adler Planetarium on the lake front in Chicago. It was the first such institution in this country to be equipped with the remarkable Zeiss projector. The star show was so far beyond anything I had anticipated or imagined that I was electrified and enchanted. Somehow I managed to weave some mention of this into one of my sports stories and, as an unexpected result, I received a kindly letter from Max Adler, the Chicago merchant who had given the money to build the planetarium and who, in his old age, had retired to California to enjoy the sun as well as the stars.

It was at the St. Louis zoo that I first saw the moat system of keeping bears, lions, tigers and other such clawed animals within bounds and yet out in the open where visitors could have a clear view of them with no intervening bars. It's a common practice in big zoos now wherever possible. I roamed through the Franklin Institute in Philadelphia and the Smithsonian Institution in Washington and a watch factory in Cincinnati, but what I really doted on was visiting the art museums in the different cities. I never tire of looking at paintings, preferably landscapes, seascapes or genre subjects. Perhaps my love of nature influenced my taste in paintings but I can appreciate a still life by a master and some of my favorite characters are portraits by Frans Hals or Rembrandt. I've known that old woman paring her nails for half a century. She hasn't aged a bit. She's still wonderful.

Washington in those days lacked the great National Gallery that the Mellon money provided later but it had the Corcoran Gallery and the Freer Gallery that included the famous Whistler room that was moved bodily from London to the District of Columbia. Washington also had the Lincoln Memorial, to me one of the most stately and impressive monuments in the world, and with the azaleas, dogwoods and cherry trees in bloom in late April or early May, it is a picturesque city to visit. Even so, Pittsburgh was my favorite city on the baseball circuit because everything in which I was interested was close at hand. We stayed at the Schenley Hotel, one small block away from Forbes Field where the ball games were played. Just down the street in another direction was the Carnegie Institute that housed a notable collection of fine art and staged an annual international show that was the big event of the art year in this country. In 1925 the international art show and the world series at Forbes Field (Pittsburgh Pirates vs. the Washington Senators) were on view at the same time and I thoroughly enjoyed both attractions. Just over the outfield fence at Forbes Field lay Schenley Park through which I roamed regularly with my field glasses at the alert. It was a good place to look for migrant warblers in May and September.

By 1925 I was working for Hearst, a step up financially but a comedown socially after being on the *Times* and the

"Trib" that catered to the "carriage trade" while the Hearst papers frankly went after the masses. I enjoyed writing for the "Trib" and I survived the merger that made it the *Herald Tribune*. But in December of 1924 Damon Runyon asked me to go down to Park Row and talk to Gene Fowler, then managing editor of the *New York American*, the Hearst full-size morning newspaper in the city. I was flattered that top men like Damon and Gene were interested in me and it didn't take me long to reach Gene's office where I accepted his offer of $150 a week — big money in those days for anybody except an established star. I signed on the dotted line quickly when Gene told me that I would have a chance to write a sports column of my own at intervals.

The promise about the occasional sports column was made good. Because I started it when I was sent to Saratoga in August to do feature stories on horse racing at the sanctuary of turf tradition, I called my column "Wild Oats and Chaff." What pleased me most about it was that I was free to include light verse when the divine afflatus swept over me. I loved to write verse — and read it, too. In my reading I knew no bounds and I reveled in poetry in three languages — English, French and Latin. If any reader is foolish enough to challenge me on this, I am apt to burst forth with "Tu ne quaesieris (scire nefas) quem mihi, quem tibi finem di dederint" or "Dictes moy ou, n'en quel pays, est Flora, la belle Romaine" and the last state of that reader will be worse than the first. But in writing I know my limitations and I stick to the lightest of verse.

In my column for the *American* it was made even lighter by some mad genius in the art department who drew waggish pen and ink sketches to illustrate my somewhat less than immortal rhymes. Indeed, all I can remember of those lyrical sallies is the conclusion of one concerning the fate of a man who was arrested for smoking at a fight in Madison Square Garden contrary to the edict of the then head of the boxing commission or, to give it a formal title, the New York State Athletic Commission. That was the famous Bill Muldoon, a reformed wrestler who became a noted professional trainer of bodies and an amateur saver of souls. He was ancient, honorable, upright and pigheaded. He loathed smoking, so he banned it at boxing events in New York State, which was ludicrous but apparently legal. At least, it went without challenge at the time.

To illustrate my outbreak in rhyme on the arrest of the offender, the office genius had sketched a thin, timid type of citizen gazing at the boxers in the ring with a cigarette dangling from his pursed lips and two burly cops in uniform charging at the miscreant with raised clubs to beat him into submission. It was lovely. My concluding lines on the episode were:

> *He might have committed a dozen crimes*
> *Untouched by the law of the land,*
> *But he smoked one night at a Garden fight*
> *And they hanged him out of hand.*
> *Yes, they hanged that man in the cold gray dawn,*
> *And they gave three rousing cheers*
> *As he plunged apace to a resting place*
> *Where he'll smoke for a thousand years.*

It was fun at the *American* while it lasted but it didn't last long. I was there only a year or so when William Randolph Hearst sent word from his barony at San Simeon that Gene Fowler had earned a vacation and should go on a nice long trip. Gene knew from the experiences of others that no Hearst editor was expected to return from any such vacation. When Mr. Hearst inquired, by wire, where Gene thought of going on the suggested trip, Gene wired back politely: "Egypt. Is that far enough?"

It was. He never came back to the *American*. I doted on Gene and had no use whatever for the character who succeeded him and who further incurred my wrath by forcing out of office by foul means my immediate superior, the sports editor. This was William J. Slocum with whom I had worked on the *Times* and the *Tribune* and who was, in my opinion, the best sports editor in the business. He was also a delightful gentleman whose friendship I prized to the day of his death. I was looking for the escape hatch at the *American* when I had word that my first sponsor back at the *Times*, Frederick T. Birchall, wanted to see me. He had succeeded the great Carr Van Anda as managing editor though they never did give him the full title; they called him "acting" managing editor. He had one of the longest runs of any "actor" in the newspaper profession, six years at full speed all the way.

I went to see Mr. Birchall about the middle of December, 1926, and he gave me tidings of great joy. In the face of the competition from the *Herald Tribune*, which offered its readers two sports columns each morning, one by Grantland Rice and the other by W. O. McGeehan, the *Times* was being forced to retreat from its austere position of almost total anonymity for members of its staff. They had decided to have a daily signed sports column and I was Birchall's nominee for the job. I picked the obvious title for such a column: "Sports of the Times." My first column appeared in the paper on the morning of January 1, 1927, and — except for annual vacation periods — I stuck to such daily labor for the next sixteen years. Incidentally, this was the first daily signed column of any kind to appear in the *New York Times*, but other signed columns blossomed soon after in other departments and now there are signed stories all over the paper.

I had no assignment except to turn out a sports column of about 1100 words every day, which made it a real "cushy billet." I could choose my own topics, go where I wanted and write as I pleased within reasonable limits. This gave me great freedom of movement and a wide choice of subject matter. Once I stretched the freedom of movement as far as a trip to England to watch the running of the Grand National Steeplechase at Aintree in early spring when

> *March made sweet the weather*
> *With daffodil and starling*
> *And hours of fruitful breath.*

On another occasion I spent three weeks in Paris, surveyed the sports activities in the area and mailed back my columns from that city of many bridges. As to subject matter, I rambled scandalously and touched on topics that rarely found their way into the sports section of any reputable newspaper. This included ancient history and modern art, organic and inorganic chemistry, popular astronomy, free translations from *L'Echo des Sports* and *Tutti Gli Sporti*, quotations from John Keats, Robert Browning and Virgil, occasional book reviews and a discussion of Heisenberg's Theory of Probabilities as applied to the game of 3-cushion billiards.

I carried on scandalously in light verse, too. I predicted in rhyme that Joe Louis would slaughter Max Schmeling when they met at the Yankee Stadium on the evening of June 19, 1936. The record books have it that Schmeling knocked out Louis in the twelfth round. I am in no position to challenge the evidence because I sat only a few feet from the ring and saw the whole thing from start to finish. To my readers I acknowledged my error in the following lines:

> *Lately I wrote in what might be called verse,*
> *Mixing my meter with banter,*

Louis would ready Herr Max for the hearse;
Burial service instanter.
That, to be brief, was the theme of my song,
Those of you know who had read it.
Query and Answer: Was I very wrong?
You said it!

Lightly I wrote that The Shuffler would bring
Maxie much damage and pain;
Lay him as flat as the floor of the ring;
I said it and said it again;
Stated it broadly and maybe too long,
Thinking I put it astutely.
Was I completely, astoundingly wrong?
Absolutely!

Two years later they were to meet again in the Yankee
Stadium, this time for the world heavyweight championship
which Louis had gathered in the interim by knocking out
Jersey James Braddock in Chicago on June 22, 1937. Apparently I had learned nothing from my earlier humiliating experience. On the morning of this second encounter I again
risked a prophecy in my column and put it stubbornly as
follows:

ON SECOND THOUGHT

They warned me of an ancient day
— Before the first Joe-Max affair —
When odds ran wild the other way
And yet the Tortoise beat the Hare.
So Schmeling would — and were they wise! —
Beat Louis down. But even though
It happened right before my eyes,
I still like Joe.

They told me that the Persian host
Who later ran to hell-an'-gone,
Were 1 to 10 in book and boast
To beat the Greeks at Marathon.

But sunset saw them on the lope,
As moonlight saw Joe Louis low.
Greek-like, Herr Schmeling crossed the dope.
I still like Joe.

They argued eke, in rising wrath,
That little David, brave and bold,
Unplayed at 8 to 1 in Gath,
Rose up to knock Goliath cold.
From this they judged — and were they right! —
That Max would land the winning blow.
But this is yet another night.
I still like Joe.

I've had due warning, loud and long,
Of what must come when clangs the bell,
And how again I will be wrong;
A state in which I often dwell;
Of how, once more, will Joe recline,
And how they'll shout "We told you so!"
But here I lay it on the line:
I still like Joe.

On this occasion my hero saw to it that I did not have to apologize. He disposed of Schmeling in the very first round. Joe and I were on such good terms that, a bit later, I even ventured to put words into his mouth without protest from him. It happened in the wake of a bout he had with a run-of-the-mill heavyweight named Arturo Godoy, a crude foreign boxer with more strength than skill. Godoy managed to go the limit of fifteen rounds with Louis in Madison Square Garden in March, 1940. He was so elated at escaping a knockout that, at the end of the bout, he threw his arms around Louis and gave him a loud kiss. The fighter spectators were astounded and so was Louis. To celebrate the event, I had Joe filch from Leigh Hunt and tell the story in my column in eight little lines of verse beginning: "Godoy kissed me when we met." Who could resist it?

To those who took their sports seriously this sort of trifling came close to blasphemy, but I persisted in it and compounded the felony by introducing the ballade, the sonnet and other rhyme schemes here and there in my lighthearted essays on sports. I loved golf, adored John Masefield and had the brassie nerve to steal from his spine-tingling "Tomorrow!" in this foul fashion:

Oh, yesterday, flushed high with hope, I stood upon the tee.
My drive I hooked behind a rock; my second hit a tree,
And all the dreadful afternoon I flubbed in misery.
But tomorrow, by the gods of golf, I'll try the game again.

Oh, yesterday my heart was torn with top and slice and hook;
The wayward path I traveled led by trap and rough and brook,
And as I missed my tenth short putt my soul in anguish shook.
But tomorrow, if I live that long, I'll try the game again.

Oh, yesterday I drenched the links with bitter scalding tears,
And what I said of golf I hope will never reach your ears.
I swore I wouldn't touch a club for years and years and years.
But tomorrow — you can bet on this! — I'll try the game again.

I seem to be getting a bit light-headed from typing out all this light verse. I must sober up and steady down. One for the road and I'll quit. When I learned that Bill Tilden, emperor of the tennis courts, had delivered a lecture to a boy's club on the virtues of early rising and plain living, I pictured him rephrasing his speech and conveying the same vital message in the general tone and the exact meter (the Alcaic strophe) used by Quintus Horatius Flaccus in his famous ode beginning "*Integer vitae scelerisque purus*" and it went as follows:

Eat but simple food; stick to early rising;
Follow out my plan, daily exercising;

Then your tennis game you will find surprising;
  So, too, will others.

Drink but water pure, not the wine that glitters;
Whiskey let alone, for it brings the jitters;
Sip not even one little glass of bitters;
  Shun it, my brothers!

Thus I reached the top and thus you must follow
If, across the net, you would beat all hollow
Playboys of the court. Though they call you Rollo,
  Stick to it cheerly.

Then upon the court, with some crafty blending,
Power, skill and speed you will have for spending.
When the wastrels sag, for a happy ending,
  Ace them severely!

Once we were beset, with the French besetting;
Threats from Anzacs, too, we were always getting;
On my upright life did they base the betting
  I would outlast 'em.

Primed with ozone rare (and with speed a trifle);
Strong on simple food (and a service rifle);
Fresh from calm sweet sleep (what a tennis eyeful);
  Say, did I blast 'em!

Place me in a land where it may be snowing,
Or 'neath tropic skies with the warm wind blowing;
Bring your young net star. When the game gets going
  I'll dust his jacket.

Thank the simple life — and a forehand stinging —
That at forty-odd, with the loud cheers ringing,
I, King William still, on the court am swinging,
  Boy, what a racquet!

I'll admit that drollery of this kind gets a sports columnist more followers in faculty clubs than in the right-field bleachers but I had fun doing it and am still unrepentant. I do not wish to give the impression that I scanted my sports chores to "strictly meditate the thankless Muse." I loved sports and I never tired of watching big league baseball, college or pro football, ice hockey at Madison Square Garden, top flight tennis at Forest Hills and big golf tournaments over famous courses. I doted on my job as sports columnist. I fully realized that it was much better than working in a coal mine. In fact, it was much more pleasant than being a news reporter. A sports writer was welcome wherever he went, and he usually went where there was something entertaining to see. News reporters often were sent to unpleasant places and more than once had doors slammed in their faces, a hint that they weren't wanted. Sports writing was the softer and the safer work. I remember what happened to Alva Johnston.

Alva, who was on the *Times* with me long ago, was one of the great reporters of those days. He was tall, brown-haired, thin-faced and "a Corinthian, a lad of mettle, a good boy" as well as a fine writer. The circus came to town and one of its attractions was a trick donkey that the management defied any spectator to ride. There was some small cash prize for any volunteer who could stick on the donkey's back for a specified time, quite brief. One afternoon a rollicking group of society playboys who acted as though they had just come from drinking lunch at Delmonico's arrived at the old Garden and heard the riding challenge. Urged on by his companions, one of them went down into the arena and stuck on the donkey's back long enough to win the money. It was a great lark. It was also a good story for the circus press agent to spread as fast and as widely as possible.

Newspaper reporters and photographers were sent to the chap's swanky bachelor digs to go further into the matter. The donkey rider and his chums by that time had changed their minds — and perhaps their drinks. They didn't want any more publicity. They turned away reporters and photographers with harsh words and threatening gestures but possibly they decided that the *Times* was something special and required different treatment. When Alva rang the doorbell and told them who and what he was, they invited him in, beat him up and threw him out a back entrance into the yard. He had to scale a six-foot board fence to make his way safely to the street again. I must add here that the donkey rider was hauled into court and made to pay for this cavalier treatment of the press. But I think I have made my point. It is the sports writer, rather than the news reporter, who can say with the Psalmist: "The lines are fallen unto me in pleasant places; yea, I have a goodly heritage."

However, the sports writers are well able to state their own case and I will not, in the Johnsonian phrase, "encumber them with help." As one retired from the field, I merely wish to register my opinion that the sports section is still the most pleasant part of the newspaper to read and that the sports columnists of today average higher in gay literacy than those of my own era. Certainly no newspaper in my time had a better pair of sports columnists than the New York *Herald Tribune* of recent years when every morning it served up Red Smith flanked by the late Joe Palmer whose untimely death was a loss to American literature.

Undoubtedly the modern athletes are better than the old-timers, too. With few exceptions, this can be demonstrated wherever the stopwatch or the steel tape is the measure of excellence. But the old boys were great in their day and I had a wonderful time watching them and writing about them. And knowing them. Naturally, I met them all — champions, runners-up, run-of-the-mill and eccentrics as well as coaches, managers, team owners and sports officials of all kinds. I played golf with Judge Kenesaw Mountain Landis and "Uncle Wilbert" Robinson, I lunched with Jack Dempsey and Gene

Tunney, I often dined with Lou Little and I roomed with Bob Jones at a golf championship. I loved dear old Connie Mack and I never missed a chance to sit with him in the back row of the grandstand while batting practice was going on before the game. I often shared a bench in the shade at the Saratoga track with "Sunny Jim" Fitzsimmons and listened to his stories about great thoroughbreds and odd happenings in turf history.

When I broke into sports one of the most colorful characters behind the scenes was Harry M. Stevens, founder of the noted catering firm and a man of whom it was written that he had "parlayed a peanut into a million dollars." He was self-educated and an omnivorous reader. He could quote Shakespeare and the Bible by the yard with the dramatic delivery of the father of all the Barrymores, whom he knew well, of course. He went to all the plays that appeared on Broadway and he knew everybody connected with the theatre — playwrights, managers, directors and actors. He lived at the old Waldorf Astoria on 34th Street and the table in his sitting room was always littered with the best books and all the current periodicals of that era. He was short, just a trifle stout, wore a derby hat everywhere except in bed, smoked long and expensive cigars and carried a cane. Somehow he took a fancy to me and I adored him. During the winter seasons when I had to cover so many night events at Madison Square Garden, I used to dine with him in his suite four or five times a week.

It was wonderful to be with him because he knew politics and finance as well as sports, English literature and the American theatre, and he loved to talk at length on these topics with fervor and a slight accent left over from his youthful days in Derbyshire, England. He was the embodiment of a Horatio Alger story — penniless immigrant, hard work, incredible energy, alert mind, upward struggle for long years crowned with well-deserved success while he was still able to enjoy it.

I remember one day when he was sitting at his desk and I was the only one with him in the office. He was well on in years then and his boys, Frank, Joe and Hal, were in active charge of the business. He often talked to me like a father and I felt like one of his family. Indeed, his sons were closer to me than my own brothers. This day the old gentleman leaned back in his chair, stared a moment at the ceiling and then leaned forward again to say slowly and almost solemnly: "John, look at me. I have all the money that any reasonable man could want —" here he brought his fist down on his desk with a bang and went on in what almost amounted to a shout — "AND NOT A DISHONEST DOLLAR IN THE LOT!"

That was Harry M. Stevens, a rare character for whom I had great admiration and deep affection.

One other notable debt that I owe to my career as a sports columnist was my first acquaintance with Colonel Theodore Roosevelt, Jr., and the long friendship that lasted to the day of his death due to exhaustion in the fighting of the Normandy peninsula. Shortly after I started the column on the *Times* I had a letter from him in praise of something I had written about the origin of the game of polo and inviting me to have lunch with him to talk things over. I leaped at the chance because I knew his deep interest in natural history and I wanted to hear all about his trip to the "Roof of the World," the Pamir Range in Central Asia, to collect specimens of the *Ovis poli* or Marco Polo Sheep.

We lunched at a rendezvous called "The Room," an informal private club — and little more than a big room with a wing containing lockers and a small kitchen — maintained by Ted and Kermit Roosevelt, C. Suydam Cutting, another explorer-naturalist, and a few friends of similar tastes. This

was during Prohibition days and each member had the obliga-
tion of providing his own liquor and a little extra in case of
emergency lest any member or guest die of thirst on the
premises. This was what the lockers were for. The place
was in the Sixties near Lexington Avenue, one flight up as I
remember it. I also recall that at luncheons or dinners or
cocktail parties at "The Room" I met men whom I had
admired from a distance — Frank M. Chapman, the great
ornithologist, William Beebe, whose tales of the South American jungle had enchanted me, Roy Chapman Andrews, who
chatted about digging up dinosaur eggs in the Gobi Desert,
and George K. Cherrie, who had traveled down the River of
Doubt with ex-President Teddy Roosevelt and whose "Dark
Trails" I still treasure. There also I had my first meeting with
Stanley Field, head of the Field Museum (now the Chicago
Museum of Natural History) and Fairfield Osborn, president
of the New York Zoological Society and, as such, the big
boss of the Bronx Zoo where I had been a regular visitor since
childhood.

I had Ted Roosevelt to thank for this — and Kermit, too,
who was a delightful companion — but I came to owe Ted a
much greater debt in time. He was one of the editors at
Doubleday & Company and, after I began to write magazine
articles on nature, he kept pounding away at me to produce a
book for Doubleday on that subject. It took some years in
the doing and it was only a small book when it came out but
it was the start on a path that I have been following ever since
with increasing enjoyment as the years go by.

As to how a sports columnist came to write an article on
nature in the first place, it was a crime as you shall see.

IV

A HELPFUL CASE OF PLAGIARISM

FROM 1873 to 1891 Kansas was represented in the United States Senate by a man now best remembered as the author of a sonnet that, in my schoolboy days, was a favorite for student recitation in tragic tones and with solemn gestures. I long ago lost track of it but recently I found it aged in the Ralph Woods anthology entitled *Second Treasury of the Familiar* and it was like meeting a boyhood chum. Being now in the public domain, it can be offered here at no extra charge. Ready; aim; fire!

OPPORTUNITY
BY JOHN JAMES INGALLS

Master of human destinies am I!
Fame, love and fortune on my footsteps wait.
Cities and fields I walk; I penetrate
Deserts and seas remote, and passing by
Hovel and mart and palace — soon or late
I knock unbidden once on every gate.

If sleeping, wake — if feasting, rise before
I turn away. It is the hour of fate,
And they who follow me reach every state
Mortals desire, and conquer every foe

Save death; but those who doubt or hesitate,
Condemned to failure, penury and woe,
Seek me in vain and uselessly implore.
I answer not, and I return no more.

I was a trusting boy and I took every word of that as gospel truth. Now I can only hope for the sake of Kansas that Senator Ingalls wasn't as wrong about everything else as he was about that. I long ago discovered that Opportunity is an incorrigible visitor and keeps rap-rap-rapping on unanswered doors just as "wisdom cries out in the streets, and no man regards it." I know that I had many visits myself and I took advantage of a few of Opportunity's cash prize offers. One of them came to me in the guise of a startling case of plagiarism in — of all places! — the staid and respectable pages of the Sunday magazine section of the *New York Times*.

Essays on anything outdoors I find almost irresistible. On this particular occasion the *Times* Magazine offered one on trees with some lovely illustrations. Some of my oldest friends are trees. I plunged into the article with eager anticipation and the opening paragraph was most alluring. At the end of the second paragraph anyone with any interest in the subject would have had to say that this was going to be good, very good. The crash came in the third paragraph where there was mention of a fictional character in Mrs. Gaskell's *Cranford*, an elderly gentleman who asked a lady what color ash buds were in March. When she pleaded ignorance, the old gentleman told her that he himself hadn't known until it had been revealed to him recently in a line of verse by a young poet, Alfred Tennyson: "More black than ash buds in the front of March."

A wonderful touch, picturesque, arresting. In fact, unforgettable. I remembered reading it years earlier in a book about trees in winter that was written by some woman whose name did not come immediately to mind. A glance at the top of this *Times* Magazine story revealed the author as no lady. The man's name was unfamiliar to me but as I went further into the story familiar passages from the old book turned up in abundance, none surrounded by the quotation marks demanded by professional courtesy, let alone the copyright laws.

The matter was mentioned the next day to Alden March, one of the *Times* senior editors on the national news side and my favorite guide, philosopher and friend. He was laden with years, wisdom and wit and it was my practice to stop by his desk almost every day to unburden my soul, ask his advice or just enjoy his companionship. When he was told about the old book and the new claimant to some of the finest passages in it, he phoned the Sunday Department and within a few days the case of plagiarism had been established. The best bits in the *Times* article had been filched from *Studies of Trees in Winter* by Annie Oakes Huntington (L. C. Page Company, Boston, 1901). The culprit was called in by the Sunday Department, confronted with the evidence and dismissed with instructions never to darken their doorstep again. I was sorry about the whole thing and quickly put it out of my mind.

Not so the editor of the Sunday magazine. About a year later he received a batch of beautiful etchings and woodcuts of trees and he needed a writer to pour a certain amount of text around them. He recalled the fellow in the sports department who had detected fraudulent dealing in an article on the same subject. If that chap knew enough about it to detect a fraud, he might be able to turn out something geniune in that field. That's how I came to write an article on trees for the *New York Times* Sunday Magazine away back in April, 1928. It was my first step into a way of life that now fills all my days to overflowing.

Up to that time the outdoors had always been my escape, my vacation land, my spare-hours hunt for buried and unburied treasure. A sports columnist was supposed to deal with more muscular matters than bird-watching, fern identification and the pursuit of wild orchids. These things had to be indulged in on the sly, so to speak, or I might be drummed out of my ringside seat at the Madison Square Garden fights on Friday nights. Too often I had to hurry back from a stroll along the river or a prowl through the miniature wilderness of the Van Cortlandt Park swamp because Duty, that "Stern Daughter of the Voice of God," was calling me to the Yankee Stadium or the Yale Bowl. In my morning walks throughout the year in the Riverdale region "I triumphed and I saddened with all weather" but seldom with a completely clear conscience. It almost seemed that these were stolen hours and illegal pleasures. But if I could become a recognized nature writer, it would make an honest man of me.

At that stage, of course, it was only a dream but it was a recurring and most alluring one. Some dreams last a lifetime and never are fulfilled. Mine lasted for twenty years and then came true. For the past ten years or more I have been walking in a dream. It can be highly recommended as good for body and soul.

The transition from sports columnist to nature writer was slow but not a bit painful. Indeed, it was joyful. I combined both pursuits for years in what seemed to me an easy and delectable way. Whenever I went to cover outdoor competition of any kind — baseball, football, tennis, golf, polo or horse racing — I kept my eyes open and saw more things than my press badge called for. I think I did best on the golf courses where the national championships were being played. Every golf course is to some extent a wildlife refuge and, since I always carried field glasses so that I could see the players at a distance, it was easy to swing the glasses on birds in the trees — or even on the fairway. As big Ralph Guldahl stood on the eighteenth tee at the Oakland Hills links outside Detroit in 1938 on the last leg of his journey to the national open championship, the fairway ahead of him at one point was being used as a feeding ground by a flock of about forty or fifty horned larks. Ralph hit his drive and walked up the fairway with the crowd of spectators streaming in his wake. Up went the horned larks in flight as the crowd pounded past. I held my ground. With my glasses I could follow the play from where I stood. By the time Ralph holed the putt that clinched the championship, the horned larks were back feeding peaceably on the same patch of fairway again.

Walking away from Palmer Stadium in the cold twilight after a Yale football victory over Princeton, I was admiring the afterglow in the western sky through the bare branches of a maple when I noticed something in the tree itself. It was a screech owl that remained undisturbed as I sauntered slowly beneath it toward the football specials in the railroad yard below. Once I was so late finishing a story of a Yale-Harvard game in the Yale Bowl that my telegrapher and I were the only occupants in the press box in the dusk. Just as we stood up to leave, a hoarsely honking V of Canada geese passed southward overhead. They were so close that we could hear the swish of their great wings. On trips to cover ball games in St. Louis and Cincinnati I learned that the western meadowlark's song is much sweeter than that of our eastern meadowlark and that there are noble mossy-cup oaks in Forest Park in St. Louis. A man would get a good grounding in botany simply by identifying all the native shrubs and trees at the Saratoga racing plant. For a full fall season there was a peregrine falcon that I used to see perched on top of one of the electric light towers at the Polo Grounds when I was there to watch the New York Football Giants in action on the gridiron below. Presumably the peregrine lived on the pigeons that tenanted the place but I saw only one chase and that time the pigeon deftly dodged the swift "stoop" of the deadly enemy. A wonderful bird, the peregrine. It's the swiftest flier in our North American skies.

Hold hard! I'd better come back to earth again. That first tree story for the *Times* Magazine evidently satisfied the literary overlords on the editorial board because I subsequently was requested to turn out many stories for that Sunday section. On different occasions over more than a decade I hailed spring in print, welcomed back the birds, praised the courage of the daffodils that "come before the swallow dares and take the winds of March with beauty," dwelt on the lure of the mountains in summer, reveled in the colors of the autumn hillsides and closed out the years with some favorable mention of snow-clad landscapes and "the long glories of the Winter moon."

Among other things, this brought me the friendship of Brooks Atkinson whose drama department headquarters were just across the aisle from the sports department. Brooks loved the outdoors as much as I did and we occasionally went on all-day excursions together in search of birds. I remember the first Iceland gull that we found on the ocean front at Jones Beach, Long Island, because it was on a cold December day just after we had entered upon World War II and everybody was on the alert for enemy attack by submarine along the coast. Brooks and I came upon this white-winged gull among a flock of ordinary herring gulls only fifteen minutes or so after we had been driven off the lower sections of the beach by a Coast Guard detail that, seeing us sweeping the offshore waters with field glasses, took us for suspicious char-

acters. Wrapped as we were in heavy rough clothing to pro-
tect us against the bitter wind along the beach, I'll admit that
we looked the part.

Some sage said long ago that the way to learn any subject
is to write a book about it. A book on nature was far beyond
my powers in the days when the Sunday Magazine was calling
on me to turn out those seasonal articles, but I was gradually
adding to my knowledge of the outdoors through the necessity of checking everything I wrote for correctness in detail.
This required poring over standard reference books and con-
sultation with the best local authorities to be found. For instance, all school children of the region knew that violets
came in three colors, white, yellow and blue, but a walk in the
May woods with a school bus driver of Westport, Connecticut, brought me the further information that there were not
three but at least thirty species of violet in the region and that
I had better be mighty careful in bandying their names about
in print.

When you begin to pry into details like that you are enter-
ing upon an endless pursuit. One thing leads to another in
an alarming way. It's easy enough to tick off the "wild animals" — meaning mammalian quadrupeds — or the native
trees or even the birds of a fairly large region but an attempt
to list the shrubs and flowers of even a ten-mile stretch of
countryside would be an appalling job. If the beginner in the
bird department thinks there are a baffling lot of warblers and
sparrows and sandpipers to be sorted out, let him give
a thought to the lot of the botany beginner trying to get acquainted with just one of the more than two hundred plant
families of the same region, the Composite Family of over a
hundred genera and some five hundred species.

An amateur needs more than patience and a magnifying
glass to make any progress through such a floral tangle. At

frequent intervals he will have to fall back upon either the three volumes of the new Britton & Brown (1952) or the 1600-page Fernald Edition of Gray, or both. If some of the technical descriptions in Gray puzzle him, he might turn to the Glossary and come upon this gem: "Anatropous (ovule). Inverted and straight, with the micropyle next the hilum and the radical consequently inferior."

There's a glorious example of defining *"ignotum per ignotius,"* a sin against logic and a crime against the innocent. It's enough to give the good old word Glossary a bad name. In the immortal word and a half of Emile Zola: "J'accuse!"

By thumbing reference books and going along with experts on field trips, I began to make some progress in botany. Indeed, I grew bold enough to hurl a challenge at one of the top figures on the *Times*, Simeon Strunsky, for a statement made in "Topics of the Times," the column on the editorial page that he conducted brilliantly — and anonymously — for many years. One day in early autumn there was registered in his column the opinion that the color of the autumn foliage around New York City was all right in its way but not quite up to the standard set on New England hillsides. It so happens that, on my daily morning walks in the Riverdale area that autumn, I had come to the conclusion that never in my life had I seen foliage more beautiful. It had been thrilling just to wander through such riots of color and it was shocking to read the "Topics of the Times" comment that it was merely so-so or second class autumn scenery. Though Mr. Strunksy was an eminent member of the *Times* hierarchy and a dweller in what we common reporters referred to as the "Temple of the Gods" — the cloistered editorial sanctum on the tenth floor — I determined to do battle for our local scenery.

I made a collection of the most beautiful colored leaves that

I could find on my home ground in Riverdale and mounted each leaf on a sheet of white paper, typewriter size. Underneath I wrote the common and scientific name of the tree that had produced the leaf — Red Oak (*Quercus rubra*), Sugar Maple (*Acer saccharum*), Rum Cherry (*Prunus serotina*), Sour Gum (*Nyssa sylvatica*), White Ash (*Fraxinus americana*), Sweet Gum (*Liquidamber styraciflua*), Sassafras (*Sassafras albidum*) and so on. I gathered the leaves of twenty species in all and when the collection was put together it made a bundle about three inches high. On top I put an indignant protest against the slur on the foliage of our fair city. Then, with a lordly gesture, I summoned an office boy to carry the bundle up to the tenth floor where, after taking off his shoes and making a deep obeisance, he was to place it on the desk of Simeon Strunsky.

About a week later a smiling Simeon Strunsky strolled up to my desk on the plebeian third floor. As he approached he held up his right hand, palm outward, and said: "Peace!" He explained that he had just returned from vacation. Another member of the cloistered community on the tenth floor — an elderly and genial gentleman by the name of Armstrong — had been writing the unsigned column in his absence and was the author of the offending phrases. Mr. Strunsky had turned over the protest and the leaf collection to the culprit and I would hear from him directly. I did. Mr. Armstrong came down with the leaf collection in his grasp, said that the evidence was convincing and admitted that he was wrong. A delightful gentleman. There's nobody I admire more than a man who admits it when he is wrong. I must try it myself some time.

V

RAPID RISE OF A RADIO SHOW

FROM the seasonal writing of nature stories for the *Times* Sunday Magazine that not only inspired but forced me to learn more about our native flora and fauna as I went along, I was suddenly and unexpectedly launched into a position where anything I said on that topic — and many others — would be subjected to the critical judgment of millions of listeners over a national radio network. It was another turning point in my case history and goes to bolster my contention that the life of the average citizen has more turning points in it than an indoor track meet.

One day in May, 1938, my desk phone rang. The man at the other end said that his name was Dan Golenpaul and he invited me to go on a radio show. I thanked him and said that I wasn't interested. The man kept talking, telling me that his was a panel show, that questions came in from the public and the members of the panels tried to answer them. A great many questions on sports came from younger listeners and he needed somebody to cover that field. He told me that Franklin P. Adams, the noted wit and popular columnist for the *Herald Tribune*, had recommended me. I asked him to thank Mr. Adams for the compliment but I still was not interested.

The caller became irritated. He informed me that I was no great attraction and that there were far more famous sports writers available. To this I agreed cheerfully and suggested that he invite one of them to go on his show. This irritated him further but he kept on talking. I couldn't shake him off. Finally he said almost in a rage: "Couldn't you even give this thing a half-hour trial?"

"When?"

"Tomorrow morning, eleven o'clock, here at NBC."

The man had worn me down. More to get rid of him than anything else, I agreed to show up at NBC the next morning. It could be done on my way to the office and that would be the last of it.

The appointment was kept in one of the big studios on the third floor at NBC and there I found Dan Golenpaul, members of his staff, various radio executives and technicians and some other candidates who were to be tested out as possible members of the panel. Clifton Fadiman was there. He was the master of ceremonies and read the questions when the show was on the air, which it had been once a week for three or four weeks past. That was why they were seeking new panelists. They had discovered that not all the starting quartet could go the distance. For one thing, only Franklin P. Adams of the original four knew or cared anything about sports and even he knew only tennis, baseball and the football fortunes of his alma mater, the University of Michigan. Somebody had to fill the gap. That was where I was to come in, on the recommendation of the literary wit and light verse poet who signed his daily columns "F.P.A." Frank and I were old friends. One of the most jubilant days in my life came when he published a verse I submitted for his column. I didn't trifle with my luck. I never submitted another.

The names of the others who sat through the half-hour of questioning that morning do not come back to mind. All I remember is that I had fun sitting there and speaking up when I knew the answers to the questions. At the end of the session Mr. Golenpaul came up to me and the conversation went something like this:

"Was that hard to take?"

"No, it was a lot of fun."

"Well, will you go on the air with us?"

"When?"

"Friday night at eight-thirty."

"Where?"

"Right here in this studio."

"I'll be here."

"We're on a budget now — sustaining. Until we get a sponsor, all I can give you is forty dollars for each show."

"That's all right with me."

I didn't add that I would have gone on for nothing, which was exactly what I had been paid for various previous performances on the air and the reason why I had not jumped at another invitation when Dan Golenpaul first mentioned the topic over the phone.

Thus I became a member of the panel of the Information Please radio program that became nationally popular in a matter of months and catapulted the regulars into public notice where we remained for more than a decade. I may be prejudiced — I'm sure I am — in saying that it was the most literate popular entertainment program ever to go out over the air on radio or television.

Aside from any contribution that I made to it, we had in Clifton Fadiman and Franklin P. Adams two of the brightest of the contemporary literary set and in Oscar Levant, who joined us shortly after I made the team, a young man of remarkable musical talent and a positive genius for making offhand cutting remarks that couldn't have been sharper if he had honed them a week in his mind. Oscar was with us every other week. When he was present, we had one guest to make up our panel of four. When he was absent, we had two guests.

Shortly after I began leading the double life of sports columnist for a daily newspaper and weekly panelist for a suddenly popular radio program I ran into an invisible obstruction. Of a fine morning I was halted by one of my fellow hirelings in the *New York Times* office and asked how I got away with it.

"With what?"

"With appearing regularly on a sponsored radio program. Don't you know *Times* men are forbidden to do that?"

I certainly did not. It was the first I had heard of any such restriction. My informant went on to tell me that Olin Downes, the noted music critic of the *Times*, had to turn down a fine offer for a radio program on music when the office had ruled against it. Apparently the point was that the good name of the *New York Times* was not to be peddled over the air by any staff member for individual profit. It sounded reasonable enough to me but I never had given it a thought up to that moment.

I went immediately to the lair of Managing Editor Edwin L. James and told all. Evidently he didn't listen to such radio shows as Information Please and seemed surprised to hear that I was a regular on it. James was short, chunky, clever and cynical. He was a chain smoker of cigarettes with a hacking cough to match. He seemed more amused than startled at my confession of guilt. He chuckled briefly, tapped the ashes from his cigarette and said: "Well, I haven't had any complaint yet so I guess no harm has been done. But you'll have to quit that radio program."

"I can't quit."

"Why not?"

"Because I've signed a contract that runs for two years."

"What in the world did you do that for?"

"For two hundred dollars a week."

This was what Dan Golenpaul was paying me for having forty-five minutes of fun with wonderful company once a week and it just matched the sum that the *Times* was paying me for working uncounted hours as a sports columnist seven days a week. I didn't go into these financial comparisons with Mr. James. I merely waited for his decision.

He stared at me, grunted, coughed, flicked some more ashes from his cigarette, looked at me pityingly as though I were the victim of some silly accident and said that he would have to take the matter up with "the people upstairs," meaning Arthur Hays Sulzberger, the publisher.

I had little more than a nodding acquaintance with Mr. Sulzberger as our paths crossed in the office, but I knew that he liked the way I wrote the sports column and would be reluctant to cast me into exterior darkness because of an unwitting infraction of the *Times* house rules. It turned out that way. In a few days I was summoned by Edwin L. James and informed of a slight revision in the *Times* house rules on radio work for staff members.

1. Since I had signed a contract, I could carry it out. But I was not to renew that contract or sign any other contract for radio work.

2. My connection with the *Times* was not to be mentioned on the air or in any advertisement of the program.

3. The general ban on radio work by staff members was to be maintained. Nobody else on the staff was to do deliberately what I had done unwittingly — but very luckily.

Within a few years these house rules were gone and forgotten. Radio had become too important to be snubbed in that fashion. When World War II broke out even the good gray *Times* had to admit the superiority of the microphone over the printing press in spreading instant news from battle zones all over the globe. The voices of Lowell Thomas, H. V. Kaltenborn and Gabriel Heatter were heard in every home. Stage and screen stars were flocking into radio, too. Everybody listened to Bob Hope, Bing Crosby, Fred Allen and Jack Benny. When our literate quiz program went to the head of its class with a rush, Messrs. Adams, Fadiman, Levant and Kieran suddenly found themselves notables in the entertainment field. Stranger things may have happened but none comes to mind at the moment.

As the fame of the program soared, the attitude of the *Times* hierarchy toward my part in it changed radically. At the expiration of my original contract to appear as a member of the cast I signed a new one to continue and nobody at the office as much as blinked. Indeed, Edwin L. James remarked to me in a seemingly casual way in the office one day that he was sure it would be all right now to have me identified on the air as a *Times* man. When I told that to Dan Golenpaul he grinned wickedly. The original *Times* attitude had roused his ire. He wouldn't even accept unconditional surrender. No mention of my connection with the *Times* ever was made on the program, but when I switched to doing a general column on the now defunct *Sun* in 1943, I was immediately announced as "John Kieran, columnist for the *New York Sun*." A small matter. It didn't hurt the *Times* and it didn't save the *Sun*. And it made no difference to me.

Until Dan Golenpaul came along with his format for Information Please, the popular quiz shows on radio featured a glib master of ceremonies directing questions at volunteer victims on a stage or persons picked at random from a studio audience. Anyone who answered a question correctly was suitably rewarded. "Thirty silver dollars to the lady with the flowered hat!" or "Give that gentleman in the gallery twelve silver dollars!" The studio audience cheered. That part of it was jolly enough. But too often the exposure of the utter ignorance of the persons to whom comparatively simple questions were put was embarrassing. The Golenpaul scheme was to reverse that process. Have the public direct questions at persons who might be reasonably expected to give a good answer.

Thus the first order of business when we went on the air each week was a recital by Clifton Fadiman of "how we play this game." Listeners could send in questions on anything under the sun. If the question was used, the sender would receive a copy of the *Encyclopaedia Britannica* Book of Maps. If the question "stumped the experts," the sender would receive in addition the 24-volume set of the *Encyclopaedia Britannica* and, through the war years, a $50 war bond. The sender of any question had to include his own idea of the correct answer — or answers in case the question was divided into different parts, as most of them were.

On multi-part questions the panelists usually were required to "get three out of four" or perhaps "four out of five," but if we hadn't been giving away enough sets of the encyclopaedia, Mr. Fadiman would calmly change that to "Get all on this," or even strain a point to call a decision against us and in favor of the sender of the question. Such an attitude won the favor of the listening audience, of course, and the *Encyclopaedia Britannica* publishers didn't balk at it a bit. For a few hundred dollars a night they gained greater identification with the Information Please program than the various sponsors who paid as much as $12,500 a performance to keep us on the air. Many topical jokes and humorous drawings of that period — some in *The New Yorker* — were based on these rewards of sets of the *Britannica* to those who "stumped the experts."

What quickly made the program exceptional and outstanding was the quality of the guests who were persuaded to appear on the panel. They came because the show was literate as well as consistently entertaining. They expected to enjoy themselves and most of them did. We had famous authors, college presidents and professors, United States senators and representatives, members of the President's cabinet, governors and mayors, top scientists and many of the stars of stage, screen and radio. Wendell Willkie first caught the attention of the general public by his apt and genial answers when he was a guest on our program and added much to his popularity when he appeared with us in two "movie shorts" of Information Please. Indeed, the release of the first of these films while Willkie was trying to get the Republican nomination for President in the late spring of 1940 won him such favorable comment that through Ed Flynn, Democratic political boss and attorney for the movie company that was distributing our "movie shorts," the second film with Willkie in it was kept off the screen until after the November election. Not that it would have made any difference, but politicians never take a chance if they can help it.

It is necessary to explain all this now because, just as in Egypt there arose a king who knew not Joseph, since Information Please went over the hill there has arisen a whole generation that never heard the program or saw the films, which, incidentally, were untimely burned to death in a storage warehouse fire on New York's West Side. Brought up on a spate of quite different types of quiz shows featuring giveaway gambling and even criminal skulduggery, this younger generation could have no idea of the intelligent entertain-

ment offered by our show and the innocent merriment it gen-
erated for listeners of all ages across the country. Getting the
right guests was the most important part of the production.
Giving a right answer was the least important contribution by
any guest or regular on the panel. It was generally more fun
when the answer was wrong, especially if the culprit tried to
wriggle out of it. An uproarious error or a brilliant bit of ir-
relevance was rated far above any dull delivery of truth.

It was Clifton Fadiman, of course, who kept things
stirred up when we were on the air. He was perfect in the
part of master of ceremonies for such a program — cultured,
witty and perfectly poised. Quick on the trigger, too.
Never thrown for a loss by an unexpected answer, and we
had some dazzlers, most of them from Oscar Levant, a composer who was never composed. Oscar couldn't sit still. He
fidgeted. He shuffled his feet, drummed with his fingers on
the table, hummed under his breath and whistled softly between his teeth. One night he answered a question on botany
correctly. It stunned the studio audience. It stunned me,
too. I was the one who was expected to answer questions in
natural history. This led to a brisk debate on one occasion.

Some listener had sent in a question on the average life-span
of different creatures. Ordinarily such questions and the answers that came with them were checked for accuracy by the
Information Please staff but apparently the office library
had no book containing figures on such life expectancies and
the card reached Mr. Fadiman's hands with the sender's figures
intact. There were four or five parts to the question. Since
little is known about the life-span of creatures in the wild,
all I could do was guess. Mr. Fadiman, consulting his card,
called every one of my guesses wrong.

The sharpest dissent was over the average life-span of the
downy woodpecker. Because of predators, storms, parasites

and other avian plagues, most of our small birds lead short and not necessarily merry lives. I put the average life-span of the downy woodpecker at perhaps three years, certainly not more than five. Mr. Fadiman informed me, on the authority of the card he held in his hand, that the average downy wood-pecker pounded tree trunks for twenty-three years before it shuffled off this mortal coil. I informed Mr. Fadiman, with-out consulting any card, that this was a lot of applesauce and asked him how many downy woodpeckers of that age he knew. Thus challenged, he admitted that he had no personal acquaintance with downy woodpeckers of any age and would defer decision on the whole question for a week, pending in-vestigation.

I spent that week thumbing reference books on the sub-ject and consulting my friends at the Bronx Zoo and the American Museum of Natural History. The experts I con-sulted agreed unanimously that the life-spans Mr. Fadiman had on his card were ridiculous and they wondered where they had been manufactured. It turned out that the sender of the question had gleaned his answers from a "filler paragraph" in an almanac stuffed with articles on astrology and studded with illustrated advertisements for patent medicines. The de-cision on the appeal was a verdict for me by the whole court. The sender of the question received a book of maps but not a single volume of the *Encyclopaedia Britannica*.

There was no other pitched battle over the facts of life on the program but I remember another official answer that I challenged because it dealt with a matter of spelling that al-ways raised my body temperature. The question concerned one of the minor horrors of war, the way English and Ameri-can soldiers in Europe mispronounced the names of cities and towns on the Continent. Ypres, for instance, was "Wip-ers" to the British Tommies in Belgium in World War I. I have forgotten the other sections of the question but what stirred me up was Mr. Fadiman's request for the proper spelling and the French pronunciation of the city that our soldiers referred to as "Reems." I put my hand up and so did Mr. Adams. He was called upon and spelled out the name of the city in six letters; R-H-E-I-M-S.

"Right," said Mr. Fadiman. "Now, give us the French pronunciation."

Mr. Adams made a stab at it and I winced.

"Don't you like his pronunciation?" Mr. Fadiman asked me.

"I don't even like his spelling."

Mr. Fadiman, who knew French and had spent a year in Paris as a postgraduate student, was taken aback. He asked what was wrong with the spelling. I said that the French spelled it "Reims," with no "h" in it. Mr. Fadiman seemed doubtful. He looked at his card. It read "Rheims" and he said so. I suggested that he look at the label of any bottle of champagne from the Reims district. He said he had no such bottle on him at the moment but would be glad to inspect one if I would provide it after the show.

The reason I knew the French spelling of Reims was that for years I had taken an irritated interest in the general slaughtering of names of foreign cities in English print. I often made cursory remarks on the subject and the word "cursory" is here used entirely for its sound effect. In the case of "Rheims," a common misprint in English, what I wanted to know was who the H — put that "h" in Reims and for what foul purpose. Take the busy French city of Lyon on the Rhone. It always comes out "Lyons" in English type. The famous old seaport of Marseille is similarly fouled up when mentioned in print here or in England. An infernal "s" is tacked on for no good reason that I ever heard.

I go even further in the matter. I do not believe that Rome, Venice, Genoa and Turin in print are any improvement over the authentic Roma, Venezia, Genova and Torino. I prefer Firenze to Florence any day in the week. Firenze has a tang that Florence lacks. Of course, this callous slaughtering goes on in all countries and all languages. Changes are understandable and often necessary where different script systems present puzzles, but there is no reason for any change in spelling from one country to another where the same alphabet is in use. Perhaps we can't pronounce the name of a foreign city the way the natives do but at least we could write it the same way when we use the same alphabet.

I make no unreasonable demands. I am ready to compromise where a cedilla, tilde, umlaut, grave or acute accent or other diacritical mark in a foreign language complicates the transliteration into English, and I never give battle over pronunciation. Even so, we often do better with pronunciation than we do with spelling. Few of us speak Spanish but most of us have no trouble with San Jose and even the least literate of the Hollywood film colony knows how to pronounce La Jolla.

That this protest is vain is certain. Reims will continue to appear as "Rheims" on our maps and in our newspaper stories. Marseille will not be able to shake off the "s," nor Lyon either. Logic is useless. Argument is futile, particularly on literate matters in a land where any observance of syntax is looked upon as pure affectation. I note that even Eric Partridge, the British philosophic grammarian, states in his *Usage and Abusage:* "In America, 'it's me' is acceptable colloquial speech; that is, it is used in good speech."

Acceptable to whom? But there again I fall afoul of Partridge for in *A Charm of Words,* a more recent opus, he ventures the prophecy that "whom" will disappear from the language, to leave "who" the only form apart from "whose." He adds that "like" will probably succeed "as" or at least to be used indifferently for it. I mourn that he may be correct. We now have on radio and television a blaring boast of a cigarette that "tastes good like a cigarette should" and a popular television panel show flaunting the title "Who Do You Trust?"

I trust nobody who murders grammar in that brutal fashion. As to the cigarette that "tastes good like a cigarette should," I suspect that the phrase was launched in ignorance and continued in arrogance. Some years ago I was in a room crowded with sports writers among whom was Ford Frick, now Commissioner of Baseball, when the door opened and the newcomer asked indignantly: "Who pinched my bottle of Scotch yesterday?"

Amid a general outcry of "Not me!" there was one loud and clear "Not I." In the momentary silence that followed the denials Ford Frick remarked with a grin: "Well, I heard Kieran."

I couldn't help it. That's the way I was brought up. My excuse is that my mother and father were trained as teachers. Our English was regularly corrected at the table. At any mistake my father's finger would go up and he would catechize the offender: "Subject? Predicate? Object?" It's laughable to note that those who say "It's me" are the same persons who say "Between you and I." Ignorance can't be the answer to a paradox like that. It must be human perversity.

There is no inclination here to be stiff and starchy about it. I am as ready as the next man to split an infinitive with a friend and I agree most heartily with the reported announcement by Sir Winston Churchill when some purist revised one of his wartime sentences because it ended with a preposition: "This is the sort of nonsense up with which I will not put!"

No one of us can afford to be captious. All of us make mistakes and English admittedly is a somewhat lawless language. But gross errors in grammar are an affront to common decency in the use of our language. The worst feature of this "old abusing of God's patience and the king's English" is the endorsement of error by those whose duty it is to correct it. We can forgive the untutored or the careless, but when "It's me," "Those kind" and "Who for?" are defended by dictionary editors and college professors on the basis of "usage," I am horrified and I call down maledictions on their heads. They are guilty of base betrayal of a cultural trust and may be indicted further for aiding and abetting manslaughter of the English language.

Probably I am on the losing side in this battle and ultimately will be overwhelmed by the apostles of ignorance but in the interim I will be firing away at the rascals at every opportunity. My model is Robert Browning's young man with a horn who said in a similarly desperate situation:

There they stood, ranged along the hillside, met
To view the last of me, a living frame
For one more picture! In a sheet of flame
I saw them and I knew them all. And yet
Dauntless the slug-horn to my lips I set
And blew: "Childe Roland to the Dark Tower came."

VI

POLITICAL PLAY IN ONE ACT

M ENTION of Wendell Willkie a few pages back reminds me of my one and only plunge into politics. I went overboard for Willkie in the 1940 presidential campaign. To mix a nice dry metaphor, you might call this my swan dive in the political pool. I never came up again.

Not that I lost interest in registering my indignation at the polls every November. Only once since I came of age did I fail to vote on Election Day and that lone exception was not my fault. Even in 1917, when I was in France with the Eleventh Engineers, we filed our "soldier votes" on the banks of the Somme and they were duly counted back in New York. But in November, 1918, still in France, I was temporarily separated from my unit. I had been sent to the Engineer Officer Candidate School at Langres where we had excellent instruction, more work than we could handle, less food than we could eat and no voting facilities at all. Beyond that, I have been as regular at the polls as the tally clerks, the party watchers and the uniformed police in the background.

Most of us come by our politics the way we come by our religion — we inherit it. My mother and father were Democrats. Indeed, my mother's name was on the ballot in 1920 as a presidential elector on the Democratic ticket, the first time women were eligible for such honor, but since Warren G. Harding, Republican, defeated James M. Cox, Democrat, on that occasion, my mother was not present when the electoral college convened. I followed the family tradition through 1932 when I cast my vote for Franklin Delano Roosevelt with extra enthusiasm for a number of reasons. One was that the Kierans looked upon him as a Dutchess County neighbor and something of a family friend. My mother and father had a speaking acquaintance with him through occasional meetings at political, social or educational functions and my brother James, a legislative correspondent for the *New York Times* at Albany during Roosevelt's terms as Governor, was intimate with the Roosevelt clan and often stayed with them at Hyde Park or Warm Springs.

I remember my mother telling me that at one gathering where the then Governor was the center of attraction, she pointed to him and quoted Miranda in *The Tempest* to his mother, the dowager Sara Delano Roosevelt: "There's nothing ill can dwell in such a temple." My mother believed that to her last days but I lived longer and changed my mind. Politically, I mean. I met him only once when he was in the White House. That was in early October, 1933, when the New York Giants and the Washington Senators were the contenders in the World Series. Clark Griffith, owner of the Senators, made arrangements for the assembled baseball writers in Washington to go down to the White House to shake hands with the President. We were identified by name and by newspaper as we filed past. F.D.R. gave me an extra shake and started to say something about my family but already the next man was upon him and he had to break it off. However, he meant to be friendly and I felt greatly honored.

Even so, by 1936 I had enough of the New Deal and cast my

vote for Alf Landon, though I knew I might as well have cast it for Paul Revere. A Roosevelt triumph was a sure thing and there was no sense in getting stirred up during the formalities preceding the election. But by 1940 there was a different story. World War II was on in Europe. A third term for any President was a big issue. Some of Roosevelt's zealous New Deal agents had been making enemies all over the place. Farmers had been in revolt. And Wendell Willkie came out of nowhere to strike the public fancy as a likely candidate on the Republican side. This might be the real thing instead of a sham battle like 1936.

Who trapped me into risking a broken head at the hustings I do not remember but it must have been a comparative stranger, because nine out of ten of my friends, cronies and co-workers in what we like to call "the creative arts" — the theatre, music, sculpture, painting, newspaper work, the writing of books and so forth — were devout followers of F.D.R. and considered it blasphemous to utter a word of criticism of him or his policies. They were astonished and grieved to discover that I was a sneak in the grass on the wrong side of the fence during the 1940 presidential campaign. If I had remained quiet I probably would have escaped notice but reticence was never one of my outstanding faults. Egged on by a group labeled American Writers for Wendell L. Willkie, I dashed off a manifesto that the group released for immediate publication. I was merely one of perhaps two dozen reckless writers who were allowed this method of rushing to their doom. My manifesto was too long, too discursive, perhaps a bit irrelevant in part. I have removed some of the excess and offer here only the essentials — without a word changed, or a sentiment, either — though in doing so I realize that once again, in the joyous phrasing of James Stephens, I may be "exhibiting myself naked to the blushes of eternity." Anyway, this was it and I still can produce a copy of the original document to prove it.

WHY I WANT WILLKIE
BY JOHN KIERAN

I want Wendell L. Willkie for President because:

I do not believe that any nation can live indefinitely on a diet of pie in the sky.

I do not believe that an increase of $25,000,000,000 in the national debt over a period of seven years can be explained away as social welfare on a large scale, even in a soothing voice.

I do not believe that the way to pull out of a depression is to pile on the debt.

I do not believe that the lot of the poor and the hungry can be permanently improved by paying farmers not to raise hogs, cattle, wheat and potatoes.

I am opposed to a Third Term, a Fourth Term, a Fifth Term and so on to the nth degree.

I believe that the doctrine of the indispensability of one man may be sound under a dictatorship, but is untenable in a democracy.

I think that Wendell Willkie or two hundred other sensible citizens could put a stop to a lot of foolishness in Washington and get us all back to honest work in the field or factory and common sense in government. But Wendell Willkie is the one who has been nominated to carry the ball, so I'm for him.

I believe that the Constitution of the United States, the code of fair play, the principles of common sense and the rules of simple arithmetic have been trampled all over by the New Dealers and we had better get back to earth before we are kicked off it.

I know Wendell Willkie. I admired him before I ever saw him. The more I know him, the better I like him. He's a worker. He's a real democrat. I believe Wendell Willkie and his cause represent the best interest of all the citizens of this country.

That's why I am for Wendell L. Willkie.

Quite a blast for a bird watcher, I'd say. The general reaction of my friends and acquaintances matched that of Macduff when he emerged from viewing the corpse of Duncan, foully slain by Macbeth: "O horror! horror! horror! Tongue nor heart cannot conceive nor name thee." All my chums on the staff of the *Times*, everybody connected with Information Please, male and female, were shocked and heartbroken at my falling from grace in this grotesque fashion.

I tried to fight back but I was overwhelmed. Dan Golenpaul, Kip Fadiman, Oscar Levant and Franklin P. Adams, enthusiasts on the other side, treated me as though I were the victim of a bad accident or a mental seizure. "Hush! Don't upset John. Don't move him unless you have to. He'll be all right after Election Day."

I heard that Elmer Davis, whom I had always admired, was displeased with my position on the Willkie side. I sent him a copy of my manifesto and asked him to tell me what was wrong with it. He sent it back with one line of comment: "I don't think it's in your best style."

I would agree to that. It could have been much shorter and better. Indeed, I thought my friend Don Herold, famous for his hilarious drawings and dead-pan humorous writing, did better than all the rest of us put together with one line in his statement of why he wanted Willkie, to wit: "I think Franklin D. Roosevelt has done this country enough good."

However, there were more than 27,000,000 voters who didn't think so. We were snowed under at the polls. I had to take it standing up. Our radio show, Information Please, was on the air election night and I stood around with others of our group in front of the big board at NBC headquarters for election returns and watched the Roosevelt tide roll in. The only one missing from our crowd was Franklin P. Adams who, as soon as we were off the air, dashed downstairs to a waiting car that carried him to Hyde Park where he was to enjoy the returns at the Roosevelt fireside with the family and a few old friends. Frank told me later that Mrs. Eleanor Roosevelt asked him how I could possibly be against her husband. She had always thought better of me than that. I think she did, as a matter of fact, from the flattering references she made to me occasionally in her newspaper column "My Day." Frank made an attempt to palliate my crime by saying: "He's against a third term."

That was polite and the truth but not the whole truth. Anyway, it served its purpose of pacifying the First Lady and persuading her that I was not a completely lost soul. The story I like best of the election was of the ebullient Roosevelt rooter who went off on a spree to celebrate the victory and, when he recovered three or four days later, confessed with remorse: "I over-gloated!"

That finished my career as a participant in active partisan politics. Liberals were in the saddle and riding high, wide and handsome. In those days "Conservative" was a dirty word whereas a Liberal was a fine fellow by his own definition. A man might better have admitted bigamy, the rifling of poor boxes and a penchant for pushing dear old ladies under speeding beer trucks than any leaning to the conservative side in politics. It came close to being a hanging offense. When charged with being a Conservative I would say "Guilty!" and run for my life. I am still a Conservative but I'm no longer running. At my age it would be undignified. I walk about quietly and no man's hand is raised against me. I sit at ease and enjoy the benefits of the semi-welfare state with equanimity. If my fellow citizens want it this way, I

can take it in stride to the end of the road in perfect contentment and this brief account of my one outburst of belliger-
ence in politics is merely a nostalgic tale of

> *. . . old, unhappy far-off things,*
> *And battles long ago.*

VII

THE GUEST LIST

Taking to the air again, it usually is somebody else who brings it up but, when it is mentioned, I am inclined to boast of the guest list we had on Information Please. In the decade that we were on the air it ran to more than four hundred notables of one sort or another and included famous authors, prominent educators, great musicians, top scientists, important government officials and, in the old-fashioned phrase of those days, "stars of stage, screen and radio." Television, so universal today, wasn't a domestic issue at the time. It had only sprouted when World War II came along to stunt its growth "for the duration." Until the fighting stopped and civilian shortages were replaced by war surpluses, men, women and children still went to the movies regularly and listened to radio religiously.

After a few daring celebrities took the plunge and came on the program with us, the rush was on. Everybody was eager to get into the act. Being a guest on Information Please became a badge of distinction, the equivalent of being tapped for skill and brains. Since I always stood in awe of policemen, uniformed doormen, income tax examiners and anybody in public office, I'll start by ticking off the names of some of the government officials who sat in with us from time to time.

From the United States Senate we had Alben Barkley who later became Vice President, Theodore Green, who lived to be the oldest member of the Upper House, Charley Tobey who sang hymns and knew the Old Testament by heart, Henry Cabot Lodge, Jr., who left "the world's most exclusive club" to join the Tank Corps in North Africa and John J. Sparkman who is still a member of the club. From the Lower House we had, among others, James W. Fulbright and Lister Hill who grew up to the senators, and Clare Boothe Luce who became an ambassadress. From Franklin D. Roosevelt's cabinet we had Postmaster General James A. Farley who directed that his fee for appearing on the program be divided into three parts and turned over to Catholic, Protestant and Jewish charities and Secretary of the Interior Harold L. Ickes who did not.

From the ranks of reigning or retired inhabitants of gubernatorial mansions we had Harold Stassen of Minnesota, Alfred E. Smith of New York, Ellis Arnall of Georgia, and dear old Wilbur Cross of Connecticut, former dean of the Yale Graduate School and four times governor of the Nutmeg State. He was a delightful gentleman with greater knowledge than all the rest of us put together but "rising eighty" when he came on the program and too slow of speech and hearing to do himself justice. He fell behind thinking up a good answer to the first question and never did catch up in our half-hour on the air that night. My heart bled for him.

To the best of my recollection we had only one mayor on the program but he was a sizzler. It was "The Little Flower," alias "The Hat," New York's famous Fiorello La Guardia. He was ready with an answer before the question was half finished. He even came up with answers that were not in question. Incidentally, the other guest on the program with

La Guardia was my brother James who was his press secretary at City Hall at the time. They had an explosive parting shortly thereafter. My newspaper friends on the City Hall beat told me it was more spectacular than the Fourth of July fireworks at Coney Island.

When the United Nations came into being we dipped into that august assembly for some special guests, the first of whom was a homebred, our own Dr. Ralph Bunche. A Canadian who made an instant hit with us and our listeners was Lester B. Pearson, now Prime Minister of his country. He enjoyed himself so much that he came back to share the fun three or four times. We regulars on the program had our favorites among the "repeater guests" and "Mike" Pearson was well up on our list. Another "repeater guest" from the United Nations was Sir Gladwyn Jebb, Britain's representative who later became a neighbor of mine in Riverdale where we went on several bird walks together. From my limited experience with titled English visitors I suspect that the first book they put in the hands of their children is a bird guide. From my point of view, a very good idea.

Musical questions probably gave our listeners more cause for laughter than any topics with which we tangled. Since Oscar Levant was with us every other week, he answered most of them and Oscar was always good for a bright response edged with acid. F.P.A. knew all the old popular ballads and he had Gilbert and Sullivan by heart. I began playing the piano by ear when I was five years old and have kept it up relentlessly ever since despite some protests from the strangest places — musical circles, for instance. I used to set A. A. Milne's verse and Mother Goose rhymes to music and sing them to my own children when they were too small to defend themselves. Indeed, I composed — words and music — a lullaby for them that was published under the title "Little

Son of Mine" by the John Church Company of Philadelphia and sung on the radio by Lanny Ross among others.

I confess now that in my youth I cheated a little in my playing "by ear." In our home we had a player piano into which we fed rolls of perforated paper that, as we pumped away with our feet, produced as far as a piano could the music of Beethoven, Bach, Rossini, Verdi and all the other standard composers. We had a large library of rolls and I played many of them until I knew them by heart. Then I would work out my own rendition of them as best I could. Where the complicated chords or the ascending or descending runs were too difficult for me to catch by ear, I would slow down the tempo of the machine and watch the exact order or the combinations in which the keys went down! That's how I learned the tough parts. There was, however, one other difficulty. Like most persons who play by ear, I favor the black keys, so I had to do a lot of transposing to fit simple selections from Schubert or Schumann or Chopin into my repertoire, such as it is — or was. My fingers aren't as nimble as they were fifty years agone. One night Oscar Levant came into the studio while I was filling in some idle time on the piano and, after listening a moment, said: "Ha! He's playing the Melody in F in F sharp!"

Guilty as charged. It was the only way I could play it at all. Our staff pianist, who was with us throughout our years on the air, was Joe Kahn, who was also the regular pianist for the NBC orchestra that had been assembled to perform under the baton of that maestro of maestros, Arturo Toscanini. Joe's customary chore was to play a few bars or a short passage from some opus and our problem was to name the piece or the composer — or perhaps we were requested to sing the chorus of some old song after Joe had played the verse.

Once Joe played a series of cadenzas and the panel was

asked to tell what well-known selection each cadenza was introducing. I remember that question in particular because, with Oscar off for the evening, Sir Thomas Beecham was our musical guest and, after answering three parts of the question without hesitation, he was stumped on the fourth — which I knew! As originally written by Tchaikovsky for the harp, it was the cadenza leading into the "Waltz of the Flowers" in the *Nutcracker Suite*. I happened to know it because I loved the *Nutcracker Suite* and often played the record on the victrola at home.

The most striking of all answers about music on our program came in response to a question that wasn't even on the card. That perfect gentleman and pluperfect pianist, Artur Rubinstein, was one of the two guests that evening and at one point Joe Kahn played brief passages from great piano compositions and it was up to Artur, who appeared with us half a dozen times at least, to identify the source of each excerpt and name the composer. One brief fast passage baffled him. He thought it over, shook his head and gave up. Reading from the card, Mr. Fadiman named the work and the composer.

"Ah, yes" said Mr. Rubinstein, "it's a piece you don't often hear — but I should have recognized it."

After announcing that a set of the *Encyclopedia Britannica* would go to the questioner who had "stumped the experts," Mr. Fadiman went on cheerfully: "Well, we missed that one, but I think we can all agree that our studio pianist, Mr. Kahn, played the passage very well. Wouldn't you say so, Mr. Rubinstein?"

The maestro considered the matter for perhaps half a second and then said firmly: "No!"

On a national hookup! The studio audience roared with laughter. Kip Fadiman, when he managed to stop laughing himself, said: "That's a conversation-stopper if I ever heard one."

By that time Mr. Rubinstein was as embarrassed as his innocent victim, Joe Kahn, but nothing could be done about it. The critical word had been heard from coast to coast. We went on to the next question.

Of course we understood and so did Joe Kahn and anybody who knew anything about music. There was Joe sitting at a piano on a stage, waiting to jump into short and complicated passages from difficult pieces of music. In each case and at a given signal he was to begin nowhere and end nowhere so to speak. Nobody could be expected to play such bits perfectly. Artur Rubinstein said he couldn't. That was enough to mollify Joe Kahn, who had quickly recovered from his state of shock.

There were no other musical crises on the program that I recall except one where I flunked out because I was armed with the wrong instrument. That evening the panel consisted of F.P.A., Oscar, Ethel Barrymore and the then sports columnist of the *New York Times* whose name escapes me for the moment. We had to be on our guard against trick questions like "How far can a Bombay duck fly?" The answer is: As far as you can throw it. Bombay duck is a fish curry dish served in India. Or another question might be: "In what part of your house would you put a set of Napier's Tables if somebody gave them to you?" On the bookshelf; they are tables of logarithms. On the musical side it might be: "The name of what opera might be construed as a command to a man to speak out?" Wilhelm, Tell! Or "What familiar operatic aria might a milkman warble in praise of his wares?" Answer — hold on to your hat!: "Ah, So Pure" from *Martha*. Often the answering panelist might be required to sing or whistle part of the answer to prove that he really knew the music.

The questions just presented were mere inventions of my disordered mind but they give you an idea of what we might expect when we sat down and faced Mr. Fadiman on the other side of the stage. I don't remember the question that brought the instrumental music into play the night Ethel Barrymore was with us but the accepted answer was the title of some popular song that all of us knew. "Play it together!" commanded Mr. Fadiman. It was a surprise to us but not to the stagehands. An extra piano was on the platform that night. Oscar took that. Joe Kahn gallantly yielded his piano to Miss Barrymore. A page boy who sneaked up from behind handed Franklin P. Adams a harmonica, on which he fancied himself a virtuoso, and another page boy deposited a full-size piano accordion beside my chair. The others started off without waiting for me: By the time I had lifted the instrument, worked my arms through the straps and settled myself comfortably in harness, the others were playing the closing chords of the musical offering. I never sounded a note on the accordion, which probably was all for the best. Oh, yes, I had one at home and played it often enough, if that's the right phrase. Eventually I grew tired of lifting the accordion and gave it to the three teen-age sons of my brother Laurence, though I was always very fond of him.

You might think that the night would be filled with music if Helen Traubel and Lauritz Melchior were on the premises but the night they sat in with us was filled with laughter. They came on thinking it might be fun and so it was, but they furnished most of it. Lawrence Tibbett was almost prim. Leonard Bernstein, just beginning his rise to fame, was eager and accurate. Alec Templeton was rollicking all the way. Yehudi Menuhin and his sister Hepzibah, the pianist, were genial and delightful. Sigmund Spaeth, tennis writer, music critic and "tune detective," was most amusing. Our all-around music man and hasty entry when expected guests had to cancel at the last minute was Deems Taylor. He was as much at home on the program as any of us.

Possibly because I was supposed to answer any questions about the birds and the bees, we had comparatively few naturalists as guests on the program. Another reason for the scarcity of wildlife experts was that Dan Golenpaul, native New Yorker, had no use for country life. Where the pavement ended, Dan was at the end of his rope. Since he made up the guest list, few naturalists slipped past his guard. However, among those who somehow made it past Mr. Golenpaul and joined us on the panel at various times were Sir Julian Huxley, the English biologist, Roy Chapman Andrews, fossil hunter and Asian explorer, William Beebe who was at home anywhere in the world but gained his greatest fame through his descents into the sea in his "bathysphere," Robert Cushman Murphy, renowned ornithologist, Clyde Fisher, head of the Hayden Planetarium in New York, Harlow Shapley, Harvard astronomer, and Donald Culross Peattie, who needs no introduction to anyone in this country who can read English.

We had a number of sports notables on in season: players, writers and sports announcers and officials. From the tennis courts we had Helen Wills, Alice Marble and Big Bill Tilden. From the prize ring — Mr. Golenpaul was a boxing buff and so was Oscar Levant — we had Gene Tunney, the "Student Prince" of the heavyweight realm, and Mickey Walker, yclept "The Toy Bulldog," former middleweight champion of the world who worked on a different kind of canvas when he retired from the ring. He took up painting and a New York gallery was advertising a one-man show of Mickey Walker canvases when he came on the program with us. We also had Colonel Eddie Eagan, former intercollegiate and Olympic boxing champion who served a term as chairman of the boxing commission in New York.

Eddie was a Yale man and a Rhodes Scholar. Brigadier General John Reed Kilpatrick was a Yale man (All-America end twice) and a French scholar, but what induced Dan Golenpaul to invite him to join us for an evening was that he was the president of Madison Square Garden and therefor one of the top sports figures of the day. At the opening of the baseball season or around world series time we usually asked some baseball official or famous player to take a seat on our bench. One was Ford Frick, then president of the National League. We like to think that he did so well on the program that they made him Commissioner of Baseball. We also had Frank Frisch, the "Fordham Flash," who turned out to be a specialist on Wagnerian opera, Tommy Henrich of the Yankees whose vice was choral singing, Lefty Gomez, who was most amusing if you didn't have to bat against him, and Moe Berg, baseball's One-Man Mystery — honor graduate of Princeton, student at the Sorbonne, world traveler, multiple linguist, barrister at law and one of the "Cloak and Dagger" OSS adventurers in World War II.

Grantland Rice was with us several times and made a wonderful guest. The "Old Master" of the sports writing clan was a poet at heart and deep student of world history. He was also about as fine a gentleman as I ever had the luck to meet. Our paths crossed briefly in France during World War I and I like to remember him as a soldier-poet and author of these lines:

> *All wars are planned by older men,*
> *In council rooms apart,*
> *Who call for greater armament*
> *And map the battle chart.*
>
> *But out along the shattered field*
> *Where golden dreams turn gray,*
> *How very young the faces were*
> *Where all the dead men lay.*

Portly and solemn, in their pride,
  The elders cast their vote
For this or that, or something else,
  That sounds the martial note.

But where their sightless eyes stare out
  Beyond life's vanished joys,
I've noticed nearly all the dead
  Were hardly more than boys.

Strong and yet curiously gentle; that was Grantland Rice. For a savage thrust on the same topic, consider Siegfried Sassoon's concluding lines on the suicide of a British Tommy in a rain-soaked, shell-shattered, rat-ridden, lice-infested trench in Flanders in World War I:

You smug-faced crowds with kindling eye
Who cheer when soldier lads march by,
Sneak home and pray you'll never know
The hell where youth and laughter go.

Quick march, now! We're on the way back from the cemetery. Here's a parade of a more cheerful kind, a list of some of the literary lions who appeared on our program. They are presented in alphabetical order to prevent quarrels over precedence or other disturbance of the peace.

Frederick Lewis Allen
Cleveland Amory
Stephen Vincent Benét
Louis Bromfield
Heywood Broun
John Mason Brown
Erskine Caldwell
Thomas B. Costain
Elmer Davis
John Erskine

Edna Ferber
C. S. Forester
Paul Gallico
Oliver St. John Gogarty
John Gunther
Ben Hecht
John Hersey
Clarence Budington Kelland
Sinclair Lewis

James Michener
Alice Duer Miller
John Marquand
Christopher Morley
Ogden Nash
John O'Hara
Dorothy Parker
S. J. Perelman
William Lyon Phelps
Quentin Reynolds
Robert Ruark
Morrie Ryskind

Carl Sandburg
Robert E. Sherwood
Jan Struther
Frank Sullivan
Dorothy Thompson
James Thurber
Louis Untermeyer
Carl Van Doren
Hendrik Van Loon
Rebecca West
Alexander Woollcott

Think of the fun of meeting that cast of characters in a game of questions and answers on almost every topic under the sun. No wonder we regulars looked forward each week to our sessions on the air. In many cases the appearance of an author on our program coincided with the publication of the aforesaid author's newest book, but there were some who liked the game so much that they turned up empty-handed (but never empty-headed) time and again. That group included Louis Bromfield, John Gunther, Christopher Morley, James Michener and Jan Struther, the dainty little English lady who wrote one book that most of us remember, *Mrs. Miniver*.

Christopher Morley was everybody's favorite, of course. He filled the night with literary lore and laughter. Louis Bromfield and I hit it off well together because of a common interest in farm life. When he discovered that I could hitch up a team, swing a scythe, handle bees and milk a cow, he and I became country cousins so to speak. He several times invited me to visit him on his famous Malabar Farm in Ohio but I never had a chance to make the trip. John Gunther, who wrote *Inside Europe, Inside Asia, Inside Latin America* and *Inside U.S.A.*, appeared with us each time he came outside, and twice just before he went inside again. James Michener, who had just bought a farm in the New Hope region of Pennsylvania, caught the bird-watching fever from sitting beside me too often. At his own request I measured him for a pair of field glasses and a Peterson's *Field Guide* and turned him loose. I warned him, however, that there was little money in it and he would do better to stick to dredging up a fortune from the South Pacific. The years proved that I was right. James went back to the South Pacific and made another great haul with *Paradise Revisited*. Solid man, Michener.

Clifton Fadiman, Frank Adams and I felt pretty much at home with these writing folk. Mr. Fadiman already had several books to his credit and F.P.A. had at least five books of light verse charged against him. I had turned out two volumes on sports and one tiny booklet on natural history. Of course, we were writing on a lower and less lucrative level — at least, I was — but we were veteran professionals at turning out printable, readable and profitable copy and were not frightened out of our wits when a best-selling author sat down to spar with us for an evening. On the contrary, we enjoyed it hugely and apparently our guests did, too.

Now for a partial list — no room for them all — of the "stars of stage, screen and radio" who spent at least one evening with us on the air. Once again the array is presented alphabetically for diplomatic reasons but added comment will be footloose and fancy free. Reader, "stand at gaze like Joshua's moon in Ajalon!"

Fred Allen
Gracie Allen
Ethel Barrymore
Richard Barthelmess

Louis Calhern
Frank Capra
Harry Carey
John Carradine

Madeline Carroll
Ilka Chase
Charles Coburn
George M. Cohan
Marc Connelly
Russel Crouse
Irene Dunne
Jimmy Durante
Faye Emerson
Reginald Gardiner
Lillian Gish
James Gleason
Ruth Gordon
Sir Cedric Hardwicke
Moss Hart
Alfred Hitchcock
Bob Hope
Leslie Howard
Ruth Hussey
Boris Karloff
Dennis King
Beatrice Lillie
Howard Lindsay

Gene Lockhart
Joshua Logan
Richard Maney
Fredric March
Herbert Marshall
Groucho Marx
Harpo Marx
James Mason
Raymond Massey
Burgess Meredith
Ray Milland
Robert Montgomery
Anna Neagle
David Niven
Walter Pidgeon
Basil Rathbone
Gregory Ratoff
George Sanders
Cornelia Otis Skinner
James Stewart
Dorothy Stickney
Clifton Webb
Orson Welles
Roland Young

Of those in the group "that from his Vintage rolling Time hath prest," all I can say is — borrowing from Bob Hope — "Thanks for the memory." Of Harry Carey in particular I recall that I asked him about a mutual acquaintance, the grim-faced, tight-lipped, hard-riding hero of so many early Western movies, William S. Hart. Carey had played with him in many films. Once I sat next to William S. Hart at some film industry luncheon and we discovered that we were companions in misery. We both were suffering from eye trouble and were under treatment by the same eye specialist.

Nothing cements a friendship faster than that. My eye trouble took a turn for the better. Hart's didn't; it was incurable. That was why I asked Harry Carey about him.

"Bad!" said Harry, shaking his head sadly. "Very bad. He's a lonely old man on a lonely ranch and he's slowly going blind. Do an act of charity and write to him."

I did write, received a friendly answer and kept up a sporadic correspondence with him until he died a few years later.

Fred Allen, Russel Crouse, Lillian Gish, Beatrice Lillie, Boris Karloff, Howard Lindsay, Raymond Massey, Gregory Ratoff, Cornelia Otis Skinner and Dorothy Stickney were frequent repeaters on our show. Indeed, Russel Crouse was our one-man rescue squad. He lived only a quarter of an hour from the studio, usually was in town and could jump in at the last moment when a scheduled guest failed to show up because of sickness or accident of one kind or another. On more than one occasion Russel filled in nobly as master of ceremonies when Clifton Fadiman was laid up for repairs.

During the war Dan Golenpaul took the show "on the road" at intervals to help the sale of war bonds or aid in Red Cross drives. Thus the program was staged in large auditoriums in Baltimore, Newark, Hartford, Chicago, Los Angeles, Washington and San Francisco where the tickets of admission went only to those who bought war bonds or contributed to the Red Cross drive. We went to Toronto on one occasion and to Montreal on another to help the sale of Canadian war bonds. Just what good cause we were helping when our show joined many others in a united program at Radio City I do not recall but I remember F.P.A.'s final fling at the close of our show. To add to the fun, Kip Fadiman came over to the answering side to join the regular Adams, Levant and Kieran trio and Fred Allen took Kip's place as master of ceremonies and tossed the questions at us.

Fred liked our show, came on with us as a guest panelist half a dozen times and, so far as I know, never accepted any money for appearing with us.

We were put through our paces on the forward section of the big stage and, instead of dropping the curtain on us at the finish, they began to lower our section of the stage out of sight behind the footlights. As a frequent cash customer in the huge theatre I often had seen the orchestra disappear in that way just before the movie of the week came on, but we hadn't been warned that we were to be lowered away and I was a bit startled when the platform began to sink under me. Not Franklin P. Adams! He stood up, waved in answer to the applause and just before our heads and shoulders disappeared into the lower depths he cupped his hands and shouted to the audience: "Don't forget to write!"

VIII

ADVENTURES WITH AN ASTRONOMER

O NE OF the best things that came out of my radio career in its early days was my acquaintance with Dr. Clyde Fisher, director of the Hayden Planetarium at the American Museum of Natural History. On a raw March day in 1939 I was pounding out a sports column in the *Times* office when the phone rang and, when I answered it, a strange voice asked whether or not I would like to see a *Bubo virginianus* on its nest. The caller announced his name, Herman Forster, said he was a neighbor of mine in Riverdale, knew from listening to Information Please that I was interested in birds, and could show me a great horned owl — the aforesaid *Bubo virginianus* — on its nest in Westchester if I would go with him the following Sunday morning.

The invitation was accepted and on the appointed day my volunteer guide picked me up at home, drove me out into Westchester and parked the car by the roadside at Wampus Pond just beyond Armonk. We circled the north end of the pond on foot, climbed a wooded cliff on the west side of the water and there, high up in a hemlock, was the big owl on its nest as advertised. It was the first time I ever had seen a great horned owl at its domestic chores and I was much in favor of keeping watch on the situation. We made an appointment for the following Sunday, each to have the privilege of bringing along a companion. On the second trip I brought my regular crony on outdoor expeditions, Fred Nagler, Riverdale neighbor, artist, lover of the outdoors and my walking companion for almost twenty years. He had the eyesight of an Indian Scout in enemy country and was tireless on the trail. Mr. Forster, who turned out to be an Assistant to the Commissioner of Water Supply, Gas and Electricity for New York City, brought along Dr. Clyde Fisher whom he introduced as the head man at the Hayden Planetarium.

This inaugurated a series of Sunday saunters that went on with few interruptions until Dr. Fisher's illness and death in 1949. He was a picturesque figure and a wonderful character. He was of sturdy build, broad-shouldered and stout-legged, with kindly features and a wide brow crowned with a great shock of thick white hair that never, to my knowledge, was sullied with a hat even on the coldest or the wettest day. It was an all-year all-weather snow-white hairdo and he carried it as dauntingly and flauntingly as ever the great Henri Quatre wore the white plume of Navarre.

Aside from that, he was an old hand at natural history and he taught me many things about plants, animals and the stars in the nearly ten years of our walks together. For one thing, he instructed me in the rudiments of systematic botany. Though he ended up as an astronomer and curator of the Hayden Planetarium, his earliest scientific honors, as well as his Ph.D. from Johns Hopkins, were won for work in the botanical field. In his later days, which was when I met him, his background was botany, his foreground was astronomy and his hobby was ornithology.

What a delightful companion he was on all those field trips! Despite his years and in defiance of his white hair, he was

full of youthful enthusiasm and, like the faithful followers of
Ulysses, "ever with a frolic welcome took the thunder and
the sunshine." He was a good storyteller and he had much to
talk about. He had been on botantical trips to the arctic
tundra and on eclipse expeditions to many parts of the world.
He had walked in the woods with John Burroughs. He had
talked with Albert Einstein. That statement clamors for a digression in which I will reveal the details of a great event in
my life.

On the afternoon of Monday October 11, 1943, the Yankees were playing the Cardinals at St. Louis in the fifth
and last game of the world series of that year. I was one of
a group of four heading for Princeton, New Jersey, in an
open roadster that afternoon and we were listening to the
radio account of the game as we rolled along. The driver of
the car was Nanette Fabray, the musical comedy star, and
the two other occupants were Dr. "Mandy" Mandelstam,
a dentist by profession but a theatrical buff and backer of
Broadway plays by preference, and Dr. Clyde Fisher who
had arranged the expedition. We were on our way to have
tea with Dr. Albert Einstein at his Princeton residence near
the Institute for Advanced Study where he was then working.

It was a most successful afternoon for traveling New
Yorkers. On the way down Miss Fabray stopped at a filling
station to phone her agent back in town. There had been
hot competition for the leading part in an upcoming musical
comedy. When she came out of the phone booth she was
jumping for joy. She had won. The Yankees also won,
bringing the 1943 world championship to New York in a
five-game series. And we four callers on Dr. Einstein had a
wonderful time with the great man.

He was busy with another visitor when we arrived and his

secretary ushered us into the garden. When he came out to greet us a few minutes later he was wearing a blue-gray sweater, gray flannel pants and comfortable walking shoes. No hat. He was proud of his plentiful gray locks and justly so, but truth compels the admission that they weren't quite up to the great white mane carried by Dr. Fisher or the famous natural snowy crop flaunted by Judge Kenesaw Mountain Landis of which Irvin S. Cobb once said admiringly: "Judge, a mouse would swim the Mississippi River to winter in a thatch like that."

Dr. Fisher, who had known Dr. Einstein for years, made the usual introductions and then whipped out a little trick camera to take pictures. Dr. Mandelstam was similarly armed with a camera and he went into action. Everybody had to be photographed with Dr. Einstein and there were group pictures in addition. The great man took it like a lamb, moving forward, backward and sidewise as directed. He was smoking a rather heavy pipe with a curved stem and at one point in the series of poses he pointed at one of the camera wielders with the stem of his pipe and observed good-naturedly: "It's a mild form of insanity in this country."

We went inside for tea and talk on many subjects, one of which was the world series result we had heard on the way down. Dr. Einstein said that he didn't understand baseball, it was too complicated for him. This from the expounder of Relativity! At the request of Dr. Fisher he tried to explain to us the continual expansion of the universe. Possibly Dr. Fisher understood him but three of us were thrown off at the first curve. Asked about his violin playing, he said he had practically abandoned the violin for the piano. He never had taken lessons on the piano. He just liked to sit down and amuse himself at the keyboard.

We lingered long in conversation at the tea table. It was

his secretary who poured. Dr. Einstein took one lump and had a dish of little pretzels to go with his tea. It was dusk when we left and our kindly host walked out to the car with us to bid us farewell. It's a great day when you meet a great man.

Back to Dr. Fisher and some of the many things he did for me. He was the president of the Explorers Club and as his guest at many of the club gatherings I met and mingled on a friendly basis with men who had been to the ends of the earth and back, mostly on foot or horseback, which was slower and harder going than by air as they do today. With his little foreign camera he was an expert flower photographer and made beautiful color slides that he used when lecturing to garden clubs. He made extra slides for his friends and I have a small but treasured collection of them. He had still another trait that naturally endeared him to me; he loved outdoor sports. He went to ball games at the Polo Grounds and the Yankee Stadium and to track meets at Randall's Island. Together we saw the swift Swedes who were the greatest milers of that era, Arne Andersson and "Gunder the Wonder" Hägg. At his death I was asked to write a short piece about him for the Bulletin of the Linnaean Society of New York, of which he was one of the oldest members. I closed the brief description of his character and accomplishments with the truthful statement: "He was an industrious student, a modest scholar, an inspiring teacher, a delightful friend and a great gentleman."

We used to meet every Sunday morning at nine o'clock at the Broadway and Van Cortlandt Park subway station, rain or shine, winter or summer. Usually there were four of us, Herman Forster, Fred Nagler, Dr. Fisher and I. But Fred Nagler was up in Massachusetts from the first of May to late October, and Herman Forster spent his weekends in

New England in summer. Now and then we had distinguished naturalists as added starters on our Sunday saunters — Dr. Robert Cushman Murphy, Dr. James P. Chapin, Edwin Way Teale and such — but more often in July and August Dr. Fisher and I were off by ourselves. Those were the days when I really learned something about botany.

Of course, we were interested in everything that we saw along the way, birds, flowers, shrubs, trees, mosses, insects, reptiles and what few wild mammals remained in the area, but Dr. Fisher always carried a knapsack into which he put any plant specimens that I couldn't identify in the field. We usually were back for luncheon at my home at one o'clock and after that he and I would go into the living room and the lesson in botany would begin. Before I met him my way of trying to track down any strange flower, shrub or tree was to thumb a field guide until I came to an illustration that looked like the leaf, the flower, the fruit or whatever other evidence I had gathered in the wild. If I couldn't find any illustration that seemed to pin down the species, I gave up for the moment. Or even for years.

That hit-or-miss method ended with the first lesson from Dr. Fisher, which didn't come until he had uncovered my ignorance and persuaded me to buy a copy of Gray's *Botany* and the 3-volume set of Britton and Brown entitled *Illustrated Flora of the Northeastern United States and Adjacent Canada*. Only when the student was armed with such books could the teacher get in his best licks. One by one the specimens would be taken out of the knapsack and placed on a long low coffee table in front of a sofa on which pupil and professor sat side by side. The instruction proceeded in Socratic style, by question and answer.

"Is this a flowering plant?"

"Certainly; very pretty flowers, too."

"The first great division in flowering plants is between monocotyledons and dicotyledons. To which division does this belong?"

"I wish I knew."

"A quick test is to look at the leaves. Are the veins parallel or are they branched or netted?"

"Branched."

"That puts it among the dicotyledons. Most of our monocotyledons have leaves with parallel veins — grasses, orchids, lilies and such. This is a dicotyledon. Now look at the flower. Does it have petals?"

"Five of them."

"Confirmation that it's a dicotyledon. None of our monocotyledons has a five-parted flower. You're sure these are petals and not sepals?"

"Yes, I can see the sepals below."

"Are the petals separate or united?"

"Separate."

And so it would go with each specimen to be identified. Are the sepals distinct or united? How many stamens? How many pistils? Are the leaves opposite, alternate or whorled. Are they simple or compound? Does the plant have a milky sap? Does it have thorns? What comes after the flowering period — a pod, a pome, a berry, a capsule or whatnot? The questions were almost endless and the student made many glaring errors of diagnosis in his early botanical schooling but over almost a decade of such training even the most stupid oaf must pick up a few grains of knowledge. I certainly knew a great deal more about botany when Clyde Fisher died than I did when he first walked into my life. What he left with me was an understanding of how to begin to track down the identity of any strange plant that I find in the wild. Now and then when I successfully do a detective job on some random little flower or roadside weed, Margaret, my wife, will say to me: "Wouldn't Clyde Fisher be surprised at the progress you have made in botany?"

I nod in agreement, and such is the bland perversity of human nature that I take the remark as a compliment.

As for astronomy, I always had some mild interest in the stars but naturally it was stepped up considerably when I became a walking companion of the curator and chief lecturer of the Hayden Planetarium. More than that, Dr. Fisher set me up in business as an amateur astronomer. He had been one of the organizers of the Amateur Astronomers Association and was in close touch with the enthusiasts who were always building, buying, selling or trading telescopes for one reason or another. In those circles the best reason for selling a telescope was to replace it with one of greater power. On the advice of Dr. Fisher I bought one that was being discarded in that fashion. It was a 3¼-inch refractor with an equatorial mounting, hour rings and three eye-pieces of different magnification. The counterweights on the equatorial mounting were heavy and often I felt as though I were in a rough wrestling match when I wrapped my arms around the upper part of the tripod and horsed the telescope outdoors to set it up on the lawn on a clear night.

I had good fun with it over the years but I must confess that I never made any notable progress in amateur astronomy. I specialized in showing astonished friends and neighbors the four major planets of Jupiter and the rings of Saturn when they were at the proper tilt for good viewing. If it was visible, I showed them the colorful "double star" Albireo. For those who were taking a first peek through a telescope, this was wonderful stuff. But a good amateur astronomer would be unfrocked for wasting the night on such trivial matters.

What I did learn was to appreciate the vastness of the universe and the comparative insignificance of a certain minor planet that means everything to us. Mark Twain long ago called attention to this little matter in a short story, "Captain Stormfield's Visit to Heaven," a razor-edged satire on "man, proud man! drest in a little brief authority." One other thing I learned was the everlasting beauty of the night skies. For years now it has been a fixed habit with me to go out of the house just before I go to bed at night for a last look upward in the dark. Even if it's raining or snowing I do it. It can be spectacularly enchanting when the wind is up and the moon is "a ghostly galleon tossed upon cloudy seas" but best of all is a clear silent night when the stars have the dark canopy overhead to themselves. You can almost hear them sparkle.

When I walk out on such a night I orient myself according to the season. In our latitude we always have most of the Big Dipper above the horizon pointing the way to the North Star but that is not what I look for. On my own lawn I have that direction fixed in mind. Furthermore, if the Big Dipper is well down, Cassiopeia is up and serves just as easily as a reference point or astronomical benchmark. When Orion slides down the western sky and Castor and Pollux ride high overhead as I go to bed, I know that spring isn't far away. Soon Regulus, anchor star of the Sickle, will be bright in the eastern evening sky and redwings and robins will be flocking back from the south. Arcturus, easily found by following the curve of the handle of the Big Dipper southward across the night, is the climbing star that presides over the warbler migration in May.

Then my stars of the late spring and long summer come on, not one by one but in groups — the lovely Corona Borealis and the great triangle made by Vega in Lyra, Deneb in Cygnus and Altair in Aquila. You have a choice with Deneb. It can be either the top of the Northern Cross or the tail end of the Swan — Cygnus — forever flying southward across the August nights. As summer slips away the night air takes on a chill and katydids and crickets fill the dark fields and woods with incessant chirping. The Great Square of Pegasus slowly hauls up to the zenith with Andromeda, seemingly caught on the lower left-hand corner, floating along like a trailing garment of starry texture. There are some clear-eyed persons who can spot the Great Nebula in Andromeda without help of any kind but I need my field glasses to find it.

Autumn is the time of great nights — and great days. Let the poets sing of spring. The English and other European bards have good reason for it. That's their best season. But in New England, "spring" is a horrid word. Autumn in New England, that's the ticket! There is no brighter or finer season anywhere in the world. The colors by hill and dale are overwhelming. The air is clear, sharp, stimulating. Blue skies are reflected in blue waters. The sunsets over a landscape of red and gold are incredibly brilliant. The moonlight nights — first the happy harvest moon, then the nippy hunter's moon — are enchanting.

Too soon come the frostier nights and the rising Pleiades that, in Tennyson's eyes, glittered "like a swarm of fireflies tangled in a silver braid." When the nip of autumn has turned into the bite of winter, Orion strides across the night sky with Aldebaran showing the way and Sirius dogging the celestial Hunter at the heels. Now of a moonless night we see "the black elm tops 'mong the freezing stars" and hear the crack of frozen branches as they toss in the teeth of an icy wind out of the northwest.

These are the great stars and constellations that provide me with a familiar astronomical calendar, one that I constantly look up to with increasing wonderment and delight. The more I learn about the stars, the planets, the comets, the nebulae and the galaxies and their interrelated movements in space, the more marvelous and beautiful it all seems to me. Now hear ye Walt Whitman on the same topic:

> *When I heard the learn'd astronomer,*
> *When the proofs, the figures, were ranged in columns before me,*
> *When I was shown the charts and diagrams, to add, divide and*
>   *measure them,*
> *When I sitting heard the astronomer where he lectured with*
>   *much applause in the lecture-room,*
> *How soon unaccountable I became tired and sick,*
> *Till rising and gliding out I wander'd off by myself,*
> *In the mystical moist night-air, and from time to time,*
> *Look'd up in perfect silence at the stars.*

For a proper comment on this I have to quote the poet again from another part of his forest:

> *I sound my barbaric yawp over the roofs of the world.*

What a plea for obscurantism! Lo, the poor poet of untutored mind who is determined to keep it so. Close the schools and life will be beautiful. The less you know, the happier you are. Impenetrable ignorance means lifelong bliss. Apparently this is the gospel according to Whitman who was never my favorite poet, anyway.

I am of a different mind entirely. I love to listen to astronomers. The first visit to a planetarium opens a whole new window on the universe. Every time I go to a planetarium I am carried away again with wonder. To me the subject is heavenly and the individuals who deal with it are supermen who live in another and far more impressive world than the one in which we ordinary mortals dwell.

I never tire of reading about astronomers and their discoveries and adventures. Copernicus is as much alive to me as my next-door neighbors. Tycho Brahe, the great Dane who steered a course between the Ptolemaic and the Copernican systems and arranged a cosmos to suit himself, was as bizarre a character in the heavenly field as Rafinesque was here on earth among the plants and animals of the world. The great astronomer Kepler practiced a little astrology on the side to fatten his income and his mother had the honor of being tried for witchcraft. A streak of astronomical genius ran through the Herschel family in England. Three of them made the big league in the study of the stars: Sir William, his sister Caroline, and his son Sir John Herschel. The double discovery of the planet Neptune at almost the same time by two different persons in two different countries — Adams in England and Leverrier in France — is a mathematical romance of the first order.

To me there is no more inspiring story than the bare biography of a man named John Alfred Brashear who was born a poor boy on the outskirts of Pittsburgh in 1840, had about as little formal schooling as Benjamin Franklin and Abraham Lincoln, and yet managed to educate himself to the point where he was able to produce some of the finest astronomical instruments in the world, was named interim head of the Carnegie Institute of Technology and acquired international prestige in certain divisions of astronomy. Apparently he was a wonderful character, known far and wide as "Uncle John" and greatly beloved by all who knew him. His wife was as keen on the study of the stars as he was and the happy couple lived to a ripe old age in just the place for such a pair — their home was an observatory. It was also their tomb. At their own request they were buried in the great stone wall of the observatory that they left as their monument and on the face of the crypt in which their bodies lie is carved the epitaph of their own choice, a line that combines modesty, majesty and eternity:

We have loved the stars too long to be fearful of the night.

There is no need to go further in explaining why I dote on astronomers, astronomy and the stars that I have looked up to all the years of my life.

IX

DOUBLE EXPOSURE

THE ONLY problem the radio success of Information Please brought to the regular panelists was a flood of personal mail that grew heavier with the steadily increasing popularity of the program. Each of us received endless invitations to deliver lectures, contribute articles gratis to college and high school publications, make speeches at breakfasts, luncheons and dinners in honor of somebody or something and do volunteer work for countless good causes. Because I answered most of the questions on natural history, I had additional requests to lead nature walks, talk to garden clubs, identify from written descriptions thereof birds, beasts and reptiles that never existed by land, sea or air, and give expert advice by return mail on the care and feeding of sick parakeets, tame turtles, pet alligators, tropical fish and other assorted livestock around the house.

Turning out a daily sports column for the *Times* had been a fair-sized job in itself. I had also written a few books and many magazine articles on the side before the radio program sky-rocketed us into public notice. In short, I had enough to keep me busy before this flood of mail came pouring down on me. Emergency measures were necessary. All those letters deserved appreciative answers.

To solve the problem I took on a part-time secretary, a good boy in the office who was a fast and accurate stenographer. For him I drew up a list of form letters that would serve as polite answers to my correspondents. Most of them were firm declinations with many thanks for the honor of the invitation. Thus I could glance at a letter, get the gist of it and toss it to the boy with the remark "No speech," "No article," "Contract forbids it," "Ask the Museum of Natural History," or simply "Don't know." Some letters were so completely baffling that no one of the stock answers would do. For these special cases I devised a letter to be written and signed by the boy himself as my secretary. I have forgotten the exact wording but I remember that I rather prided myself on it at the time. Beyond a courteous acknowledgment that the letter had been received, it was a plea in avoidance of a direct answer coupled with a hint that Mr. Kieran was not in the best of health at the moment and couldn't go into the matter. The code phrase for that answer when I tossed a letter to the boy was "Mister Kieran is dead."

Handling correspondence in that fashion solved some of the problems that came with the success of our radio show but not all of them. A man called up one day and threatened to take legal action because I hadn't acknowledged receipt of his letter containing valuable material of some kind. I had no recollection of any such letter as he described. He insisted that it was a very important letter and I must have received it. I replied that I was an unimportant person and had never received an important letter in my life. I gained the impression that he believed only the first half of my declaration. But he took no legal action.

There were, of course, invitations that had to be accepted. They went with the well-paid job. You had to write articles or speak or just put in appearances at luncheons or dinners for charity, art or education. As a sports columnist I had been attending many sports luncheons and dinners and social gatherings of various kinds. Now we were launched in a new profession — radio work — and found there were social obligations and professional duties in that field, too. Most of it was pleasant enough but my life was becoming too crowded. I was a sports columnist, a writer on natural history and a radio performer. I was hurrying in three directions at once. I never had time enough. Labor and Management were discussing the 40-hour week when what I needed was a 40-hour day.

At that point things got worse. We began to make movie shorts of Information Please. Up to that time we had been only voices in the night and nobody recognized us on the street next day. But when the films began appearing on movie screens from Broadway to the Golden Gate, our faces were exposed to public view and we were in for trouble. In no time at all we were being halted by strangers who had something to say about the program or our parts in it. Usually the stranger began by stating frankly: "I have a question that will stump you." Almost every time the stranger was right. Even when the answer was supplied I was still stumped. I had no interest in the question and tried to forget the answer as quickly as possible.

There was one week when three different Information Please shorts were running in Broadway movie houses. That was when I gave up eating lunch alone in any downtown restaurant or hotel. Some stranger was sure to sit down at my table and either toss a question at me, invite me to join some society, ask me to speak at the annual breakfast, luncheon, or dinner of some organization or try to persuade me that astrology and dowsing are the only exact sciences known to man. Worse than spoiling my lunch or dinner, this sort of thing cut into my reading hours. I always went about with a book in my pocket and pulled it out when I sat down in a bus or a subway car. You can get in two acts of *Hamlet* or thirty pages of *La Rôtisserie de la Reine Pedauque* between Times Square and 242nd Street on the Van Cortlandt Park line. But not when strangers recognize you and come over to discuss Shakespeare and the musical glasses.

Up to that time the only trouble I found with reading in the subway was that I often became so absorbed in my book that I rode past my station. In an effort to save my reading hours on the rapid transit system from interruption, I always tried to get into the last car and as near the last seat as possible. It was only partially successful but it was better than a total loss of good reading in a bad light. Of course, I realized that those who wrote or spoke to me were the radio followers whose interest in the program made possible the salaries we were getting for going on the air, probably the easiest money anybody ever earned. I always tried to be polite to strangers who came up and spoke to me and I answered every letter that bore a legible name and address.

The strangest letter I ever received was from a woman who delivered it by hand at the reception desk on the third floor of the *Times* office. The letter informed me that any continuation of my attempts to kill her by putting poison in her food and cigarettes would force her to place the matter before the district attorney. I thought the letter was a joke but when several more of the same tone followed I knew I had to do with a mental case. I asked the boys at the desk what the woman looked like. They said she was fairly young and attractive. She never made any fuss. She came early in the morning before I was there, asked to see me in person, and left the letter quietly when she was told that I wasn't in. She was well dressed. She never raised her voice. Her name and address were in the upper left-hand corner of the envelopes.

A sports columnist knows most of the police officials in his home town through meeting them at the ball park or the track or the championship fights. I phoned one of my friends at Police Headquarters for help. In an hour or so a man appeared at my desk in plain clothes and introduced himself as Detective Jacobs from the local precinct. I remember the last name very well because he told me that he was a brother of Joe Jacobs, the manager of Max Schmeling, the fighter who won the world's heavyweight championship lying down and lost it standing up. (He was awarded the title when he was fouled to the canvas at the Yankee Stadium by Jack Sharkey in 1930 and lost it by a decision to the same Jack Sharkey in a bout in Long Island City two years later.) I had known Joe Jacobs for years. But I wish I could remember what Detective Jacobs gave as his first name. It was a very fancy one for a West Side detective in New York City — Lancelot, Marmaduke — something like that.

I told my story to Detective Jacobs and gave him the lady's letters. He was back the next day to tell me that he had gone to the home of my correspondent. She lived with her family — mother, father, one sister, one brother — quite nice quiet people, he said. She had been a secretary in a Wall Street office but had lost her job in the depression that began with the crash in 1929. She admitted that she didn't know me but she always listened to our radio program and she had seen me in the movie shorts of Information Please. She promised that she wouldn't write any more threatening letters and her family said they would see to it, too. They conceded that she was a bit weak mentally but they were sure she wouldn't cause any trouble. I thanked Detective Jacobs heartily for his help and he left.

The following week I received another letter from the lady and this time it was registered. In it she accused me of still poisoning her cigarettes and said she was going down to the mayor's office unless I stopped immediately. I phoned Detective Jacobs and handed him the letter when he popped into the office. He put it in his pocket without a word and walked out. A few hours later he was back with the information that he had confronted the lady and the family with the letter and announced to them: "One more letter and off she goes to Bellevue!" Solemn promises were given.

"I really think it will stick this time," said the detective, "I laid it on the line."

Apparently he had because I never received another letter from the lady. But about two years later I had a phone call from the desk sergeant of the local precinct. He asked me whether or not I knew any woman by the name of — I don't remember now — I didn't remember then, either, because I said I didn't know any such person.

"I thought not," said the sergeant. "I think she's a little wacky. She came in here and told some story about you trying to kill her. I eased her out."

"Wait a minute," I said in alarm. "Now I remember. That's the woman who pestered me a couple of years ago and I called headquarters. They put Detective Jacobs from your precinct on the case. He knows all about her. She's crazy. Jacobs can tell you all about it."

"Detective Jacobs died six months ago," said the desk sergeant.

"Oh, no!" I wailed. "What do I do now?"

"Well, if we hear any more from her we'll let you know," said the desk sergeant. "And if you hear any more from her, let us know."

That was the last I ever heard of the unfortunate young

lady who accused me of trying to poison her, but I'm sure of one thing. She knew me by sight from watching the Information Please movie shorts. If she had waylaid me at the front door of the *Times* office and flung acid in my face, nobody in the world would have believed that it was our first meeting.

I wouldn't have blamed them. Some occurrences are almost incredible. A boy had won a scholarship in a radio contest and I was asked to make the presentation on the program that promoted the contest. I was in the sponsor's advertising office on Park Avenue discussing the details of my appearance on the show and was about to leave when the public relations man for the program said the usual thing: "I'll bet you have the craziest questions thrown at you wherever you go."

I agreed. They wouldn't believe how impossible some of them were.

"Like who was the first man to put sugar in blocks," said the publicity man.

How did he come to think that one up? I was embarrassed and everybody in the room must have noticed it. I finally stuttered apologetically that I happened to know who was the first man to put sugar in blocks. They all stared at me in amazement.

"Wait a minute!" I said. "I can explain. There are extenuating circumstances."

I told them that I never miss a chance to visit a good art museum. Before I ever set foot on English soil I knew that the Tate Gallery in London had the greatest collection of Turner paintings in the world. When I was in England in 1935 covering the Grand National Steeplechase at Aintree, the Oxford-Cambridge boat race on the Thames and some lesser sporting events around the countryside, I found time to spend a few hours in the Tate Museum where it fronts the Thames in London. I went over all the works of James Mallord William Turner on exhibition there and decided that I liked his watercolors better than his oils. I still feel that way about his work.

Some time later in random reading I ran across an item about a Tate scholarship endowment fund at Liverpool University. Still later I learned of a Tate medical foundation. I began to wonder whether or not these Tates were all the same man and, if so, how he amassed the money that he had distributed in such worthy ways. I picked up the SORD to TEXTILE volume of my set of the *Encyclopaedia Britannica* and found my man. Tate, Sir Henry (1819-1899), prosperous merchant in sugar, knighted for his many charities. He piled up a fortune by putting sugar in blocks and marketing it all over the globe as "Tate's Cube Sugar." If I hadn't been so much interested in art I never would have had the faintest idea of the identity of the man who first put sugar in blocks. My explanation was satisfactory to the men in the advertising office and I was released on parole.

I had another experience of somewhat the same kind but on this other occasion I was not a bit embarrassed. It was my questioner who was practically stunned. Whenever I went to a ball game at the Polo Grounds or the Yankee Stadium I always ended up in the counting room of my friends the Stevens brothers, the concessionaires. On this day the ball game at the Yankee Stadium had been called on account of rain in a late inning. I went down under the stands to the Stevens office and waited for Frank Stevens to wind up his chores for the day. We were to have dinner together at his home on Riverside Drive. We were driving away from the front entrance of the stadium in the rainy dusk in Frank's limousine when I noticed three forlorn figures — two men and a woman — standing outside the Stadium Club exit, apparently waiting for a taxi. They might as well have been waiting for a camel caravan. They had lingered too long in the Stadium Club aloft. There would be no taxis in sight until the next afternoon. They were isolated in the steady rain and the growing darkness. Suddenly I recognized the taller man.

"That's Jess Sweetser!" I said.

"Friend of yours?" asked Frank.

Old friend, good friend, former national amateur golf champion. He had won the British amateur championship, too.

"Back up," said Frank to the chauffeur.

I called to Jess and he came down to the car with his two friends, all of them glad to be rescued. The first order of business was to get them into the car and out of the rain. Introductions were exchanged as the car rolled ahead. The strangers with Jess were Mr. and Mrs. Something from Baltimore. When Jess identified me for the benefit of the couple the man, who was in the jump seat just in front of me, whirled around and said: "John Kieran? Say, I've got a question for you!"

"Good God, no!" cried Jess, "The man has just saved our lives. Have a heart!"

"No!" said the man. "This really is something. You would think that almost any intelligent person would know about this and nobody does. I've asked lawyers, judges, newspapermen, Congressmen, college professors — nobody knew the answer."

"I probably won't either," I said. "But just for the fun of it, go ahead and ask."

Jess put his head in his hands and groaned at the gross ingratitude as the man turned on me again and said in a loud challenging tone: "What Vice President of the United States resigned his office?"

I answered: "John C. Calhoun in 1832."

The man's mouth opened but no sound came out. He was dumfounded. To make up for it, Jess Sweetser roared with laughter at his friend's blank discomfiture.

How I happened to know the answer was that among the old books in our home in my youthful days was the first volume of the two-volume set of Thomas Hart Benton's memoirs published in 1854 under the title *Thirty Years' View*. This was the documented inside story of Washington politics from 1820, the year in which "Old Bullion" took his seat as the first United States Senator from Missouri, until he retired from that office in 1850. Several modern historians have ransacked that rich storehouse of American political lore to great advantage. I was fascinated by some of the stories in the book, including the tale of how President Andrew Jackson discovered that his Vice President and trusted friend, John C. Calhoun, had lied to him about the part he played in a proposal to court-martial Jackson for his conduct as commanding general in the Seminole War in Florida in 1818. At that time Calhoun was Secretary of War in Monroe's cabinet. He assured General Jackson that he was his friend and defender. Ha! The court-martial proposal was rejected, but not through Calhoun's good offices. Publication of letters a dozen years later proved that it was Calhoun who started the whole thing.

Naturally, Old Hickory and his Vice President had come to the parting of their political ways but Calhoun played it craftily. He remained in office until he became Senator-elect from South Carolina in 1832. He was a "lame duck" Vice President when he resigned on December 28, 1832. It was a mere formality, since he had no further duties to perform as the presiding officer in the Senate. Its only importance — if it has any — is that it is the only such resignation on record. Even Aaron Burr didn't resign as Vice President after he had killed Alexander Hamilton in their famous duel. Burr merely ran away and hid until after his term had expired.

The most fun I ever had in answering a question came during an informal session at the University of Michigan. Franklin P. Adams had spent a year or two there as a student and some old acquaintance at Ann Arbor had asked him to help in a campaign to raise money for some new building needed on the campus. The idea was to put on an Information Please show or reasonable imitation of it out there and charge admission. Kip Fadiman was to be master of ceremonies, as usual, and two university professors would sit with Frank and me to make up the panel of four. Frank, Kip and I were to be paid all expenses and a reasonable fee.

It was a nice trip and we had a wonderful time. I spent a whole morning in the Museum of Biology with the late Dr. Josselyn Van Tyne going over birdskins and listening to his stories of field trips in the mountains of China, India and Tibet. We had a full house — some 2500 persons — for the show that night. I knew there would be questions on intercollegiate sports because of student enthusiasm. Michigan had long ranked at or near the top of Big Ten competition and the Wolverines were riding high on the gridiron at the time. However, I counted on Alumnus F.P.A. to handle that end of the program in case I flunked out.

We had the usual run of questions on history, geography, politics, English literature and assorted other topics and the audience seemed to be enjoying our answers and our errors. It was toward the close of the program that Kip Fadiman picked up a fresh card from the table in front of him and said to us on the panel: "Gentlemen, this is a three-part question.

First part: what was the date of the first Rose Bowl football game?"

All four hands went up and one of the Michigan professors gave the correct answer: 1902.

"Right," said Kip. "Second part: name the teams that played."

Frank knew that one: Michigan and Stanford.

"Very good," said Kip. "Third part coming up. There was something very odd about this game, something that rarely happens in football, something extraordinary. What was it?"

I hadn't the faintest idea. Frank looked blank. The two professors were stumped. Suddenly I had an inspiration and my hand shot up.

"Yes, Mr. Kieran," said Kip. "What was extraordinary about that game?"

In a good loud voice I said: "MICHIGAN WON!"

I turned sideways, slapped my knee and bent over double with laughter at my own joke. The audience let loose with a hearty laugh, too, but the students almost immediately realized that the jest was sacrilegious and the laughter changed to a chorus of booing that I had every reason to expect. The right answer to the third part of the question turned out to be that Michigan was leading Stanford 49-0 when Stanford ran out of substitutes to put in for wounded men so the game never was finished officially. I never heard of it before — or since.

Another feature of that trip was an unexpected view of a peregrine falcon fairly close at hand. It was in December and snow was falling heavily the next morning when one of the university professors drove Kip and me to Detroit where Kip was to board a train for New York. Frank was staying over a few days with friends in Ann Arbor. I had a plane reservation at the Detroit airport. Considering the snowstorm, I had phoned the airport from Ann Arbor and was told that the flight, starting from Chicago, was still on. Just to be sure while I still had a chance to take the train with Kip, I phoned the airport from the railroad station in Detroit. To my surprise, I was told that the plane was expected to arrive and leave on schedule. When I reached the airport I had the distinction of being the only expectant passenger in the waiting room.

After checking in I went outside on the apron and wondered how a plane could find its way down through such a whirling snowstorm. That was over twenty years ago before planes had all the navigational gadgets that are standard equipment now. As I stood there with my collar turned up and the snowflakes slanting down around me, I saw a bird sitting on the roof of the nearest hangar. I thought at first that it was a pigeon with its feathers fluffed out because of the cold but suddenly it took off and came sweeping down the wind past me and I saw that it was a peregrine on the prowl. I watched it dash in among a flock of small dark birds that rose from the snow ahead of it but pursuer and pursued went out of sight around a corner of the airport building and I never knew the result of the chase. But for me, an encounter with any peregrine falcon is a memorable occasion.

Oh, yes, the plane came in quickly and quietly through the falling snow and taxied over to near where I was standing. Several persons got off. I was the only one to board it. Ten minutes later we were up ten thousand feet in clear sunshine and I was home in Riverdale in time for lunch.

X

THE PLOT THICKENS

SOMEWHERE on some occasion there must have been somebody who said of the Schicklgruber boy in Bavaria the German equivalent of "That fellow will never set the world on fire." But he did in 1939. Nobody in the civilized countries escaped some of the stress and strain of putting the fire out. A war beats even politics for making strange bedfellows. The next thing I knew I was working with or sitting beside notables that I never dreamed I would meet. I was encountering them at luncheons, dinners, cocktail parties, bond rallies, radio studios, committee meetings, hospital visits, benefit auctions — all of it intended to aid in the war effort or alleviate the suffering caused by the colossal conflict.

We of Information Please were in on all this because the radio program and the movie shorts of the show had made us drawing cards at the time and our names on a program could help to sell tickets, gather an audience and bring in contributions for the campaign of the moment. One of the first I attended was a dinner and auction of contributed objets d'art at the Plaza Hotel for the benefit of "Bundles For Britain." The man who organized that affair was the famous wealthy, witty and almost happy-go-lucky book collector, Dr. A. S. W. Rosenbach. The auctioneers of the evening were amateurs at that game but professionals in their own fields — authors, actors, singers, musicians and public figures of note. The lady who sat beside me on the dais was Kitty Carlisle, singer and actress whose playwright husband, the late Moss Hart, I knew as a two-time guest on Information Please. What she auctioned off I do not recall. I sold the original manuscript of Elizabeth Barrett Browning's "A Musical Instrument" — the one that begins "What is he doing, the great god Pan," an old favorite of mine — for about $250 or so. The other auctioneers did much better with their wares and "Bundles For Britain" gathered a great bundle of cash that lively evening.

I almost became a buyer there myself. There was an Eilshemius landscape of about 20 × 30 stalled momentarily at $200 and I jumped right into the bidding at that inviting level. However, the real collectors present ran it up swiftly beyond the modest confines of my available spending money and I lost sight of it when it passed the $500 mark. Aside from the fact that I liked the picture and knew that the artist was represented in many of the great museums here and abroad, I once had a personal encounter with Louis Michel Eilshemius, the self-styled "Mighty Mahatma," "Grand Transcendent Eagle of Art," and "Supreme Parnassian," these being among the titles he gave himself in writing hilarious letters to the editor of the *Sun* (New York, long deceased) over a period of years, much to the amusement of old subscribers.

I was one of the many who made merry over those letters but my friend and walking companion, Fred Nagler, took the matter more seriously. He had known Eilshemius for years, admired his work very much, and was fond of the eccentric old gentleman. One hot day in August I had a letter from Fred, who was in his cool retreat in the Berkshires: "Do call on old Eilshemius, will you? Poor Louis, he writes me that he is sick and alone, tied to his cot. Drop in and say a few kind words. Tell him I sent you."

The call was duly made at noon the day after I received the letter. Eilshemius lived in an ancient, narrow, three-story house on East 57th Street, south side, between Lexington and Third Avenue. A man who looked like a janitor answered the bell and, when I announced my mission, he yelled upward into the interior darkness with a heavy Italian accent: "Meesta Louie; somebody heez for you." A cracked voice came back: "Send him up." I went up one long straight flight upstairs into the gloom. Nobody there. "Come on — come on!" was the impatient call from somewhere above. I went up another long flight of stairs to a dark landing. A door was opened at the front end of the hall.

"Here I am," called the Mahatma from beyond the open door.

Even so, it was hard to locate him in the gloom. It was a large room fronting on 57th Street but the tall windows had heavy draperies over them. Finally I saw the old gentleman and a strange sight he turned out to be. An army cot was stretched along the wall just a few feet inside the door. The great Eilshemius was lying there under a blanket in mid-summer. Only his bare arms and his head were exposed. And his straggling whiskers.

I told him who I was — friend of Fred Nagler, who had asked me to call. The Mahatma perked up and began to orate immediately. Painting? That was easy; nothing to it. He could do that with one hand tied behind his back. He was a musician, too. Beat Beethoven all hollow. And a crack athlete in his days at Cornell — fine ball player — great man at track and field — jumped two feet higher than his head. But that was a minor matter, too.

"Poetry — that's the thing!" said the Mahatma. "I've written more poetry than any other man alive — and better poetry, too. I'll show you. I'll let you be the judge. I'll give you one of my volumes and autograph it for you. Take one from that shelf there — one of those green books."

The Mahatma had been lying there so long in the gloom that his eyes were accustomed to it. I was new in the semi-darkness and had to peer where he was pointing to a book-shelf on the wall near the foot of his cot. I leaned across the cot to get at the shelf, and I had trouble picking out the book he wanted.

"Not that one — to the left a little more — there, that one," he said.

I reached for the indicated volume and just as I extracted it the Mahatma gave a terrific shriek — then another one — then a third for good measure. I fell back in amazement and stared at the blanketed figure on the cot. His skinny arms were upraised with fingers extended. His eyes were wide open, glaring at me. Even his whiskers were quivering.

"You touched me! You touched me!" he yelled at the top of his lungs. Then he subsided and explained that he was in agony if anybody as much as brushed his toes as I had done accidentally. But he recovered quickly, bore no malice and autographed the book for me with a firm enough hand. It was time to go, so I moved toward the door with the ex-pressed hope that he would soon be up and around in bloom-ing good health. He shook his head, whiskers included, with evident disgust at my lack of perception.

"I'm dying," he said.

Dying; oh no. Couldn't be that bad.

"Yes, I'm dying!" he insisted fiercely.

He looked angry enough to get up and do battle stark naked in defense of his opinion, so I merely contented myself with the observation that he showed more energy in dying than most people did in living.

"Well, anyway," he said more quietly, "I'll never get up again."

And as far as I know, he never did. I read his little book of verse when I arrived home that evening. The only good thing in it was the autograph, "Louis Eilshemius, Supreme Poet of the Universe."

Bundling for Britain and lending a hand to other such good causes kept us fairly well occupied until we got into the war ourselves. Then the pressure was on from all sides and I practically lived on the run. Even so, I ran into some nice people doing the same thing. I was going into a recording studio at NBC one day to cut a platter for the Treasury Department — a plea to buy war bonds — when a well-groomed, rather small, not young but distinctly attractive woman with alert eyes came out of the studio, smiled quietly at me, said "How do you do, Mr. Kieran" and walked away. When I entered the studio I asked the man there who the lady was. Helen Hayes! I had an inclination to run out, try to catch her and tell her how wonderful I thought she was. Luckily I did meet her later on and had a chance to treat her with due deference.

I went up to Providence one time to speak for the Treasury Department at a bond rally that was held in the city art museum and found that one of the other speakers was the British Ambassador in Washington, Sir Gerald Campbell, noted as a wit and scholar as well as a diplomat. We rode together on the train back to New York the next morning and somehow the topic of the Youth Movement in this country came up. It was quite the thing at that time. Mrs. Eleanor Roosevelt was one of the big backers of the movement and I recalled a huge Youth Movement dinner in New York at which Mrs. Roosevelt, Archibald MacLeish and I and others were speakers. My turn came late in the program and my only noteworthy contribution to the oratory of the evening was a story about some children I knew and their parents. At that point I interrupted myself to say: "Parents! I have been listening to speeches about the youth of America all evening and this is the first time that parents have been mentioned. Whatever became of parents in this country?" I was not carried off on the shoulders of a cheering audience.

But Sir Gerald Campbell seemed to relish the retelling. Just for that I promised to send him a little masterpiece entitled *Plea for an Age Movement* by the Harvard philosopher, Professor Ralph Barton Perry. I had bought a half dozen copies to distribute to friends and well-wishers. At this point I beg to quote from that little literary jewel this sparkling facet:

> The institution of the school was originally created in order that the young might learn from the old, who had when young learned from *their* elders. The idea was that the infant was a vegetable, the small child an animal, the adult a human being, and the aged adult a wise human being with a touch of deity. On this theory the individual learned at each stage from a superior who had something to give. Progressive education (though why progressive is not clear) reversed all this. The child being a genius and the adult a fossil, nobody taught anybody anything. The child unfolded in accordance with his own creative impulses and the adult provided the tools and conveniences. Meanwhile, as the child grew to manhood, he himself gradually fossilized until he became a dodo in his own right.

I sent the booklet, which was really a reprint of a speech that Professor Perry had made at the forty-fifth reunion of his college class at Princeton, to the British diplomat as I had promised and I still have the note I received in return from the British Embassy in Washington. It ran as follows:

Dear Mr. Kieran:

How very friendly of you to send me the reprint of Professor Perry's speech which is quite delightful. My wife and I read it last night and enjoyed it enormously, and I shall keep it as a comforting souvenir of the visit we both paid to Providence and of the journey back. With all good wishes to you, I am,

Sincerely yours,
(signed) GERALD CAMPBELL

I was glad to have written proof that such a distinguished scholar and gentleman was on my side in my high appraisal of Professor Perry's little masterpiece. I knew another Harvard professor who was slightly skeptical of Progressive Education, too. That was Earnest Albert Hooton, the noted anthropologist. He was on Information Please one night and we were having a sandwich and a drink after the program when somebody brought up the topic of Progressive Education. I probably was the culprit because it seemed to me that allowing or inviting a child to go its own way in education was about as sensible as leaving it up to a colt to break itself to saddle or harness. In any event, when the topic came up Dr. Hooton chuckled and said that he recently had delivered a lecture in Philadelphia on that very subject and he had titled his talk "Progressive Education or the Decline of Literacy."

Because education is so important, it's easy for me to run a temperature when speaking or writing on the subject. Or is that too specific? Long years ago, when I was standing beside the desk of my dear old friend and mentor Alden March of the *Times* fulminating on some matter of the moment, he looked up at me with the light of added years and wisdom in his eyes and said: "I wish I could get as excited about anything as you do about everything." I still think there are worse faults — but I'm afraid I have them, too.

Back in 1939 President Cowley of Hamilton College asked a number of persons interested in the subject to write down their ideas of what the essence of a college course should be, what the instructors should try to instil or produce in the student mind. There was the chance to put the matter in a nutshell but in my case I ran all over two pages of typescript, single spaced. Too long, O Catiline, especially for one who cherished an arresting passage in the autobiography of Thomas Riley Marshall, Vice President of the United States under Woodrow Wilson, the paragraph in which he described his first appearance in court as a young lawyer: "On this occasion I said all I had to say — and a great deal more."

Confiteor! But I stand by some of the shorter sentences in that letter. I believe that, on the average, the teachers know more than the students. I think that the swing to elective courses has gone too far. We have made "marvelous progress" in human affairs and certainly there are changed conditions and new values, but the human mind has not improved perceptibly in three thousand years. I look around now and find no one wiser than Socrates, Plato and Aristotle, and in education I am opposed to experiments based on the premise that the wisdom of the ages is an old fraud. I'll go quietly now. There's no need to call the police.

One of the most pleasant interludes of the war years was a series of weekly dinners given by the Lambs Club to visiting service men of different units from the beginning to the end of our term in the war. A member by the name of Joe Buhler organized the whole thing and financed it in some mysterious way — possibly out of his own pocket. The club lent the premises and there was room for about two hundred uniformed guests at a time. They came from all branches of the service — Army, Navy, Marines, Air Force, Coast Guard and U. S. Merchant Marine. It was all for enlisted men but occasionally a commanding officer might be included in a unit invitation. Or even as a guest speaker. One night the man who sat on my right at the speakers table was Admiral Nimitz. Another time it was Lieutenant General George C. Kenney, commander of our air forces in the Pacific. It was wonderful company for me considering that at one point in my military career with the Eleventh Engineers in France I held the rank of saddler in a regiment that didn't have a horse.

Since the purpose was to entertain the troops as well as feed them, most of the after-dinner speakers were drawn from the club itself and included such professionals as Harry Hershfield, "Senator" Ford, Joe Laurie, Jr., "Colonel Stoopnagle" of radio fame, Peter Donald, the old comedy team of Smith & Dale, and so on. You can see that, for me at least, going to one of those affairs was as good as a vaudeville show. All I had to do was to get up and tell one story. I had all the remainder of the evening to enjoy myself. Since there was always a fresh audience at each dinner, I told the same story every time I went there which, according to the account rendered by Joe Buhler when the series ended after the surrender in the Pacific, was thirty-two times.

Of course, Joe Buhler had to listen to that story thirty-two times but, curiously enough, he didn't object. In fact, he insisted on it. He demanded that story and would accept no substitutes. It was a war story and always good for a laugh from the troops. It was the waiters who objected. They were club members who volunteered for the duty. They didn't mind carrying in the food and carrying out the empty dishes but when they sat down and fraternized with the guests later they stared in horror when I rose to tell the confounded story again. They did more. They groaned and booed and shouted such rude remarks as "Not that chestnut!" "Put on a new record," "Call the cops!" or with a haughty British accent, "Withdraw, sir! Withdraw." Joe Buhler always gaveled them down and I went ahead relentlessly with my oft-told tale. Indeed, I gave it an extracurricular telling on a famous occasion at the club. It was a black-tie affair, a dinner preceding a Lambs Gambol. The Shepherd of the Lambs, Fred Waring, was the toastmaster and the guest of honor was a man just home from the wars, General Eisenhower. He laughed.

I suppose I am honor bound to tell the story here though I know it will come out as flat as this page without the *viva voce* flavor, the necessary gestures to portray a major general on horseback coming from full gallop to a sudden stop at the sight of a forlorn private in a ditch, and the dramatic change of voices to represent the short and snappy dialogue between the two characters. Therefor I enter a Shakespearean plea and ask you to eke out its imperfection with your thought.

The youngest, shortest, fattest, brightest and jolliest student in my class of 1912 at Fordham was John C. Egan, "Jack" to one and all, dead, alas, these many years. He was a ragtime wizard on the piano. After graduation he became a popular song writer and an inmate of "Tin Pan Alley." He wrote lyrics as well as music and had his share of hits. When World War I broke out in 1917 Jack was twenty-four years old, five feet five inches in height and weighed about three hundred pounds. He was shaped like a vast beach ball, probably a glandular case. How they came to draft him into the army I will never know, but they did and sent him overseas with the 77th Division. Jack was a rear rank private, an aide de camp to one of the company cooks.

The division was marching up to take a front line position in the Chemin des Dames sector. It was to be their baptism of fire. The rain was pouring down on the column, the road was a wreck from artillery pounding and it was dreadful going for the marchers in the mud with their soaking packs, their rifles and their cartridge belts heavy with ammunition. For my 300-pound rotund classmate it was torture and eventually it was impossible. He collapsed in bulk on the side of the road.

That was an old-fashioned war in some ways and the divisional commander, Major General McAlexander, was a dashing figure on horseback. This stormy day he came splashing along the line of march on his gallant steed like a Stonewall Jackson, giddy-yap, giddy-yap, giddy-yap — whoa! He had arrived at the spot where Private John C. Egan was a motionless mess on the roadside. The stern major general leaned over his horse's neck and roared down at the fallen figure: "That I should live to see the day when an American soldier, on coming within range of enemy guns, would fall out of ranks and hide in a ditch like the yellow-bellied coward he is!"

Private Egan somehow managed to lurch upward far enough to utter these immortal words in the very teeth of the glaring major general: "The man who says I'm a coward is a blankety-blank liar!"

The gallant major general roared back twice as loud this time — and jubilantly: "THAT'S THE SPIRIT I LIKE TO SEE! GIDDY-YAP, GIDDY-YAP, GIDDY-YAP!"

This might be a good place to pause for refreshments.

XI

FIRST PRIZE
AND OTHER SEA STORIES

THE FIRST time I went to Europe by boat I slept in a wooden bunk three decks down and I never saw the captain during the entire voyage. That was when the old SS *Carpathia*, the ship that brought in the survivors of the *Titanic* disaster, carried the Eleventh Engineers on the first leg of our journey to France in July, 1917. My next trip abroad came in 1934 on the SS *Champlain*, French Line, New York to Le Havre, and this time I made the captain's table. Not under my own steam, however. I was traveling with my father and, as the president emeritus of the largest women's college in the world, which Hunter College was at the time, he rated it.

The celebrated Abbé Dimnet (who lectured widely in America on his best seller "The Art of Thinking") was aboard and one night Captaine Victor Barthélemy had the Abbé, my father and me for dinner in his own quarters behind the bridge. The Abbé, on the invitation of the Capitaine, mixed the dressing for the salad according to his own formula for which he said some women's magazine in America had offered him $1000 if he would put it in writing. We had it free. All I remember is that he used pepper, salt, beef juice, a touch of garlic (ugh!) and melted butter! The Capitaine's eyes opened wide when the melted butter went into the bowl. The garlic was what disturbed me. I might say that all this was in December when passengers were few and there was little competition for the honor of sitting at the Captain's table or dining with him in his quarters.

However, I always loved sea stories and admired shipmasters and I was always glad to meet one afloat or ashore. I met a noted one in an odd way. The first American ship taken prize in World War II was the SS *City of Trent* (Joseph A. Gainard, master) out of Baltimore, bound for Manchester, England, with a cargo of flour, tobacco, apples, lard and other such innocuous material when it was halted on the Grand Banks by the German pocket battleship *Deutschland* (later renamed the *Lützow*) on October 9, 1939, and a prize crew put aboard to take it to Germany. Before the battleship pulled away thirty-two survivors from the sunken British ship SS *Stonegate* were also put aboard the SS *City of Trent* to be carried to Germany as prisoners of war.

The pocket battleship disappeared. So did the merchant vessel. All that was known of their encounter on the Grand Banks was that the SS *City of Trent* was missing at sea. It was a front page story in this country and something of a sensation weeks later when it turned out that Captain Gainard of the SS *City of Trent* had outwitted the German prize crew, had brought about the release of the British "prisoners of war" when he put into the neutral Norwegian port of Tromsoe to take on fresh water and finally, by a brilliant coup involving the "violation of Norwegian neutrality" and the removal of the German prize crew by the Norwegian navy, regained possession of his ship. The SS *City of Trent* was free again and Captain Joseph A. Gainard was the hero of the day. He received a hero's welcome when he returned here.

He has been dead these twenty years. Who remembers him

now? I do, and I'll tell you how and why. One day in the office I received a phone call from a member of the New York Yacht Club. Among the honors thrust upon Captain Gainard for his exploit was to be a dinner at that ultra-posh club. To me that was something of a sensation in itself — the millionaire amateur sailors doing homage to a master mariner of the merchant marine. Very interesting. However, it seemed that the guest of honor had made one condition in his note of acceptance to the dinner. That was what brought about the phone call to me from the New York Yacht Club. Captain Gainard insisted that I be there to introduce him when it was time for him to stand up and give an account of himself.

I was astonished. *Que diable allais-je faire dans cette galère?* There was no visible or logical connection. But I accepted eagerly. I wanted to meet the man and hear his stirring story firsthand. I have no doubt that the bar at the New York Yacht Club that night was well stocked with some of the best wines, whiskies and liqueurs that were to be had for love or money. When I was introduced to Captain Gainard he was seated with a group of the dinner committee at a round table near the end of the bar and he was drinking a ten-cent bottle of pop! Who said that a hero must drink brandy? (Doctor Samuel Johnson; that's who. I just took time out to look it up.) I called for a martini to help me absorb the shock.

The next order of business was to find out why in the world the guest of honor had wanted me to introduce him at the dinner. It turned out to be a simple matter. He was a sports fan and, in particular, a rabid baseball rooter. He was a regular reader of my sports column in the *Times*. When he was off on a voyage his sister — he was a bachelor and lived with his sister in the Boston area — cut out the daily columns and saved them for him. He would take the collection to sea with him on his next voyage and read them at leisure. Under such conditions it's easy to understand that our meeting that evening was the beginning of a beautiful friendship. For the next two years any time his ship was in New York harbor he would stop by the *Times* office to have a chat with me. Of course, I was always delighted to see him — a lean man of middle height and middle age with a weather-tanned face and a touch of gray in his hair. He had been to all the great ports of the world, had a working knowledge of three or four foreign languages, a good grounding in Latin and apparently he had read all the books he could find on naval history.

Then came Pearl Harbor and the next time I saw the man he had lost one of the four stripes on his sleeve. He was no longer Captain Gainard of the merchant marine but Commander Gainard, U. S. Naval Reserve, recalled to active duty. He had some kind of hush-hush anti-submarine assignment that sent him out in command of what looked like the perfect target for a U-boat but was really a bait ship trying to lure enemy submarines into coming to close quarters. I took it to be something like the British Q-boats that were playing the same game in the English Channel. At the last minute the "innocent victim" turned out to be loaded for bear. There lingers in mind the impression that Commander Gainard referred to his ship as a "hedgehog" and said that, instead of dropping depth charges one at a time over the stern, it fired an extensive pattern of them all at once from a masked battery. Somewhere in navy files there must be an official report on this venture. All that Commander Gainard offered in comment when he was next seen ashore was: "We got some." He wouldn't say how many. But he was promoted captain and assigned to take a 20,000-ton attack transport to the war in the Pacific.

Before he left I had him to dinner in town with two other navy men and a young artillery lieutenant who showed up wearing the first "Eisenhower jacket" that met my eye. The artillery lieutenant was Quentin Roosevelt who had been wounded in North Africa and had been sent back to Halloran Hospital on Staten Island for treatment. He was sound of wind and limb again and was leaving the next day to rejoin the First Division in the African theatre. One of the navy guests was Commodore Frederick George (Red) Reinicke, Jr., U.S.N., who was a big redheaded guard on three Navy football teams away back yonder and whom I had come to know well when he served a hitch as graduate manager of athletics at Annapolis. Red was now Port Director in New York, one of the big shipping jobs of the war and he took me around his watery precinct on several inspection tours. It was most impressive — ammunition ships here, oilers there, food ships in another place, freighters anchored in line all the way from the submarine net at the Narrows to beyond Yonkers up the Hudson. When a convoy left at night each ship had to up anchor wherever it was and hit the submarine gate at the exact minute or a monumental traffic jam would foul up the harbor.

The fourth guest at the dinner was Red's "opposite number" in the Royal Navy, Captain Arthur Marsden, who was the British Admiralty man in charge in the area. Not only were there many British merchant ships loading in the harbor but some of their warships put in now and then for repairs at the Brooklyn Navy Yard or elsewhere. I had met Captain Marsden at one of the Lambs Club dinners and found him a delightful companion. Aside from his naval duties he was a Member of Parliament on the Conservative side of the aisle. He had been a junior officer on a destroyer in the Battle of Jutland in 1916 and his ship had been sunk not long after midnight. He was in the water until dawn and was the sole survivor of the ship's company.

I know when to listen and the dinner that night was the place for it as far as I was concerned. Red Reinicke had been on an American destroyer in World War I. Captain Gainard had been a "rating" on one of our warships during the same period. All three were familiar with many African, Asiatic and South American ports of call. The name of a ship or a captain or a port would start a chain of stories from these three deep-water veterans. A goodly company, a great night. Quentin Roosevelt took off for North Africa the next day and Captain Gainard headed for San Diego where his attack transport was to be fitted for the struggle in Pacific waters. He never made it. He died suddenly in a naval hospital on the Coast, of what I never knew. He was quite a man.

Another seagoing gent was responsible for a book that I wrote and he illustrated. That was *The American Sporting Scene* published by Macmillan in 1941, at which time the artist's smock had been tossed aside and his naval reserve uniform taken out of mothballs. He was Lieutenant Commander Joseph A. Golinkin, recalled to active duty just before the book appeared in print. My fondness for art led to the production of this book. I saw in the papers a notice of an exhibition of oils, watercolors, lithographs and charcoal sketches of sporting scenes at a gallery somewhere in the Fifties and I went around to have a look. I was delighted with the exhibition and particularly with the beautiful watercolors of action in many fields of sport — sailing, horse racing, baseball, football, ice hockey and practically everything else on the calendar.

In my sports column I commented enthusiastically about the art exhibition and a few days later the artist dropped anchor by my desk to suggest a bit of teamwork; I to write about the sports events I had seen and the champions I had known, he to ornament the text with watercolor paintings and crayon sketches of games in progress and competitors in action. Since the book has been out of print some years, nothing that I state here can have any mercenary motive. All that I insist on at this late date is that the illustrations alone were worth the price of admission. The publishers did a handsome job of printing and it was a lovely book to leaf through even if you couldn't read.

One reason we never did another book together was that I soon gave up writing sports and the artist didn't swallow the anchor for many years. He led destroyer escort divisions in battle in the Mediterranean and in the Pacific, had four stripes on his sleeve as he stood on the deck of the battleship *Missouri* and watched the Japanese sign the surrender papers, remained in the Navy after the war and was retired as a rear admiral a few years ago. I'd call that pretty good going for an artist, a fellow who is supposed to starve quietly in a garret.

Looking for something else the other day I came across a letter from another old salt, Bob Bartlett, arctic explorer, skipper of the famous schooner *Morrissey*, aid to Peary in his successful search for the North Pole in 1909, and a wonderful character in his own right. He was as rugged as his schooner and he had a voice that could outroar the elements. It was flavored with a thick Scotch-Irish brogue honestly come by from his Newfoundland ancestors. Hearty and jovial as all get out — oh, a lovely, lively man was Bob Bartlett! And what hair-raising tales he had to tell of glorious adventures in the arctic seas.

Apparently he had asked me to identify some biblical quotation and I had failed to find the source. I offer his letter here because it shows Bob plunging ahead with his pen the way he drove the *Morrissey* butting into the ice floes west of

Greenland. He wrote it in longhand on lined paper and I
give it in his own words and punctuation:

> Sch. Morrissey
> East Gloucester.
> Mass. Jany, 20/44
>
> Dear John:
>   Thanks for letter. I found it. It's in "The Psalter." The
> Thirteenth Day, Morning Prayer. Psalm 68. Exsurgat Deus.
> 6 Verse. Instead of Psalm quotation from King James; which
> reads, "but the rebellious dwell in a dry land": — The Psalter
> Says: — "but letteth the runagates continue in scarceness."
> By God, it took a woman to find it. A friend of mine's wife;
> at the Coffee House, bagged it. It's from Mountain Meadows,
> last Book of John Buchan.
>
> > Forgive me for bothering you.
> >   Sincerely, Bob Bartlett

Bob had many friends on the *Times* staff and I often encountered him in the office. One day I met him as he was
about to enter the entrance on 43rd Street and I asked him
some question about walruses. In two minutes we had a big
crowd around as Bob's booming voice filled the street with
walrus lore. With magnificent gestures he had the Labrador
Current sweeping in from Broadway, the ice piling up toward Eighth Avenue, the heaving deck of the *Morrissey* under our feet and a herd of bewhiskered walruses in the doorway of the *Times* Annex. For the moment it probably was
the best show in town.

The last time I saw Bob he was speaking at the annual dinner of the Explorers Club and telling of his love of life at sea,
especially in the Arctic with the midnight sun turning the ice-
bergs into gorgeous sparkling spires. It was a paean in praise
of the ocean — he called it the "awshun" — and it sprang
from the depths of his great heart and his huge lungs. Like

the roar of the sea itself came the thundering peroration that I wish I could give as he rolled it out in his broad brogue, but cold print is a poor substitute for the warm voice of the grand old man who was Bob Bartlett. You will have to lend a hand here. This is as near as I can come to remembering his final words:

I'm an alld man and I know I'm gawn to die soon and I'm gawn to heaven, I hawp, but I'll tell you wan thing — if there isn't an awshun there, I won't stay!

XII

IN THE GARDEN
OF THE CELLULOID GODS

W<small>HEN</small> a man dies he usually leaves behind him a few unfinished odds and ends that were on his schedule. When Alexander Woollcott died on January 23, 1943, I fell heir to his chance to become a movie actor. (Those Information Please movie shorts didn't count, even though we had to join the Screen Actors Guild to make them legal. What we did was, as guaranteed, spontaneous and unrehearsed. It wasn't acting.)

Some weeks after Alec's death I had a phone call from the Hollywood office of a pair of noted film directors, Charles Brackett and Billy Wilder. Because Alec was a mystery story fan in his off-duty hours, he had agreed to appear in a prologue to a mystery play that Messrs. Brackett and Wilder had on the fire. They wanted me to fly out to Hollywood and replace Alec in the prologue. When I said that I couldn't go out there, they asked me whether or not I would do it if they filmed the scene in New York. It was only a short bit — about three minutes on camera and a few lines to deliver to set the scene and the tone of the mystery film that was to follow.

I didn't know what I was letting myself in for when J

agreed to do it. When Billy Wilder arrived in New York he came to see me at the office and decided to film the scene in the living room of my house in Riverdale. He showed up there one day with a mobile unit consisting of a big truck and a crew of about a dozen men, all told, including the Paramount Pictures' local lawyer in New York who turned out to be Boris Kaplan, a classmate of mine in college. Meeting Boris was the only happy incident of the day. The rest was confusion sprinkled with chaos.

The first thing they did was to run half a dozen electric cables into the living room for the lights, the sound track and the motion picture camera. Then they set up a blackboard on which my brief lines were chalked. Next they moved all the furniture around — several times. Each time they moved a bit of furniture they moved the lights again. They tried me sitting in different chairs. I had a handsome Airedale by the name of Spike whose disposition wasn't as good as his pedigree. He was surly and selfish. Billy Wilder had Spike sit beside me while I ran through a rehearsal of my lines but the dog couldn't keep a civil tongue in his head. He snapped at one of the crew and was dismissed to the kitchen with an official reprimand. It took a long time to adjust the sound track to the right point. We had any number of "runthroughs" and something always was wrong with them. Either I fumbled my lines or the camera jammed or the lighting was wrong or the sound went sour. It was noontime before we knew it, nothing had been accomplished and everybody was hungry.

We adjourned to the dining room for cold cuts, potato salad, tea or coffee and some kind of dessert. This was in wartime, of course. Meat was rationed — and we had a hungry crew of twelve as our guests. In one hour they ate up our meat ration stamps for the whole month! About mid-

afternoon we finished the brief bit that I had to do and the
camera, the lights, the reflectors and the cables were hauled
out of the living room. Billy Wilder and truck and crew de-
parted and I assumed that I was to be packaged off to Hollywood to appear in a prologue to an English mystery story
filmed under the title *The Uninvited*. Some months later the
film was released. There was no prologue. I was nowhere to
be seen. Apparently I couldn't act any better than a dog —
my dog Spike, I mean. We both had been dismissed, but at
least I had been paid for my services.

Until I saw the picture I knew nothing about the story or
who was in it. To my surprise, I knew three of the leading
figures in *The Uninvited*. All three had been on Information
Please more than once. Ray Milland was the hero who
saved the young heroine from being frightened to death in
the haunted house on the English coast. Cornelia Otis Skinner was the villainess who did the fake haunting. Dorothy
Stickney was a fey character who added local color to the
plot. I admired all three very much and I wish I could have
appeared in the picture with them. All I lacked was talent.

Not long after that film flop on my part Dan Golenpaul
took Information Please on a bond-selling tour that carried us
as far as the West Coast where we broadcast the show from
Los Angeles and San Francisco. By that time so many Hollywood figures had appeared on Information Please that we
regulars on the program looked forward to something like
an alumni reunion in Beverly Hills. Safari Leader Golenpaul,
who knew the movie colony longer and better than we did,
arranged the schedule so that we stayed about ten days at the
Beverly-Wilshire Hotel, had a round of parties of all kinds
and penetrated a few of the big movie studios.

One of the first affairs we attended was a buffet luncheon
at the home of Charles Brackett where I had the privilege of

meeting Olivia de Haviland and of asking my host, Mr. Brackett, why he had made me the face on the cutting-room floor. Billy Wilder had told me that it was his partner who had sentenced me to movie oblivion. The Brackett explanation was brief and complete. He looked at me with something like indignation and demanded: "What did they photograph that through — a chimney?"

Even in Beverly Hills and with all the parties that we went to I stuck to my custom of getting up early and going out to inspect the birds, trees and flowers of the area. Beverly Hills is full of canyons with modest to palatial homes tucked away on the wooded slopes. My old friend Frank Craven, veteran actor and playwright, had a nice little home only five or six blocks from our hotel. I was on his doorstep every morning at 8 o'clock and we would go walking together up Coldwater Canyon or some nearby region. I was armed with my field glasses for the spotting of birds and Frank carried an ancient pair of opera glasses through which I took one look and then advised him that he might as well put a stone over each eye as try to see anything through those glasses. He remained unconvinced and would peer solemnly through them as I directed his attention to a hooded oriole, an Audubon's warbler, a black-chinned hummingbird or — one that was new to me — a phainopepla, a shining little black bird with a sharp crest and white patches in its wings.

As we were rambling along one morning a taxi came tearing down the canyon road and suddenly screeched to a halt on the far side of the road from us. The driver was a woman wearing the conventional chauffeur's cap. The woman taxi driver was another evidence of a country at war. Out of the halted taxi came a fairly large, bold and brisk gentleman who strode across the road toward us, held out his hand to me and said warmly: "My dear friend, how are you? I saw in the papers that you were in town. Why haven't you been to see me?"

It was the great Sam Goldwyn himself, in person, and quite a picture. In a jiffy I can explain how I became his "dear friend." It was he who had produced a movie based on the life of Lou Gehrig, the great Yankee baseball star who had died untimely of a creeping form of paralysis called "amyotrophic lateral sclerosis." Not only did I know Lou well as a Yankee player but he was also a neighbor of mine in Riverdale and I used to visit him frequently when he was housebound and finally bedridden in the last stages of his illness. I was probably the last member of the sports fraternity to see him alive. When he died I was asked by his wife, Eleanor, to make the announcement to the newspapers.

The motion picture based on Lou's life was called *Pride of The Yankees* with Gary Cooper in the title role and half a dozen big league ball players, including some of Lou's Yankee cronies, playing bit parts to make the action more realistic in the baseball scenes. The premiere was at one of the big Broadway movie theatres on a warm June night and, of course, it was to be quite an affair. Late in the afternoon I had a phone call at the *Times* office from Christy Walsh who handled the business affairs of Babe Ruth, Lou Gehrig and other sports stars and sold syndicated articles written under their names, mostly "ghost" jobs. Christy was helping with the advance publicity on the *Pride of The Yankees* film. He said that there would be onstage preliminaries to the presentation of the movie, including the appearance of all the members of the Yankee ball team led by Manager Joe McCarthy. Producer Sam Goldwyn would consider it a great favor if I would act as master of ceremonies and introduce the ball players individually.

What in the world made him pick me? How did he know who I was? He never read the sports pages.

"No," admitted Christy Walsh over the phone, "but he listens to Information Please every week and he's one of your fans. How about it?"

All my life I've been like *Maître Corbeau sur un arbre perché;* I fall flat for flattery. I dashed home to Riverdale, put on a black tie and a white dinner jacket, and rushed downtown again to go through the process of standing on the stage in front of a microphone and presenting the Yankee teammates of the late Lou Gehrig, each with a few more or less appropriate words, to the packed house on a sweltering evening. If there was air-conditioning in the place, it didn't affect the climate behind the footlights. I was dripping when my chore was done. But *Pride of The Yankees* turned out to be a good picture and Mr. Sam Goldwyn was delighted with the way everything had gone. He invited me to have luncheon with him the next day at the sunken garden restaurant — the skating rink in winter — in Radio City.

I remember the luncheon well for several reasons. One was that the two other persons at the table were Paul Gallico and his wife, the former Baroness Garaboldi. Paul had written the script for *Pride of The Yankees* and they couldn't have picked a better man for the job. Aside from his writing ability in wider fields, Paul had been sports editor and columnist for the *Daily News* (New York) in his younger days and he and I were old friends. At this stage of his career he wasn't often in New York and I was glad to see him. Another reason to remember the luncheon was Sam Goldwyn himself. He lived up to all his advance billing. Of course, I knew that the monstrous malapropisms charged against him were a false front that he enjoyed as much as anybody else. To me, at close range, he seemed to be a man of energy, intelligence and even vision. As to the vision, at the end of the luncheon he had left some dollar bills on the plate for the waiter. He was discussing politics and economics with Paul Gallico and finally

he said: "Let's not fool ourselves, Paul. If things keep going
as they have been going in Washington" — here he picked
up a dollar bill from the plate and let it drop back again —
"that won't be worth twenty-five cents."

Check the prices of that day against what you can get for a
dollar now and you will realize that Mr. Sam Goldwyn, at
the luncheon, was a man of 20-20 economic eyesight or practically perfect vision. Anyway, he thanked me profusely for
my small contribution to the previous evening's entertainment. That was how I became his dear friend. As to calling upon him at his office in Hollywood, I wouldn't think of
it. Why, everybody in the area wanted to get into his office.
He was infinitely too busy to be bothered by casual visitors.

"I am never too busy to see my friends. Promise me you
will come to my office. Please, my friend."

Who could resist him? He looked so earnest and honest
and kind. I said I would. He shook hands, went back across
the street to his taxi and rolled on down the road. But I never
went to see him. I figured that I would be doing him a second favor by not bothering him at his office. And there was
always risk of being killed in the crush.

Frank Craven and I resumed our interrupted ramble up
the canyon, pausing here and there to peer at a bird or ex-
amine a flower. One morning when we returned to Frank's
residence he took me out back to show me his cultivated
flowers and his vegetables. He had a great store of both,
especially vegetables in the "Victory Garden" that we were
all urged to cultivate to alleviate the food shortage during
the war period. His was the strangest "Victory Garden" I
ever inspected. He had flowers and vegetables in alternate
rows — a row of geraniums, then a row of parsley; a row of
begonias, then a row of string beans; a row of lilies, then a
row of strawberries. He had some vegetables I never ate

and a few I never had heard of. I wondered at the infinite variety.

"Tell you how I did it," said Frank modestly. "I'm a simple man myself and I like to eat in the kitchen when nobody is around but one of these big movie magnates took me out to a swank restaurant for dinner and I swiped a menu. Then I went to a seed store and said I wanted a package of seed of every vegetable on the menu. That did it. Is there anything missing?"

Well, he had artichokes and onions and eggplant, all of which I preferred to keep at a distance, but I saw no asparagus, one of my favorite dishes.

"Follow me!" commanded Frank, leading me into another area masked by a grape arbor. There he had a fine stand of asparagus, several fig trees and an avocado tree about fifteen feet tall. Pointing to the young fruit that covered the avocado tree, Frank said: "Just wait until they ripen! Melt in your mouth."

Unfortunately, they wouldn't be ripe for another month and I couldn't wait that long. The morning walks with Frank were the most restful part of our stay in Beverly Hills and vicinity. Dan Golenpaul put on dinners for our friends in the movie colony and they retaliated with other dinners, cook-outs, buffets, receptions and catch-as-catch-can cocktail parties. Boris Karloff had us out to his chalet tucked high up over a valley and there I met A. J. Cronin, the British novelist, and saw my first "monkey-puzzle tree" or *Araucaria araucana*. I knew its near relative, the Norfolk Island Pine (*Araucaria excelsa*), from my visits to Bermuda where it is a stately and decorative addition to the landscape of the island.

I was a real movie fan and I was delighted to meet some of my favorite movie actors in the flesh. At Jimmie Gleason's party for us I found myself talking to Danny Kaye who had just come off the movie lot and was still wearing his costume, war paint and a red wig. When Gregory Ratoff had us to lunch at the big M-G-M commissary, I sat next to Gene Kelly and saw Spencer Tracy quietly eating at the next table. Later in the day we went to the set where Director Ratoff was filming a scene of *Song of Russia* with Robert Taylor playing the lead. It was the last scene of the movie and the last bit of acting that Robert Taylor was to do for several years. We met him as he walked off the stage to head for duty with the United States Air Force.

Lillian Gish was doing a film over at Universal City. We had promised to visit her on the lot and found her playing the mother part in some New England family drama. Her stage husband was Richard Dix and her stage son was the then budding Donald O'Connor. On another set nearby I found my friend Pat O'Brien being directed by Frank Borzage in a light comedy called *The Butler's Daughter*. The daughter in the case was Deanna Durbin. While they reloaded the cameras we all sat around and talked baseball. Sitting beside Director Mervyn LeRoy one day on the M-G-M lot when he was filming *Madame Curie* with Greer Garson in the title role, he turned to me between shots and said that he was worried. I was surprised. Everything seemed to be going along very smoothly.

"Oh, everything's fine here," he said. "I'm worried about the Yankees. They're in a bad slump. I don't know that they'll make it this year."

Director LeRoy needn't have worried. They made it and won the world series. But the real rooter of the Beverly Hills brigade was the taller member of the team of Kalmar and Ruby, songwriters and scriptwriters extraordinary. Outside of their professional collaboration, they were as disparate a pair as the famous English partners of Crosse & Blackwell, "Purveyors to Her Majesty the Queen," one of whom was the most famous lay preacher in England and the other the owner of a whippet that won the Waterloo Cup, the Epsom Derby of the dog racing world. I never can remember which was which but I knew the oddities of the Kalmar and Ruby pair. Away from the piano or the writing desk chunky little Bert Kalmar was one of the best amateur magicians in the country. Taller and thinner Harry Ruby was a noted book collector and had in his Beverly Hills home a paneled library filled with precious first editions of Keats, Thoreau, Milton, Poe, Thackeray, Dickens, Goldsmith and more — all upholstered and boxed to preserve them from the touch of unworthy intruders and the ravages of time.

It was Ruby who was the record-breaking baseball rooter. He rooted for every team in the two big leagues! He went far out of his way to make friends with players and managers and at one time or another he had put on the uniform of fifteen of the sixteen big league clubs and played the infield during batting practice before games during the regular season or at the southern camps during Spring training. The only big league uniform he hadn't worn was that of the New York Yankees — Mervyn LeRoy's favorite team. It wasn't for lack of trying. Ruby had begged Manager Joe McCarthy to let him don the uniform and get out there with the Yankees as he had with all the other teams in the two leagues but Manager McCarthy was, as Harry put it, "repulsive" to the idea.

"You'd get hurt," explained McCarthy, "and I'd get blamed."

"Look," pleaded Harry, "I'll even pitch batting practice if you want."

"Batting practice!" said McCarthy with horror. "The way we hit you'd get killed out there!"

Some months later the team went into a tailspin when all the Yankee sluggers slumped at the same time. Groucho Marx wrote out a telegram that he advised Ruby to rush to McCarthy. It read: "The way your team is hitting Baby Snooks would be safe pitching batting practice." (Baby Snooks was a character made famous on radio by the late Fanny Brice.)

Ruby still had hopes and refused to ruin them by sending an insulting message to Manager McCarthy. However, he might just as well have sent the telegram. He never made the team.

To show how long ago all this was, we made the trip to the West Coast and back entirely by train. Who would do that now? However, train travel has some advantages over the jet planes. You have a better chance to fraternize with fellow travelers. On the train we took from Chicago to Los Angeles we encountered Artur Rubinstein and in a quiet conversation in the observation car he explained to me the advantage of playing the piano rather than any other instrument in the orchestra.

"It's healthier," he insisted and went on to give evidence. He said that violinists usually quit in their seventies and woodwind players earlier. But Paderewski, Saint-Saëns, de Pachmann, Moritz Rosenthal and others played in their eighties and he himself had heard Francis Planté, the great Frenchman, play when he was ninety-seven. And play well, too. I asked him what was at the other end of the gamut, the most dangerous instrument to play. Perhaps the harp. A man might develop heart disease just carrying the thing around. I once heard a chap sing — to a piano accompaniment — a song entitled "I Took My Harp to the Party and Nobody Asked Me to Play." It was a tragic ballad.

"No, not the harp," said the pianist. "Many a harpist grows

to a ripe old age at his work — or at her work. Often the harpist in an orchestra is a woman. And I don't think the kettledrums are dangerous, either. In fact, it looks like good exercise to me and that ought to keep a man in good health. Doctors recommend regular exercise, don't they?"

He was narrowing the field down to the brasses and the woodwinds. At times it did look as though some enthusiastic slide trombonist was going to blow himself up in his struggle with the mouthpiece.

"No, it isn't a brass," said Rubinstein, and looking around to make sure that nobody was close enough to overhear, he whispered, "it's one of the woodwinds, but I won't say which one. Some of my good friends play the deadly instrument and they are very happy. Better they should not know."

A very kindly gentleman, Artur Rubinstein, and thoughtful. Nobody could take any exception to his remarks except some narrow-minded person like a manufacturer of woodwind musical instruments — and who cares about him?

But we were talking of the quaint old custom of traveling by train. When we concluded our tour with a broadcast from San Francisco, Mr. and Mrs. Golenpaul went to Mexico, Mr. and Mrs. Levant went back to Hollywood, and Messrs. Adams, Fadiman and Kieran boarded a train heading eastward. On the train we found an Information Please alumna, Dorothy Stickney, who had just closed out an engagement in San Francisco. That called for a slight reunion and some social activity on the way to Chicago. At Chicago we had to shift trains and when we boarded the Twentieth Century Limited we found we were Pullman neighbors of Gertrude Lawrence and her leading man returning from a tour that ended in Los Angeles. We took down the movable panels between adjoining compartments and had a lively general

cocktail party. It was wonderful fun, but when I boarded the
train in San Francisco I had no idea that there would be gay
luncheon parties and sounds of revelry by night on the way
to New York and I had neglected to pack enough cash to
fit the occasion. I managed to hold up my end but it was a
close squeak. When I tipped the Pullman porter and walked
off the train in Grand Central Station the next morning I had
just fifty cents in my pocket. However, I was only two
short blocks from my financial filling station, the dear old
brownstone Fifth Avenue Bank of those days that is the Bank
of New York now in a shiny new building. I preferred the
famous brownstone edifice with its real wood fire in an open
fireplace in front of which elderly dowager depositors occasionally had tea. I wish that they had kept the old building as it was. It had a Victorian or even colonial flavor. And
if they had to change the name of the bank, in the wake of
Point of No Return I think they might have preserved its
literary and historical identity by calling it the John P. Marquand Memorial Bank and No Trust Co.

XIII

C'EST LA GUERRE

IT WAS the war that finally did me in as a sports columnist. Until the Pearl Harbor horror I managed to keep going as a full-time worker for the *New York Times* in the field of sports and do some other chores on the side such as the radio show, the movie shorts, random speeches and occasional magazine articles. But when we joined the shooting war I was swamped with additional obligations that estopped me — I love that word "estopped," borrowed from Blackstone (the English jurist, not the Chicago hotel) — from putting in my regular hours of duty in the press box at the Yankee Stadium, at the ringside in Madison Square Garden, on the clubhouse lawn at Belmont Park and other such delectable haunts.

Everybody lent a hand in the war effort in one way or another and sports writers were by no means exempt. The American Theatre Wing of the Red Cross organized a sports committee that sent out parties of writers and athletes to entertain the inmates of service hospitals and army and navy installations in the area. I was a charter member of that visiting team and kept making rounds with the sports group until long after the end of the war. One of my prized possessions is an onyx electric desk clock — it is three feet from the tip of my nose as I type this — that was presented to me by the patients in a veterans' hospital on the Hudson near Beacon, New York, because I made so many visits there to talk about sports. Or perhaps it was because of one particular trip to the place.

These were all excursions after dark or, at least, after-dinner entertainment for the service men in camp or the patients in hospitals. When the camp or the hospital was at a distance from town, our sports troop would start out in the afternoon. We tried to have four or five in the party, writers, athletes, fight managers, coaches, umpires, referees or sports officials of one kind or another to give the troops a balanced diet. Baseball and boxing were the favorite sports of our captive audiences. One day I was a member of a group of five scheduled to take an afternoon train out of Grand Central Station, debark at Yonkers, meet a Red Cross car and driver there and ride to this hospital for tubercular veterans up the Hudson. I saw nobody I knew on the train and when I walked out to the Red Cross station wagon at the Yonkers station I was still alone. The driver was a girl in uniform. I explained that apparently the others who planned to make the trip had to cancel. Many who meant well were not masters of their own time and perhaps other duties had called.

"Are you going up there alone?" she asked.

"I will if you'll take me."

"Get in," she said.

It was a very skimpy show the patients had that night but by that time I was looked upon as an old friend and we rambled on about sports — give and take — as old friends do when they get together. Even so, I was embarrassed by the absence of the others who had been scheduled to appear and I think the old-timers in the audience felt sorry for me. It was on my next visit — happily with sufficient teammates — that they gave me the clock.

These sports expeditions were easy to take in stride but on top of that I had to answer the American Theatre Wing calls for help from the entertainment field in which they placed me as a member of a popular radio show and a series of movie shorts. I made the round of camps, canteens and hospitals in that guise, too, usually with companions who were much more entertaining than I was. And better looking, too, which is faint praise. There was also work to do for the Treasury Department in the matter of writing appeals or putting in appearances to spur the sales of war bonds. There were articles to be written and broadcasts to be made for the Office of War Information, too. Over one stretch I did a series of weekly broadcasts to South Africa for the OWI with a notable couple as my teammates, Fredric March and his actress wife Florence Eldridge. We used to "cut the platters" at the OWI headquarters on West 57th Street in mid-afternoon and then adjourn to a nearby restaurant for tea and talk. The announcer who opened and closed the show in the Afrikaans language was Jo Marais, the concert hall singer of South African folk songs who, I am delighted to learn through the newspaper reports, is still on the entertainment circuit with his wife, Miranda, a dancer.

All this took time but it was in good company and I enjoyed it. I kept running into old friends and meeting new headliners of the day. Going into a studio to do a sports broadcast for the armed services radio network, I found that my partner on the broadcast was Paul Douglas, the stage and movie star whom I had known in earlier years when he was a radio sports announcer. On a broadcast to Australia for the OWI the man sharing the microphone with me was Beardsley Ruml, the hefty and handsome financial wizard who thought up the scheme of having employers withhold a portion of all salaries and wages to make sure that Uncle Sam received his share in the form of individual income taxes. It was an act of distrust of our intention or ability to pay later on demand. In short, an insult to our national character — and thoroughly justified. It made millions for the government. Naturally I stood in awe of a money magician like Mr. Ruml but, for all his imposing appearance, he was as easy as an old shoe and as friendly as a bartender.

But doing these things, and many more that I have forgotten over the intervening years, made it impossible for me to keep abreast of the sports activities of the day. I fell behind fast. The *Times* deserved a full-time sports columnist who would know what he was talking or writing about and I could no longer qualify. I had too many other activities that filled my days and nights. I quit the *Times* with regret in December, 1941, and went down to the *Sun* on lower Broadway to write a shorter general column six days a week. Not only was the word count considerably less but in a general column I could put to good use my adventures and encounters in the strange new world into which I had been projected — radio, movie shorts, charity drives, military propaganda, Treasury Department war bond sales promotion, OWI broadcasts, hospital visits, Red Cross work and assorted other good causes. Very little of that could have been poured into a sports column though there were occasional sports items picked up in strange places.

I have forgotten whether we were selling war bonds or helping a Red Cross drive when Information Please was broadcast from Atlanta, but during our stay in that town F.P.A. and I went out to speak in the recreation hall of some big military hospital. Frank gave his usual humorous talk and left everybody laughing. I told a few sports stories, just what was expected of me, and then volunteered to answer questions. The first question thrown at me from the third row back was a cinch to handle. Was Luke Appling any good as a ball player?

I was about to launch into high praise of Luke Appling, fine shortstop of the Chicago White Sox and twice the batting champion of the American League, but before I could open my mouth a roar of laughter swept the hall. You have to be careful when among strangers. At another hospital a soldier rose in a hall and asked my opinion of a prizefighter. I said truthfully that I thought the fighter was terrible. "Thanks," said the questioner. "He's my brother." This time in Atlanta I merely stepped to the front of the platform, peered around and asked: "Is Luke Appling in the house?"

He was. Some soldiers pushed him forward from where he had been standing in the doorway. He was now Sergeant Appling, infantryman, engaged in the physical training part of the rehabilitation program at the hospital. A good lad as well as a fine ball player, I was delighted to see Luke again. And since it was Atlanta, I couldn't miss seeing an old friend I had followed for years around golf courses while he was gathering one championship after another, Bob Jones. He and the late John B. Kelly, father of Princess Grace of Monaco, were the sports champions with whom I had the longest acquaintance. I had known Bob since he appeared as a fourteen-year-old competitor for the national amateur golf championship at the Merion Cricket Club in 1916. I met Jack Kelly a year earlier on my first official out-of-town assignment as a *Times* sports writer.

By "official" I mean that I was sent over to Philadelphia to cover the 1915 Labor Day rowing regatta on the Schuylkill and the *Times* paid my expenses. That made it official. Weeks before that I had covered the national amateur rowing championships at Springfield, Massachusetts, but I was allowed that privilege only because I told the sports editor that I planned to be there anyway and would be glad to file copy on the two-day competition. My former boss on construction work, James Pilkington, was the long-time president of the National Association of Amateur Oarsmen and he was driving up there in an ancient and decrepit Panhard to preside over the proceedings. He offered to take me along. I could help with the driving and the necessary emergency repairs to the car en route. However, riding to the regatta with the famous president of the rowing association was a wonderful break for a rookie sports writer on his first big story. I was bound to get a good seat at the races.

Hold Jack Kelly in the wings a minute; I must digress. This was the time the boys from the Duluth Boat Club came out of the woods to sweep the river. That was because they had been most bountifully backed by a rich merchant out there by the name of Julius Barnes who was later named "Wheat Dictator" by President Woodrow Wilson during World War I. A rowing enthusiast, Barnes put up the money to help his home town gain fame in the rowing world. He set up a training program. He paid for new shells, gigs, oars and all other needed equipment. He brought his elegant motorboat *Bobbie B* — named for his son — to Springfield for the championship regatta and it was immediately designated the "official boat" with the referee of the regatta, James Pilkington, aboard. I sat in the front seat with Mr. Pilkington, Julius Barnes and the driver of the shining and luxurious vehicle. I never had it better in my life.

The Duluth success at Springfield led to a sustained interest in rowing out yonder and the subsequent emergence of a Duluth Boat Club sculler by the name of Walter M. Hoover who won the national singles in 1921 and capped that by winning the great Diamond Sculls event the following year at Henley, England. There was a civic demonstration when he returned from that signal triumph and the parade was followed by a dinner in the oarsman's honor. A local poetess informed the committee that she had composed an ode in

praise of the great Hoover and would be delighted to read it
at the dinner. It turned out that she was slightly mixed in
her Hoovers. Another man of the same name had come to
public notice when he was appointed to ladle out wheat and
other foodstuffs to the hungry Belgians and Russians in the
wake of World War I. He later became President of the
United States. When the poetess rose to read her ode at the
rowing dinner her opening line was:

Oh thou who fed'st the starving millions . . .

Now we can get back to Jack Kelly whom I approached
that September day in 1915 by way of a walk from the North
Philadelphia station down through the woods to the group of
boathouses along the Schuylkill River. I remember well the
walk through the woods because I heard a bird whistling in
notes that were new to me and I investigated. I tracked the
whistler down and thus saw my first cardinal. In those days
a cardinal was practically unknown around New York,
though now they are settled residents in the region.

When I reached the river I strolled along and saw a tall
young fellow working over a shell in one of the boathouses.
I walked in and introduced myself as Kieran of the *New York
Times*. The tall young fellow held out his hand, said his
name was Jack Kelly and added that he was rigging his boat
for the singles competition that afternoon. I forget now
whether he won or lost that afternoon but he won many a
race after that, including the national singles championship in
1919 and 1920 and the Olympic singles championship at Ant-
werp in 1920.

He had, however, one stunning reversal. His entry for the
Diamond Sculls was refused because he wasn't a "gentleman"
under the English code of those days when athletes were
divided into "gentlemen" and "players" who, though they

could compete in common, had to enter clubhouses or playing fields by separate doors or gates so marked. What marked
Jack Kelly as no "gentleman" was that he had been a laborer,
he had worked with his hands during a summer vacation
when he had laid brick for his father, a prosperous contractor.
For this he was barred from the Henley classic.

It rankled. But the whirligig of time brings in his revenges
and John B. Kelly lent a helping hand. He brought up his
son John B., Jr., as an oarsman of the first water. He made
sure that the boy would qualify at Henley as a sculler and a
gentleman. He was never allowed to soil his hands in manual
labor. In 1949 John B. Kelly, Jr., with his father looking on,
won the Diamond Sculls at Henley and Jack Kelly's Thirty
Years' War with the English rowing and social set had ended
in triumph.

That was on a Saturday. The next morning I went over
to New Rochelle to take a walk in the woods with my friend
Joe Stevens who lived on Stratton Road. As I came up the
driveway I found Joe on the lawn with the *Times* sports
section in his hand. Before I could get out of the car he
waved the paper in the air and said: "Hey, how about Jack
Kelly's boy? Isn't that great? Come on inside and let's see if
we can get Jack on the phone."

We got him. He had left Henley but we tracked him
down in a London hotel. The transatlantic conversation was
not epic, it was merely heartwarming. We were very fond of
Jack Kelly — as, indeed, was everybody who knew him. His
last will and testament was typical of the man; fair and forth-
right, but naught set down in malice and all in the best of
humor. I'm glad that I walked down through the woods that
long ago morning and met a good tall lad rigging a shell in a
boathouse on the Schuylkill River. Pleasant memories are
private treasures that moths cannot corrupt nor thieves break
in and steal.

But there are memories not so pleasant. As the war went on I kept working around the clock and dashing from one engagement to another. I was worried about my son, John Jr. who, when I last heard from him, was a first lieutenant with the 18th Infantry, First Division, in Sicily. He had been acting as forward observer for the heavy weapons company — I had reason to believe that there was some slight risk attached to the job — and I hadn't heard from him in months. Long after the fighting had ended in Sicily I had a letter from Ted Roosevelt in England where he was training for the invasion of Normandy. By that time Ted was a brigadier general in charge of the infantry of the Fourth Division. He wrote that he had been down to visit his old division — the First — and everybody in the 18th Infantry was sorry about what had happened to "Red," which is what we both called John Jr. in those days. It was Ted who managed to extract John Jr. from the Tank Destroyer Corps in North Africa and have him assigned to the First Division where he could keep a friendly eye on him. While Ted remained with the First Division I had more frequent news of John Jr. through him than I did from the young man himself.

This letter about everybody being sorry "for what happened to Red" was no help to me or the other members of the family. As far as we knew, he might be dead, captured, sick, missing in action or court-martialed for some high crime or low breach of military discipline. I didn't mention Ted's letter around the house because his mother was going through the last stages of an incurable disease and worry about John Jr. could only have made her condition worse. Probably because he had been a very sickly child, he was her favorite of our three children. I kept the bad news — whatever it was — from her and did the worrying for us both.

In an effort to stay in good physical shape to go on with my busy schedule, I used to sprint at intervals in my regular morning walks in Van Cortlandt Park or wherever it might be. One morning during a sprint I suddenly had a paralyzing pain in my chest and had to sit down on the side of the road. I thought it was merely what we used to call "getting a stitch" when we were boys — momentary shortness of breath from too much exertion — but over the next few days I had a series of such "stitches" and called the doctor. He listened to my story and knew the answer before I had finished. It was a plain, ordinary, open-and-shut case of angina pectoris brought on by a combination of overwork, little sleep and constant worry. No more running along the roads, said the doctor. No more dashing to catch a bus, a taxi or a subway train. Slow up, calm down, take it easy — or as easy as possible. And I was always to carry with me a little box of nitroglycerin tablets. When a pain grabbed me, one or two tablets put under the tongue to dissolve would ease me in a minute or two.

The real big shock was the command: No smoking! I had learned to smoke in World War I and had cultivated the habit with enthusiasm when I resumed civilian life. I never smoked in the morning and I never smoked in bed or underwater but, aside from these restrictions, I smoked incessantly from noontime to bedtime. I had a routine. I smoked cigarettes before lunch and dinner, cigars after such meals and a pipe at all other smoking hours. In fact, I was such a slave to my pipe that I couldn't read a book with comfort or use a typewriter efficiently unless I was puffing on a pipe at the same time. I never quarreled with those who said that cigarettes were a nasty habit and I readily admitted that expensive cigars were a luxury, but I would have no nonsense about pipe smoking. To me a pipe was a necessity. This I firmly believed.

Like many of my firm beliefs, this one I discovered was

false. I managed to get along very well without a pipe. I made other discoveries, too. I learned that I could be undignified in public with equanimity, a difficult combination for a stuffy conservative like me. The intermittent angina pains usually came when I was taking my customary morning walks in the woods and fields. On such occasions I would simply lie down on the flat of my back and breathe slowly until the pain left me. This was no disturbance of the peace. But when our Information Please group went to Toronto to broadcast the show I felt the dagger in my chest while enjoying an early morning saunter along one of the main streets of that city. I didn't want to make a spectacle of myself by lying down on the sidewalk. I looked around for something on which I could lean or sit — the steps of a bank or church, the window ledge of a store, or a handy fire hydrant. No luck. I had to totter to the edge of the sidewalk and sit on the curb with my feet in the gutter.

To my great relief, nothing happened. No crowd gathered. Nobody called a cop. Men, women and children merely glanced at me in passing and went right along. I never was a fancy dresser. Perhaps they thought I looked natural there. No matter. Two pellets of nitroglycerin under the tongue and ten minutes of rest on the curbstone put me on my feet again. The attacks continued at varying intervals at home and abroad — *domo militiaeque* was Caesar's phrase — but I took them in stride until they began to leap at me while I was sitting down, which I thought was foul play and against the rules. The doctor had warned me against violent exercise or undue exertion and I tried to obey his warnings. Never up to that time had I considered tapping a typewriter "violent exercise" or "undue exertion" but I had to revise my opinion when the pains hit me while I was typing. Perhaps I pounded the keys too fervently, or worried too much about the quality of the copy. Either way, when I had to get up from my typewriter and lie on my back on the floor beside my desk, I realized that my career as a columnist for the *Sun* was in jeopardy and, indeed, I closed it out in December, 1944.

By that time our immediate family had begun to disintegrate. It was Swinburne who wrote that

> . . . *marriage and death and division*
> *Make barren our lives.*

The first break in our little family circle of five — myself, my wife Alma, and our three offspring — came when our older son, Jim, married above his station. When he was graduated from Yale in 1941 he also took with him a commission as second lieutenant, artillery, in the reserve corps, the reward for four years of ROTC work. But as a medical student he was forced to resign his commission and take a rating of private first class as long as he was in medical school. All medical school students were inducted into the service that way. He was still a student and a private first class when in April, 1944, he married Lieutenant Evelyn Fenton of the United States Navy. I had known Evelyn's father for years as a co-worker on the *New York Times* and our families had summered together on Fire Island. We were all in favor of the marriage.

Shortly after Jim's wedding John Jr. came home a disabled veteran and only then did we learn what had happened to him. He had sustained a severe head wound during the fighting in Sicily and, after a long stay in a hospital in England and a short stay at Halloran Hospital on Staten Island, had been mustered out. His explanation for keeping it secret was that he thought we might worry if we knew that he had been hit. I worried all the more because I didn't know, and by the time he walked in the front door of our home his mother was past the worrying stage. A month or so later she lapsed into a coma and never regained consciousness. Up to the very end she was still black-haired, beautiful and gentle. Her funeral marked the last time that our little family of five was ever together in one room.

Within two years I was alone in our Riverdale home except for an elderly cousin, Jane Kelly, a widow, who had been with the family for years as a housekeeper — and beloved relative. John Jr. was in Cambridge studying law at Harvard under the G.I. bill. Jim was a medical officer with the Air Force in the Philippines. My daughter Beatrice had married a West Pointer, Roger Hendrick, and, after the shooting stopped, had gone out to join him in Japan where her first two children were born. The Kierans certainly had been scattered by World War II and its aftermath. Indeed, on a USO trip with our Information Please show around the American Zone of Occupation in Europe in the summer of 1945, I myself wandered as far east as Salzburg, Austria.

XIV

IN THE ZONE OF OCCUPATION

ALL THROUGH the war I kept getting letters from men in uniform whom I had known through their previous activities on or around the sports field. This included amateur and professional athletes, coaches, managers, publicity men and sports writers turned combat correspondents in the different branches of the service. In the early spring of 1945 I had a letter from Lieutenant Commander William Sullivan of the U. S. Navy inviting me to take a summer cruise with Admiral Marc Mitscher's task force in the Pacific.

I have had better offers. There could be no guarantee of peace and quiet on the cruise and I am not only timid by nature but subject to horrible seasickness on the slightest provocation. Also, I knew that I would have to work my passage in some fashion, probably by speaking of sports to the crews during idle moments while I was aboard and speaking or writing favorably about Navy activities when I returned to solid ground. I had met Billy Sullivan some years earlier when he was a student at Boston College and drum-beater for the B.C. football team.

I told Dan Golenpaul of this invitation to view activities at first hand in the Pacific.

"Whoa! Wait a minute!" said Brother Golenpaul. "I've offered Information Please to the USO for the summer and we're trying to set it up now. I think we'll be going to the European front — or what there is left of it. I'll let you know. In the meanwhile, don't sign up for anything else."

I wrote to Billy Sullivan to ask for a rain check until I knew whether or not I would be going to Europe that same summer with Information Please. If the European trip fell through, I'd be glad — what a lie! — to accept his kind invitation to get seasick and scared to death with Admiral Mitscher's famous task force in the Pacific.

It wasn't long before I learned that Information Please was to go to the ETO as soon as we had closed out our regular season on the air in late June. We began to get suited up for the trip. We were to wear army officer uniforms without insignia — one trench coat, two tunics, one light and one heavy, and four slacks, two light and two heavy, all fitted and tailored to the king's taste, the king being Mr. D. Golenpaul who paid the extra money for the deluxe material and fittings.

Incidentally, the USO had a standard salary of $75 per week plus service food, board and travel accommodations for all performers on USO tours but, of course, this salary was inconsequential to most of the "stars of stage, screen and radio" who made USO tours during the war — performers like Bob Hope, Jack Benny, Bing Crosby, Dorothy Lamour, Ingrid Bergman and others including Al Schacht, the "Clown Prince of Baseball," second only to Bob Hope and Joe E. Brown in mileage covered to entertain servicemen scattered all over the globe. Task Force Commander in Chief Golenpaul of the Information Please Overseas Expedition decided that his performers were as good as the best and should be in a position to look upon the standard $75 a week salary as quite unimportant. He paid us our full salaries all through the trip just as though we had been spending the summer on the air in New York instead of on the ground in France, Germany and Austria. When it came to money there was nothing small about D. Golenpaul. He threw it around with a lavish hand and put on some wonderful parties during the long run of Information Please.

Once the trip was decided upon, the next thing to do was to line up a couple of guests to fill out our panel of four on the answering side. Oscar Levant couldn't make the trip because of other engagements throughout the summer. Groucho Marx said he was crazy to go with us and then reworded it; he would be crazy to go with us, he had too many other chestnuts in the fire. How he snared them I don't remember but Dan Golenpaul came up with two panelists who were pluperfect for the trip as entertainers and cheerful traveling companions; Beatrice Lillie from Broadway and Reginald Gardiner from Hollywood. No need to say anything about Bea Lillie. Reggie Gardiner, famed for his light comedy roles on the screen and the stage, turned out to be a delightful addition to our troupe. Both had been guests on Information Please before the trip was planned and they knew what they would be in for on the tour.

Bea Lillie was in London and was signed on by phone. Reggie Gardiner came from Hollywood to be on our last regular broadcast of the show in June, get fitted for his uniforms and take all the prescribed "shots" for persons going overseas. This reminds me of one trifle that I almost overlooked. On May 7, 1945, the Germans surrendered and the shooting war in Europe was over. Somehow this pleased me very much. Other things being equal, I'm for a quiet life. There's nothing better than peace with asperity.

I still have the official score sheet showing the "shots" we

had to take before we were allowed to go overseas. We had
one for smallpox, one for yellow fever, two for tetanus,
three for typhus, and three for typhoid-paratyphoid. We had
to pass a preliminary physical examination before we were
treated to the first injection. We didn't lose a man. We had
quite an expeditionary force when we were all assembled but
our last man didn't catch up with us until we were in Bad
Nauheim, Germany. We went over in detachments. Golenpaul went first with one of his office staff, Joe Freeman, to
confer with the USO and Army officials in Paris on where we
were to go and what he needed to put the show on the road.

Spick and span in our nice new uniforms, Kip Fadiman,
Reggie Gardiner, Franklin P. Adams and I reported at Fort
Totten, Long Island, on the last day of June for a final check
by Army authorities and assignment to the first available seats
on a MATS (Military Air Transport Service) plane heading
for Paris. It was a coincidence that it was from Fort Totten
that I had left to go overseas in World War I. Our regiment
had trained there for seven weeks before we boarded the old
Carpathia and sailed to England. This was to be a much
shorter stay for me overseas. We had to go through a "ditch-
ing drill" at Totten in case the plane came down on the water
and after that had little else to do except wait until there was
room on a plane. It was a sweltering day and I was in particular misery because of eye trouble, which was nothing new
in my life. For years I suffered recurring attacks of a virus
infection in my left eye. The doctors told me that it was of
the "herpes" type, a nonfilterable nuisance that causes, among
other things, "cold sores" on the lips. The eye gets very red,
feels sore and vision dwindles — on one occasion almost to
the vanishing point. Through the bad eye I couldn't see a
man standing five feet in front of me.

This time the attack came in April and the eye specialist

had "curetted" the eyeball — that is, he had scraped off the thin transparent outer layer, the epithelium, hoping that he was removing the nuisance with it. The little beasties begin gnawing on that layer and then dig in if they can. It was the third time I had undergone such a scraping job under local anesthetics and, while there is no great pain in the process, it is difficult to keep from flinching instinctively when a man runs a thin little piece of steel over the pupil of your eye. Anyway, on this occasion, the beasties had gotten through the epithelium and were doing business below. The doctor gave me a tube of opthalmic penicillin to apply to the surface of the eye at stated intervals. The infection was still lingering while we were at Fort Totten.

Since it appeared that we wouldn't get off before midnight at the earliest, the commanding officer put on a party for us at the Officers Club. I was wearing dark glasses because the less light that fell on the bad eye the better I felt. A colonel in uniform walked up to me and said: "You seem to be in trouble. What is it?"

I told him that I had a herpes infection in my left eye.

"Maybe I can help. I'm the post surgeon and it so happens that I'm an eye specialist, too. Come on over to my office."

This was about ten o'clock at night. We went out into the darkness and across a lawn to the building where his office was located. He turned on the lights, looked at the eye in the raw and then through a "slit lamp," washed the surface with a weak solution of carbolic acid, covered the whole eye with a wad of gauze, sealed it tight with tape, gave me a big shot of penicillin in the rump and told me to see an eye doctor as soon as I reached Paris. It was good medicine. But what luck that he noticed me at all at the party and then turned out to be an eye man. I was fairly comfortable all the way to Paris, and we didn't get there as fast as we thought we would.

It was about midnight when we had word that we were to board a plane at nearby La Guardia Field. It was a "plush job," a regular 4-engine passenger plane, and we took off for Newfoundland about 2 A.M. where we expected to stop for fuel and breakfast. We dozed off in our seats and when we woke up we were on the ground in Presque Isle, Maine. The MATS airport on Newfoundland at Stephenville was fogged in. So we had breakfast at Presque Isle and made Stephenville in time for lunch. And what a lunch! The lieutenant who ran the officers' mess turned out to be an old friend, a "bit actor" who had worked with our group in turning out the Information Please movie shorts. He heard that we were coming and had set aside some special goodies for us — individual sirloin steaks! The men around us were eating the regular chow — cold cuts, baked beans, canned fruit salad and such fodder.

Gather ye sirloins while ye may. Our friend saw us off at 2 P.M. heading southeast for the Azores under a clear sky. He also saw us when we trudged back into his mess hall at 6 P.M. for supper. When we were two hours out the inboard engine on the right side sprang a bad oil leak and we had to return to Stephenville. Our friend was not armed with extra sirloins to meet this unexpected return. We had to take the regular table d'hôte dinner along with the common people. I felt sorry for our friend, he looked so crestfallen when we showed up for supper after the farewell feast he had given us at noon.

We took off again in the dusk and made the Azores about dawn in wonderful weather. The huge airfield was as busy as Grand Central Station — planes landing and taking off every few minutes, workers in khaki and denims strolling in and out of hangars and barracks, straggling platoons of men in different uniforms, all laden with baggage of some kind, coming from or heading for the flight line, and steady traffic through the long one-story building that offered a traveler every convenience, including a washroom, post exchange and huge cafeteria. We shaved and had breakfast there. By mid-morning we were on our last leg of the trip. As far as sight-seeing from the air was concerned, we might as well have made the flight in a telephone booth. Most of the time we were above a cloud layer and even when we could look down and see water we didn't see a ship until we were approaching the shores of France.

The pilot and co-pilot were Information Please fans and we took turns spending some time up forward with them. I had the last watch. I sat in the co-pilot's seat as we circled Mont-St.-Michel to give all the passengers a close look at the famous edifice and then followed the Seine all the way to Paris. I noted that every one of the regular bridges spanning the river had been destroyed until we reached the Paris area. The only crossings were by pontoon bridges and other temporary wooden structures. We had a fleeting look at Omaha Beach and other parts of the Normandy battleground and then we slid down fast over the "toits de Paris" and circled to a landing at Le Bourget in the twilight to find a worried Golenpaul waiting for us at the passenger gate. We were over a day late. He had a car and a chauffeur assigned to him and he drove us to the Ritz where he had arranged quarters for us. The hotel had been taken over by the American army and was the headquarters caravanserai for big Army brass and top USO troupers.

Paris was still a military camp. Most of the shops and private houses were boarded up when we arrived. Americans in uniform were all over the place on foot and in army vehicles. We lingered in Paris for a week while Dan Golenpaul and USO officials and army authorities worked out the details of our trip around the American Zone of Occupation. For one thing, Dan insisted that he couldn't set out without two missing staff members who were still back in the United States when we left. They were Joe Kahn, our program pianist, and Irving Kolodin, music critic, who handled all the musical questions for the program and acted as a general assistant to Golenpaul in arranging the shows. Both men were in the army. Joe Kahn was due for an immediate discharge from the band at West Point and he was to be sent over as a USO export. Sergeant Irving Kolodin wasn't due for discharge but, through military channels, he was assigned to accompany us on a duty status.

However, it took time to unwind the red tape involved in these human shipments and Kip Fadiman, Reggie Gardiner, F.P.A. and I walked all over Paris while we waited. The first morning we were there I went down to an army hospital near Malmaison to have my bandaged eye looked after. They had an eye specialist, a young captain, who knew his business and gave me the full treatment, slit lamp and all. He handed me a salve to rub in my eye four times a day and drops to enlarge the pupil for some reason that I forget now. Frank Adams, who was my roommate throughout the trip, used to put the drops in my eye as required. He didn't have a very steady hand with the dropper and I complained audibly when he missed the target. Two of the USO roomers at the Ritz were Alfred Lunt and Lynn Fontanne who were playing *O Mistress Mine* at one of the neighborhood theatres. We met them every day downstairs in the hotel or on the sidewalk in front and Miss Fontanne was concerned about my eye with the patch over it. When she heard my critical reference to Frank's marksmanship with the eyedropper, she volunteered for the job on several occasions and never let a drop go to waste. Getting such attention from Lynn Fontanne was the only good thing that ever came of my eye ailment.

To wind up the medical report, I had the patch over the eye through our entire stay abroad except when we were onstage doing the show. At such times I removed the patch and wore dark glasses. As we moved about, I was passed along from one army eye specialist to the other and had to make many side trips from the main expedition to get treatment from a specialist and a fresh supply of penicillin and drops. The eye never was healed or even comfortable — it felt as though there were fine sand in it — until we landed back in New York in late August. What I grieved over most was that I couldn't do any bird watching of importance with only one good eye. And there were so many entrancing and unfamiliar birds to see when we were walking, as we did on occasions, in the open country.

Bea Lillie joined us at the Ritz the day after we checked in and, since that completed our panel, Golenpaul offered to put on a show in Paris, which we did on July 9 at the Olympia Theatre to a crowded house. Our pianist, Joe Kahn, was still missing but Bea Lillie's accompanist, a small thin British Army veteran named Norman Hackforth who walked with a limp and a cane, took over the required piano assignments. Then Irving Kolodin — Sergeant Kolodin, officially — arrived to help Golenpaul with all the staff work and it was decided to take off for the provinces and let Joe Kahn catch up to us when he could. Norman Hackforth would hold the pianoforte for him until he arrived.

It's curious that few persons realized how many individuals were needed to put a show like ours on the road under conditions that prevailed in the American Zone of Occupation. Entertainment of the troops was controlled by a branch of the Army known as "Special Services" and many of the officers assigned to such work had little experience in the entertainment field in civil life. One officer into whose area we were

Schoolteacher on horseback, Dutchess County family farm, 1913.

Timekeeper and general handy man on New York City sewer work, 1914.

Three sergeants of Eleventh Engineers, AEF, on leave. Casino garden, Aix-Les-Bains, August, 1918. Left to right: Kieran, Pope, Jones.

Hunting bag at Camp Bryan, North Carolina, November, 1932. Left to right: Babe Ruth, Frank Stevens, and *New York Times* sports columnist.

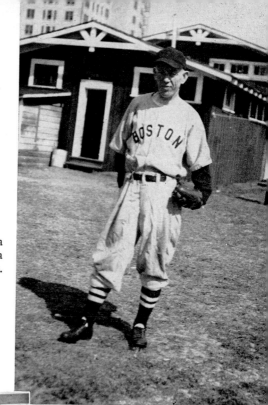

Ready for exercise in a
Red Sox uniform, Sarasota
training camp, 1939.

After switching caps
with Manager Joe McCarthy
at Yankee training camp,
St. Petersburg, 1940.

Covering a football game in the Yale Bowl, 1940.
Sports writer Bob Kelley, left.

Bill Bingham of Harvard starting skating race between "Speed" Saltonstall and "Slowpoke" Kieran, The Country Club, Brookline, January 30, 1941. Background, left to right: A. Larrivee, Joe Cronin, Joe Stevens, Tom Carens, F. C. Gray, James Lowell, Ted Stavarides, M. T. Kelleher, Mrs. Kelleher, Mrs. Gray, Mrs. Saltonstall, Dan Lynch. *Photo by Arthur L. Griffin.*

Playing it by ear. Listening for warblers in Riverdale woods.

Scene from movie short *Information Please*: panelists Kieran, Adams, Christopher Morley and Levant ponder question posed by hired stranger. *Pathé Studios.*

Another part of the movie forest. Kieran, Adams and Levant watching Clifton Fadiman not striking a blow at guest panelist Gene Tunney, former heavyweight champion. *Metropolitan Photo Service.*

Franklin P. Adams, just before interrupting to say: "A likely story!"
Metropolitan Photo Service.

Selling war bonds at Symphony Hall, Boston, 1942. Regulars Levant, Kieran and Adams, with guest panelist Henry Cabot Lodge, Jr., third from left, Emcee Fadiman hovering rear. *WBZ, Boston*

Autographing for fans after the ball was over. A regular **job.**

With an *Information Please* alumna, Lillian Gish, on our Hollywood visit. *Universal Studios.*

Commander G. C. Simmons, USN, with frightened passenger, about to take off in jet fighter-trainer (Lockheed Shooting Star) at Pensacola Naval Air Base, April, 1952. *United States Army*.

Where there's smoke,
there's the great
Dr. Einstein. Princeton,
October 11, 1942.

Putting a Cape Ann
wildflower through the
third degree. *Doris
Berthold.*

Author and wife Margaret proffering latest Kieran opus to stuffed eagle at autographing party, 1959. Eagle apparently disapproves. *Charles Rossi.*

A low sun, a long shadow and one last look before starting home.
Photo by Brooks Atkinson.

going and who had to prepare to receive us had arranged board and lodging for what he considered the proper number. He had often listened to Information Please and he knew what to expect when it arrived at his post — Kip Fadiman, the master of ceremonies who posed the questions and the four panelists who tried to answer them. Total, five persons. He was stationed in Linz, destroyed by bombs, and was managing a wrecked hotel with no doors, all the windows blown out, half the roof gone, most of the walls cracked and the only available light supplied by naked electric light bulbs dangling from loops of insulated wires crudely strung along the halls, up the stairways and into the bedrooms.

When our party trooped into the bare lobby some time after midnight the young officer, who had waited up to greet us, stared at us in horror. We were fifteen in number! He disposed of five of our fellow travelers at once by sending them down the road to the barracks for enlisted men, which they were. To put on our show in a big hall or on an open hillside we needed microphones, loud speakers and electrical power to make them effective. For that chore the Army sent along with us five enlisted technicians who had a mobile generator on a big truck and a lot of additional electric equipment in a smaller truck called a "weapons carrier." Incidentally, they were fine lads and did a wonderful job for us on the tour. On this occasion they left the hotel quietly and went down the road to find their bunks in the barracks.

That still left ten of us standing our ground in the hotel lobby. There was Group Commander Golenpaul, plus his two staff assistants, Joe Freeman and Irving — pardon, Sergeant Kolodin. There was Bea Lillie's accompanist and our own regular staff pianist, Joe Kahn. And finally the five performers the young officer had expected, Bea Lillie, Reggie Gardiner, Kip Fadiman, Franklin P. Adams and a short man with big ears and a bad eye whose name was Kieran. The young officer had to dig up five extra cots, ready a couple of linen closets for unexpected occupancy and shift everything around before we could be bedded down for the night.

Information Please on the air was a half-hour show, commercials included. On this USO tour we did a two-hour show with no commercials and added attractions. We started with a brief piano recital by Joe Kahn — selections from Brahms, Beethoven and Chopin as well as George Gershwin, Irving Berlin and Dick Rodgers. Then Reggie Gardiner would step out and run through a few of his old vaudeville routines — the startling effects of different wallpaper designs on a man sick in bed, the contrasting sounds of British and French railroad engines starting out of a station and other such capers. It was very funny and always warmed up the audience. Next came the "show-stopper," Bea Lillie, with her own accompanist, doing songs and recitations. She was just as wonderful on a crude platform in an open field in Bavaria as ever she was on the Broadway or London stage. We closed with Bea and Reggie joining Frank and me as panelists for a regular Information Please show with Kip in the driver's seat putting the whip to us. Since our whole purpose in going abroad was to entertain the troops, we didn't take the questions too seriously and, if we had a choice, we gave the answer on the lighter side.

When we went by air from Paris to Augsburg to open our tour, Frank Adams and I looked down on territory where we ourselves had been soldiers a generation earlier. And no sooner had we landed in Augsburg than I met the first of many friends in uniform whom I had known through covering sports for so many years. This was Brigadier General G. H. Davidson, Chief of Engineers of the Seventh Army, far more familiar to me as "Gar" Davidson when he was

stationed at West Point as the head coach of the Army football team over a five-year stretch from 1933 through 1937.
The emissary he sent to invite me out to his baronial headquarters — most of our army brass was quartered in cas-
tles or "schlosses" — was his "Public Relations Officer,"
Colonel Marshall Newton, a refugee from the city editor's
staff on the *New York Times* and naturally one of my old
cronies. I could see that I was going to enjoy this tour immensely.

And the scenery in Bavaria in summer! The first thing Gar
Davidson said to me was: "John, these people must have been
crazy to start a war. They had the most beautiful country in
the world — and look at it now!"

Even the wrecked cities — and they were mostly heaps of
rubble — couldn't hide the beauty of the countryside or the
quaintness of some of the little medieval towns left untouched
by the holocaust that had swept over the region. We put on
our show in a riding hall in Augsburg. The next day we went
to Ludwigsburg where we were quartered in an empty museum that once had been the palace of the reigning duke of
Württemburg. We did an afternoon and an evening show
there for small audiences and the next day moved on to
Heilbronn, a city of tragic story. The inhabitants had become
accustomed to hearing and even seeing our bombers going
over at night to drop their wares on more important targets.
Then one night the target was Heilbronn and, with perhaps
half the inhabitants gazing upward from the streets, the car-
nage was terrific. When we arrived thousands of corpses
were still buried in the rubble.

We played afternoon and early evening shows there in an
open field alongside a meandering stream, a recreation area
for one of our artillery groups. It was at Heilbronn that I
had my one and only flight in an artillery spotter plane. A

young pilot offered to take me up and I accepted. The little planes were tethered out like cows on a flat pasture. We were just walking out to his plane when the pilot said: "Wait a minute. We'd better get parachutes."

Parachutes? What for?

"I'd like to show you what this plane can do up there. It's really nifty."

This proved that the young man didn't know me at all. The very idea of doing flipflops away up yonder almost caused me to swoon. No parachutes, please. No tricks. Just easy up and easy down. I merely wanted to see what it felt like to fly in a small plane with an open cockpit. The pilot looked at me impassively but probably was thinking "What a clod!" as he led the way, sans parachutes, to his plane — an LC-5, if I remember correctly. He unleashed the moorings, climbed into the front seat, saw me safely strapped into the other seat directly behind him, started his motor, trundled into the clear, gave it the gas and, after a short and bumpy run, we were upward bound.

We cruised around for fifteen minutes or so at about five thousand feet and I was enjoying the view until the pilot turned around and said: "Here's how we took evasive action when we had an enemy plane on our tail."

Before I could shriek a protest he had us in a perpendicular dive toward the earth at full throttle. I stared down in horror, clutched the sides of the cockpit convulsively, closed my eyes, and hung on for dear life. Probably turned as white as your shirt, too. Or, as the old vaudeville gag had it after a second look at your shirt — whiter. I could feel the impact of some swift swerves one way and another but I didn't dare open my eyes until I knew that we were riding along on an even keel again. Then I looked over the side and saw that we were only a few hundred feet in the air and coming in for a landing. I

was immensely relieved and even recovered enough presence
of mind to thank the young man for the ride. I made my
official report of the trip to Franklin P. Adams, who was
waiting for me on the ground.

"It's a nice safe little plane" I assured Frank, "but the pilot
is dangerous."

From Heilbronn we moved along to Schwäbish-Gmünd,
a little town right out of Grimm's Fairy Tales or Disneyland.
Walking the streets was like being a character in some costume play of the Middle Ages. There were carvings over
doorways and second-story balconies jutting out over little
narrow cobbled streets. We stayed there two days to give
shows for the Sixth Corps troops. Our next stop was at a
place that I never since have been able to find on the map.
It was called Jugenheim or Benscheim indifferently and we
gave a show in an open field for the 42nd Field Artillery.
But what I remember most vividly about it was that the
billeting officer told the owners of a big estate there that
they would have to move out of their palatial home for the
night and let the Information Please travelers sleep and eat
there. The owner was an elderly lady by the name of Merck,
one of the famous pharmaceutical family. We came in as she
was packing up to leave and she most obligingly told us that
she had brought up half a dozen bottles of champagne from
the cellar and put them on the buffet in the dining room for
us. The champagne was doubly appreciated when we found
that the main course at the dinner dished up by the army cook
was a powdered egg omelet.

I never missed an opportunity to get in a walk along the
country lanes or the local woods and I did so at the Merck
estate without going outside the gates. There were extensive
lawns, gardens, orchards, groves and pastures in all directions.
I was out in the early morning with the dew on the grass and

on the velvety turf in an orchard of small ornamental crab
apple trees I saw hundreds of large snails that I took to be
the famous *Helix pomatia* that I once had served up to me in
a Paris restaurant as *escargots en coquille*. Just once. They
were garnished with garlic. I cherish the famous dictum of
my old friend Bugs Baer: There is no such thing as a little bit
of garlic.

I was sorry to leave the Merck estate but I didn't know
what luxuries were awaiting us at our next *étape*, which was
the famous spa, Bad Nauheim, with the 19th Corps in residence. They sent out a half-dozen light planes to meet our
motorcade and give us an aerial escort into town. In the main
square we were greeted by a brass band that blared ahead of
us all the way up the street to the casino where there was a
formal reception for us by the local military authorities armed
with a standing microphone over which we made little
speeches of thanks for the honors thrust upon us. We played
to an evening audience of 2100 officers, enlisted men and Red
Cross nurses in the band shell there. When we walked off the
stage after the performance we walked right into Joe Kahn
who was almost ready to weep with joy over catching up
with us after a chase of weeks. We were just as glad to see
Joe as he was to see us.

We stayed two days at Bad Nauheim and took the baths
both days. Wooden tubs and bubbling warm water. They
were possibly healthful, certainly pleasant. On our second
day at Bad Nauheim we made a sortie to a place called Gies-
sen to give an evening show in a theatre. All I remember is
that after the show one of the soldiers who came up and
spoke to me was Ernie White, a big left-handed pitcher for
the St. Louis Cardinals before he went to war. I didn't have
much time to chat with him because one of the medical
officers at the infirmary there was an eye specialist and he
was waiting in his office for me to come in and give my body

up to science. He reloaded me with fresh drops and more ophthalmic penicillin.

We moved on to the city of Marburg where army intelligence officers were gathering all the secret Nazi papers that were presented later in court at the Nuremburg trials. One of the features of our two-day stay in Marburg was a general check by Military Police of every alleged American in the Zone of Occupation. This included the few civilians in the area on economic missions, all USO groups, Red Cross personnel and all servicemen. They were looking to round up deserters, spies, criminals and men who had gone AWOL. It was a house-to-house and barracks-to-barracks check and nobody was allowed to leave his or her quarters until the local check was completed by the Military Police. We passed the test with honors.

Another feature of our stay in Marburg was an early evening outdoor show before what was practically a captive audience of five thousand soldiers. It was a huge "tent city" housing at least a big part of what was officially designated the Third Reinforcement Depot. For the benefit of those who were never in the army — and even those who were in the army but luckily never separated from their units — a "Reinforcement Depot" is a polite name for a casual camp and a casual camp differs from a jail in that the food usually is better in a well-run jail. And the lodging, too. The "casual" is the outcast of army life, the waif and stray in uniform. I know. I was in a casual camp for weeks in World War I. It was in Le Mans, France and consisted of barracks constructed to house four thousand French soldiers. When I arrived there on Thanksgiving Day, 1918, there were twelve thousand American soldiers inside the walled "caserne" or cantonment. We inmates referred to it as the "Pigpen Madhouse of Europe."

My heart went out to the casuals in this "Third Reinforcement Depot" and I spent some time talking to a number of them after the show. One poor fellow gave me an almost incredible story of the way he and his group had been kicked around in the mishmash of changing assignments after the shooting stopped. I asked him what brought his outfit into such straits. I'll never forget his answer. It was right from the heart and I could almost see the tears in his eyes when he said:

"We lost our colonel. He died of wounds. When we lost him, we lost God."

We moved on to Kassel, a manufacturing city to which our bombers had paid many nightly visits because it was turning out airplanes and other important implements of war. It was also a railroad center. Only a few of the main streets were passable by auto. The others were all blocked by rubble. When the 30th Infantry of our Third Division came in to occupy the town, they had a hard time finding a headquarters habitation with a roof that would keep out the rain. We stayed there for three days, giving a show each day in a hospital theatre that seated about 1200.

From Kassel we flew down to Bamberg in a "bucket job," a C–47 with the seats ripped out, benches along each side of the cabin and baggage and freight in a jumble in the center. Our enlisted staff with the mobile generator and other equipment had to make it over the roads on the double to meet us there in time for a show the following day. We landed in the twilight and, without equipment, were on the town for the evening. Frank Adams and I went for a short stroll and when we returned to the hotel — run by the Army — Dan Golenpaul asked me did I know a General Stokes. I was flattered by the soft impeachment but I said "No."

"He says he knows you and he wants you to have dinner with him."

Stokes? Stokes? The only army man I ever knew by that name was "Trench Mortar" Johnny Stokes who was — when I last saw him — a young lieutenant and assistant football coach at West Point.

"Well, he's coming around to take you to dinner so, if you're hungry, you'd better recognize him."

He came around on the dot. It was Johnny, grown older, and wearing the one star of a brigadier general, but just as bright and cheerful as ever. He, too, had his headquarters in a "schloss" like most of our military brass, but his was only a small one befitting a "buck general" as he liked to call himself. He not only invited me to dinner but told me to bring three of our group with me. He had a staff of three and four outsiders were all he could feed in his dining room at one time. Golenpaul was busy. Kip and Reggie Gardiner had made other plans. I took F.P.A. and our two pianists, Joe Kahn and Norman Hackforth. Everywhere we went we were served champagne with "Wermacht" stamped across the label. It was wine that the Germans had "captured" in France and the Americans had "liberated" as they moved into Germany. It was a most successful dinner and the two pianists provided music later on the Bechstein piano — the Steinway of Europe — that they found in the living room.

We stayed in the army hotel at Bamberg for three days and, after giving a show for the 15th Corps Headquarters troops in the local riding academy, we made side trips to several other areas. One was Bayreuth, the Wagnerian shrine where we played in the famous Festspeilhaus, a great barn of a place with a huge stage that befitted the Wagnerian choruses and galloping Valkyrie. Yet the acoustics were so good that Bea Lillie discarded the microphone and had no trouble sending her rollicking notes to the far corners of the big theatre. One of the features of our trip to Bayreuth was that the army

officer in charge of the motorcade that took us there and
back — almost! — was a certain Major Ralph Houk who became much better known later as the manager of the New
York Yankees.

Because transportation was a problem, the Army had con-
scripted all civilian cars for military purposes. It didn't make
much difference to the Germans because they had no gaso-
line, anyway. About half of our motor trips were made in
German cars and most of them were in marvelously poor
shape. Ralph Houk showed up with four coughing wrecks
that caused several halts for repairs on the way over. It was
during one of those halts that Kip Fadiman, who rode in the
lead car with Major Houk, came back to the car in which I
was riding and told me that the leader of the expedition was a
baseball player, a Yankee farmhand in Kansas City. I walked
forward to meet him and we talked of mutual acquaintances
in big league baseball. Major General John Leonard, commander of the Ninth Armored Division for whom we played
in Bayreuth, told me that Houk had made a fine record with
his outfit. Incidentally, one of Houk's commandeered cars
resolutely refused to start for the return trip and General
Leonard had to lend us his own car to get us safely out of
town.

The next day we had a long "field trip" to a place called
Hammelberg to play outdoor afternoon and evening shows
for the Twenty-sixth Division that was encamped in the area.
I made a special trip to Nuremburg — eighty miles there and
back — to see an eye specialist before the main trip started at
11 A.M. after a snack of sandwiches and beer to stay us until
dinnertime. Which reminds me that one of the features of our
army-run hotel at Bamberg was free beer for all inmates and
visitors at any time of the day or night. I took it that our
troops had "liberated" a nearby brewery when they took
over the town and the hotel.

As was to be expected on all such trips, the roads were terrible. You might ride along blissfully at high speed on one of the famous autobahns for ten miles or so and then would come the problem of going down into a gulley, a gulch or a valley to resume travel on the far side of every stream or river that ran under the autobahn. There wasn't a bridge of any respectable dimensions left standing in the region. And the streets and roads were all pitted by bomb craters only hastily filled in. Over some stretches we were lucky to do ten or fifteen miles an hour. I don't know how far we traveled on this particular motor trip but at midnight we were creeping back in pitch-darkness — no street lights, of course — through Schweinfurt, a town of dreadful memory to our air force, and finally rumbled back into Bamberg at three o'clock in the morning. Even so, I think that probably it was our best day over there. We played to four thousand soldiers in the afternoon and forty-two hundred in a twilight performance that ended in the dusk.

We flew from an airfield near Bamberg to Regensburg and there gave an outdoor afternoon show for the 12th Corps in what for me was a sentimental setting — on a green bank beside the Blue Danube! It was a bright summer day and rippling waters of the wide river were sparkling in the sunlight. I grew up in an era of Lehar light opera and Strauss waltzes and standing of a summer day beside the Danube was a memorable moment for me. Furthermore, I knew that Regensburg in Bavaria was the "Ratisbon" of the Napoleonic legend and I had every right to stop Franklin P. Adams on the river bank and fling in his face, from the first line to the last, the Browning schoolboy classic that opens, "You know we French stormed Ratisbon" and ends thirty-nine lines later with "Smiling, the boy fell dead!" Indeed, Frank caught fire and the recitation finished as a duet.

On we went to Weiden, where we played for the 90th Infantry and to Kielheim where our victims were the 4th Armored Division. I remember little of either stop except that at Weiden an M.P. sergeant came up to me with the announcement that his name was Sullivan and that everybody at Yale knew him as "Sully, the campus cop." He asked news of my two sons whom he had known as students there. I brought him up to date — John Jr. invalided out after being wounded with the First Division in Sicily, and Jim a medical officer with the Air Force. He said to give them his best, which I eventually did and learned from them that "Sully, the campus cop" was a favorite figure in New Haven.

When we reached Munich on Aug. 1 we were on the home ground of the Armed Forces Radio Network and thus were able to do a live show over the air while at the same time entertaining an audience of fourteen hundred servicemen in the Prinz Regenten Theatre. Naturally we had to look the town over — not much of it was intact — and visit the beer hall in which Herr Hitler began his infamous career as a disturber of the peace. Indeed, we had beer there — without disturbing the peace. The officers mess in Munich was installed in what had been one of the great art galleries of the world, the famed Pinakothek, before the war. The most valuable paintings had been taken down and hidden away before our troops arrived but lesser canvases were recovered from storerooms and put back on the walls of the main gallery in which three meals a day were being served to American army officers and their guests. I never ate in a more art-filled dining room.

This tour got better as it went along. We lived in comfortable barracks in Munich but at our next stop we were all lodged in a lovely villa beside a lake with the Bavarian Alps as a backdrop in the distance. The town was Starnberg, just below Munich, and the adjacent large and lovely lake was the

Starnsee. The local yacht club had been taken over as a recreation center for American soldiers and there were plenty of sailboats rigged and ready for those who could handle them. When we were summering on Fire Island before the war I had leased a little gaff-rigged sloop each season and everybody in the family soon became competent at the tiller. The chance to go sailing on the Starnsee was too good to miss. The sky was clear and the breeze was light when I took Frank Adams with me as a passenger for a cruise of an hour or so in a nice little marconi-rigged boat of about Star size. However, I must admit that my hand was rusty and I nearly lost Frank overboard when I made a fast turn into the wind at the last to bring the boat to the mooring.

Well, there we were, sailing on the Starnsee, living in a villa with wide lawns and a view of the Bavarian Alps across the lake. There was a formal garden with statues along the paths. Some of our lodgings along the way had been on the rugged side but this was living in the lap of luxury. A musical note; the villa next to us had been occupied by the great Johannes Brahms for some time and was the show place of the lakeside. We made the villa our headquarters for three days as we ranged the countryside. We gave one show in Starnberg for the 20th Corps Headquarters, another in Augsburg for the Seventy-first Division and a third in Garmisch-Partenkirchen where we performed for the Tenth Armored Division in what had been the Olympic hockey arena in the winter games of 1936. The show was put on in the long twilight of summer, with the towering peaks of the Bavarian Alps all around us. The setting was indescribably beautiful. As we were drawing near Garmisch on the auto trip over I saw a road sign pointing south at a crossing and on it was written "Oberammergau, 10 Kil." We were in historic country.

The villa by the lake was the last we saw of luxury until we got back to Paris at the end of the trip and took up lodgings at the Ritz again. We made a trip to Linz, the birthplace of Hitler, to entertain men of the 65th Division in a huge hanger on the airfield there. The American and Russian Zones meet at Linz with the Danube as the dividing line. American soldiers guarded one end of the bridge over the river and Russians the other. Frank Adams and I were allowed to walk across the bridge to talk to the Russian warders at the other end. The interchange of statements was paltry and need not go down in history. Fact is, I don't remember a word of it. I do remember that everybody grinned amiably and no blows were struck.

We had a long, hard motor trip to Salzburg, the home of Wolfgang Amadeus Mozart, but it was worth it just to walk around the streets of that quaint little city in bright sunlight the next morning. We inspected the Mozart Memorial Concert Hall and found it not nearly as impressive as the old bishop's castle atop an enormous crag overhanging the Salzach River that runs through the town. For some reason we had only a small audience when we played in an open field for the 2nd Corps troops just outside Salzburg, and a still smaller one the next day when we did another outdoor show for the Forty-second Division in the little town of St. Johann in the Alps about forty miles below Salzburg. Perhaps the troops weren't told that we were coming. Or perhaps they had been warned and stayed away. I hardly think so, though, with Bea Lillie in the show.

Anyway, that finished our tour and we went back to the barracks in Munich where we were to wait for a plane to take us to Paris. Bad weather set in and flying was at a minimum. We had to wait several days during which we answered three or four false alarms that a plane was waiting for us on the airfield. We hastily grabbed up all our gear, rushed out in various cars to the airport, discovered that the expected plane hadn't come in, hung around for an hour in hope and retreated to the barracks to unpack. We had just returned from one of these false alarms when we had another summons to return to the airport immediately if we wanted to get to Paris. We wanted, so we rushed off in mad haste and this time we made it. There actually was a plane waiting for us and it took off as soon as we were aboard. The weather was poor and the trip was bumpy but who worries about the going when the next stop is Paris-sur-Seine? Of course, we had to wait in Paris for transportation to the United States by air but waiting in Paris was no hardship, especially as we were lodged at the Ritz and meeting all comers like Bob Hope, Ingrid Bergman, Jack Benny and other official boarders including some of my Army acquaintances from the field of sports.

We did one show in a theatre near the Arc de Triomphe while we were waiting for a plane and Frank Adams and I went out to speak at a baseball dinner at Reims for the champion team of the corps area. But our tour was over and our happy family was breaking up. Our enlisted crew, who had done wonders for us, had parted from us in Munich. Bea Lillie and her accompanist Norman Hackforth were heading for London. The rest of us were bound for New York with Reggie Gardiner going on from there to Beverly Hills. We took off of a clear midnight, were at the Azores in the dawn, in Newfoundland in the afternoon and I was at home in Riverdale at ten o'clock that night. Not bad flying time for those ancient days.

As for the tour itself, I enjoyed it hugely and I do hope that our audiences did the same. Bea Lillie alone was worth the price of admission. She was a delightful and tireless trouper all the way, never complaining, never demanding, always giving and always cheerful. We all adored her, and so did everybody else who met her along the way. I hope she won't mind if I say that she was the only baggage we had with us to match the beautiful scenery of the Bavarian Alps.

XV

AN AUTHOR BY INVITATION ONLY

To go back a bit, when I was new on the *Times* I nourished the youthful dream of most neophytes in newspaperdom; writing for a newspaper was merely the first step on the road to a literary career. I had it all planned. I would become an author of note. I would begin with short stories for the magazine editors and then move along to longer and more serious manuscripts for book editors and respectable publishers.

I never got around to the longer and more serious works of fiction but I wrote half a dozen short stories that in my unbiased opinion were ingenious in plot and entertaining in style, though perhaps a trifle lurid in spots. The death rate among my characters was high; few lived to see how things came out in the end. The magazine editors to whom I submitted these little masterpieces rejected them with revolting speed. The only person on whom they made any impression at all was my brother-in-law, Paul Reilly, an artist who did humorous sketches for the gay *Life* of that era. After reading the manuscripts Paul did a sketch of "The Author At Work" — a pen and ink drawing of me banging away on my portable typewriter in a cemetery with the surrounding tombstones bearing the names of the many characters in the stories who had met death at my ruthless hands.

The whole thing had such a depressing effect on me that never again did I think up a plot for a short story or a long book and attempt to foist it on any magazine editor or book publisher. I always waited to be asked. Curiously, I was asked quite often to do magazine pieces and I don't recall turning down any good offers until I became so involved with Information Please and other activities during World War II that I had no time for such exercises on the typewriter. Since I wrote sports, the demand at first was for sports articles for magazines, but after I was launched as a nature writer in the *Times* Sunday Magazine, I had requests for articles in that field, too. Over the years I wrote articles of one kind or another for most of the popular magazines of the day.

The first book I wrote was on sports. It was the story of the Olympic Games from 776 B.C. to A.D. 1936, inclusive. In a manner of speaking, I did this by double request. The first came from my good friend John Hutchens, who was to reign for many later years as daily book reviewer for the *Herald Tribune*. Back in 1932 John, who had been on the *Times* with me, had a friend in a publishing house that wanted a history of the Olympic Games in a hurry. The winter sports section of the Olympic Games that had just been completed at Lake Placid had been a spectacular success. The upcoming outdoor Olympic Games at Los Angeles probably would be a similar smash hit. A good story about the games up to and including the festivities at Los Angeles might find a ready market. John Hutchens suggested to the publishing house that I be asked to write the book.

I accepted the nomination. The first thing I discovered was that I was a pioneer in the field. There was no book in French, English, German, Italian or Spanish that covered the

series of modern Olympic Games from Athens in 1896 to
Amsterdam in 1928. The nearest thing to it was a small book
written and printed in England on the games from 1896 to
1908, when they were held in London, but it was a lopsided
and incomplete account. I had to start from scratch, which I
did by going back through the *New York Times* files to the
published stories on the Athens inaugural in 1896 and all subsequent renewals of Olympic competition.

I knew a great many track and field coaches who had been
Olympic champions or competitors in their younger days.
Before I finished my groundwork I had talked with men who
had competed in every set of Olympic Games beginning
with 1896 and from them I gleaned a wealth of firsthand information on the subject and innumerable personal recollections of stirring events. I chatted with James B. Connolly,
the salty historian of the Gloucester fishing fleet who also
was the first of modern Olympic champions. The hop, skip
and jump was the first event concluded at Athens in 1896
and the lithe, little, black-haired Bostonian was the winner.

My tall quiet friend, Raw Ewry, winner of ten Olympic
jumping championships told me endless tales of the happenings from Paris in 1900 to Stockholm in 1912. Harry Hill-
man, coach at Dartmouth, Paul Pilgrim, coach at the New
York A.C., Lawson Robertson, coach at Penn, and many
other track and field veterans who had been to the Olympic
wars were my friends and readily provided grist for my mill.
Came the day when I had the manuscript finished except for
the Los Angeles games, which were just ahead. That was to
be the last chapter. Alas, the head man at the publishing house
didn't like my manuscript. He turned it down. John Hutchens was more upset than I was. One little item that might
have swayed the editor's judgment a trifle was the unexpected
appearance on the market of a paperbacked history of the

Olympic Games from 1896 to 1928 put out by the Los
Angeles organizing committee to stimulate interest in the 1932
Games on the Coast and bring a big attendance at the gate.
The book sold for 50 cents and was a good rush job by a
good man, Bill Henry, then a Los Angeles sports writer, now
far better known as a fine newscaster on radio and television.

That probably cut heavily into the market for the proposed book that I had worked on. Anyway, I took the rejected manuscript and put it away for nearly four years.
Then a follower of my sports column, a friend named Jack
Winters who was a book salesman for the Frederick A. Stokes
Co., asked me one day why I didn't do a book on sports. I
told him that I had done one and it didn't take. I had the
manuscript to prove it. He asked for it and I dug it out and
gave it to him. He phoned a few days later to say that he
liked it and had just turned it over to the head of the firm, the
venerable Frederick A. Stokes himself, who was drawing
close to his eightieth birthday. Jack said that the old gentleman was taking it home with him that night. The next day
at noon Jack phoned to give me the astonishing news that
Mr. Stokes had read it overnight and was ready to publish it.
All I needed to do was to complete the Los Angeles story,
add a final chapter on the 1936 Olympic Games at Berlin that
were just ahead and the book would be up to date for late
fall publication.

That's how I became an author in the first place. The book
came out on schedule and did reasonably well on the market.
The next book I did was so small that it is hardly worth
mentioning. Ted Roosevelt practically took a stick to me to
make me write it. He insisted that I do a book of some kind
on common birds, flowers and wild animals for the ordinary
person who is fond of Nature but knows little about it. I
said that I didn't have the time but the cunning fellow devised

a scheme. He somehow arranged for me to write a short
nature piece — 250 words — each month for the *Woman's
Home Companion* over a term of years. They were to be of
the kind he had mentioned and the magazine would not only
present them as a regular feature in a "box" but would have
the articles illustrated by the artist Fritz Kredel. When the
series had run on long enough, Ted would get permission
from the magazine to reprint them in a booklet and Doubleday would publish it.

The scheme worked, the articles ran for something over
four years in the *Woman's Home Companion*, Fritz Kredel
did a fine job of illustrating the little stories of common
birds, flowers, trees, insects and "wild animals" and fifty of
the magazine pieces were bound into a little book that
came out in 1938 with the following well deserved dedication:

> *This book is affectionately dedicated to the man who drove
> me to it, Colonel Theodore Roosevelt, who like Hamlet,
> knows a hawk from a handsaw when the wind is southerly.*

The story of my third book, *The American Sporting Scene*,
illustrated by an artist who rose to be a rear admiral in the
United States Navy, already has been told. All that is necessary to add here is that I stood my ground as a reluctant
author. It was the illustrator who asked me to write the
book. The next hard-cover opus that came out with my
name on it was *Poems I Remember*, an anthology that Ted
Roosevelt set me to compiling and a book that he never saw
as far as I know. By the time it came out in 1942 Ted was
overseas with the First Division (Infantry) and remained
there until he died of exhaustion two years later in the Normandy campaign. I knew that he always carried little limp
leather or paperbound books of verse in his pocket wherever
he went and would read them at odd moments but I doubt

that he could burden himself in a war with a rather bulky hard-cover anthology that ran to 564 pages, as mine did. Or should I say "his," for Ted was really responsible for the collection that, slightly revised and under the title *Poems To Remember*, is still selling as a paperback in the book marts.

By the end of 1945 the war was over, I had retired from newspaper work, my family had been dispersed and, for the first time since I was graduated from college in 1912, I didn't have a daily job to which I owed allegience and promptitude. I could pick and choose. I still had Information Please once a week through nine months of the year and now and then I went by invitation on other radio shows. This was seldom but, looking back, not seldom enough. I had nothing to gain from such exploits except the money, and I didn't need the money. Indeed, the income tax collectors were in agreement with me on that point and took three-quarters of the extra money away from me. At the top in those days I was paying 69% surtax on my federal return and 7 percent to the New York State tax collector in Albany.

However, I simply couldn't resist an invitation to write another book. In fact, it turned out to be three books. Bird watching was getting to be a popular sport in the United States, as it had been in Great Britain for several centuries, and bird guides were selling at least as well as cool cakes. The standard field guides contained fine color plates of birds and detailed technical descriptions of size and plumage and general behavior of each species, but the beginner in bird watching could easily get discouraged or even lost amid the wealth of the supplied material and the unexpected number of different species that the book reported on his home territory. Van Cartmell, at that time head of one of Doubleday's many divisions, decided that there was a market for a beginner's book on common birds and he asked me to write one. Doubleday was putting out the *Audubon Bird Guide* with text by Richard H. Pough and color plates by Don Eckelberry and thus there would be no problem of illustrations for a beginner's book. We could borrow the Eckelberry color plates of the common birds that I might select for the projected work.

I picked a hundred common birds across the country, favoring the northeast not only because I knew the birds of that region better but also because the same area is the best market for bird books. New England contains more bird watchers to the acre or the mile of shore line than any other area of similar size in the western hemisphere. When a rarity appears in the vicinity the local bird watchers block public roads and invade private property to track it down. Only a few are wealthy but most of them are "comfortably fixed" and all of them can read. That is why *An Introduction To Birds* when it came out in 1946 in "picture book" format (8 by 11 inches) contained noticeably more portraits of — and pure reading matter about — birds that you would expect to meet around Concord, Massachusetts, than those you might come across on the desert outside Phoenix, Arizona.

Van Cartmell was right. The book did well; so well that I had an invitation from Doubleday to do a similar book on wild flowers for beginners. Van had moved on "to fresh woods and pastures new" but the invitation came from his successor as head of the Doubleday division, Ferris Mack, who promised to supply color plates by Tabea Hofmann if I would pick the flowers and do the blooming text. The debut of that opus was delayed when it was discovered that I could write about flowers faster than the lady artist could turn out water color pictures of them. To keep me from getting out of practice on the typewriter, Ferris Mack came up with an interim idea. When I was writing that general column in the *Sun* in 1943 and 1944 I fell into the habit of making my Monday column a report on my Sunday rambles in the wildwood with my regular trio of companions, Dr. Clyde Fisher, Fred Nagler and Herman Forster. Ferris suggested that the material in those columns, with more recent observations added, could be expanded into a book. I expanded as requested and *Footnotes On Nature*, published in 1947, was the result. There were lovely woodcuts by Nora S. Unwin to dress up the pages in which my faithful companions were rather thinly disguised as the Astronomer (Dr. Fisher), the Artist (Fred Nagler) and Herman the Magician (Herman Forster). Some irregulars received similar treatment but at this distance it is safe to identify the Dramatic Critic as Brooks Atkinson, the Falconer as George Dock, Jr., and the Medical Student as my son Jim, now well past the student stage and assistant professor of clinical medicine at the University of California Medical School.

This book was easy to write and apparently not hard to read because one Sunday it very modestly made last place on the nonfiction best seller list in the *New York Times* Book Review Section. Unfortunately, the publishers were not prepared for such popularity and the first run had been limited to 7500 copies, all of which had sold in the process of lifting the book from nowhere to the bottom rung of the best seller list. With no copies to be had for the asking, the public appetite for it passed and though a second printing of 7500 was rushed to the market, it was too late. Never again did the book attain even so much as honorable mention. In fact, the only later list made by *Footnotes on Nature* was the one under the heading OUT OF PRINT. That's the potter's field of publishing and three of my books are buried there. *Nature Notes, Footnotes on Nature* and *The American Sporting Scene. Requiescant in pace.*

I grieve now over the slow death and quiet interment of
Footnotes. Frankly, I liked the harmless little book, probably
because it was my own *recherche du temps perdu*, a recollection of joyful days afield with good companions. I think
it was my favorite literary offspring but, when it came out in
1947 I could not know that it was not long for the book
world and even if I had known, I wouldn't have cared particularly because I had something much more important
on my mind at the time. I had just been thrown off balance
by the revelation to me of the advanced age of a person
whom I had long looked upon as a very attractive young
woman. It was another one of those "turning points" in my
life that I kept running into so often.

Away back in 1940 Francis C. Gray, Boston banker,
chairman of the board of trustees of Massachusetts General
Hospital, ditto for Radcliffe College, and bird watcher of mediocre caliber on the side, was heading the annual community
chest drive in Boston or, as it was then called, "The Red
Feather Campaign." Through mutual friends I was inveigled
into going to Boston to "kick off" the campaign with a speech
at Mechanics Hall on Huntington Avenue to the volunteer
workers who were to invade business offices, ring doorbells
and beat the bushes for contributions. As part of all of this,
I was subjected to an interview by a feature writer on the
Boston Herald, a certain Margaret Ford. I had been warned
about her.

Everybody in the book publishing business knows Anne
Ford — and many persons in the theatrical world know her,
too. This brisk and attractive lady was advance agent for
Theatre Guild productions on the road before she took to
publicizing books and authors. Plying her book wares, Anne
was in and out of newspaper offices all across the country.
A real baseball rooter, when she was in the *Times* office on

business with book reviewers, she would often stop by my desk to discuss the rivalry of the Red Sox and the Yankees. Now and then she presented me with a book, which didn't hurt her standing in my league. I was always glad to see her. One day she said to me: "I see that you're going to Boston to open the Red Feather drive in our town — and you're going to be interviewed by my sister."

Who?

"Margaret Ford of the *Boston Herald* — she's my little sister. Be kind to her."

I promised. It was cold weather when Margaret Ford of the *Herald* came to interview me at the Lenox Hotel in Boston. She was fairly tall, quite dark and very attractive. I would have guessed that she was in her twenties. The interview went off in friendly fashion but I never did see what she wrote of me because it was for the Sunday paper and I was back in New York by that time. However, I went back to Boston three or four times to speak at the *Boston Herald* "Book Fairs" and Margaret Ford was always one of the staff hostesses at such gatherings. I came to know her fairly well and my respect and admiration for her grew with each meeting. When Information Please was broadcast from Symphony Hall in Boston I remember meeting Margaret later outside the hall on Huntington Avenue where she was standing with some friends. I asked her jokingly whether or not she was married yet and when she smilingly answered in the negative, I said somewhat indignantly: "What's the matter with the young fellows around Boston?"

I really did wonder that such a bright and attractive young woman wasn't married, but beyond that it meant nothing to me and I went my way. I thought no more of the matter until this spring day in 1947 when Anne Ford was visiting at my home in Riverdale and happened to say that her sister Margaret had just celebrated her forty-second birthday. I was astounded and incredulous but Anne insisted and gave the statistics: Margaret Ford, spinster, born in Winthrop, Massachusetts, 1905, now resident of Brookline, currently feature writer for the *Boston Herald* and editor of the children's page, forty-two years old in April of 1947 if there was any virtue in simple mathematics and the Gregorian calendar.

Even over the distance that separates New York from Boston, I began to see Margaret Ford in an entirely different light immediately. I had been a widower for three years and never had given any thought to marrying again. I was fifty-four years old and quite comfortable at home with my cousin Jane as the housekeeper, which she had been for more than twenty-five years. However, with the children married and off on their own, the house did seem empty and lonely at times, particularly when I came home late at night and there was nobody to greet me. Jane always went off early to her room on the third floor. If anything was in the back of my mind, it was a determination not to be "an old fool" and marry a young girl. But a clever newspaper woman of forty-two was long out of the "young girl" class. I gave the matter some thought. The fact that Margaret was beautiful as well as bright didn't discourage me at all. It was a small matter and I could put up with it if she could put up with me. To make a short story longer, five months later I had tricked her into marrying me and now, seventeen years later, you couldn't tell us from Darby and Joan or Philemon and Baucis — that is, without a scorecard.

All this, of course, was the long result of my short trip to Boston to aid the Red Feather Fund drive of 1940 and my meeting with a *Boston Herald* feature writer who wanted to do a story to aid the charity drive. Otherwise I might never have met Margaret who, incidentally, kept the appointment with white-booted figure skates slung over her arm. Which reminds me that one other happy consequence of that same charitable campaign grew out of one of the worst mistakes I ever made in my life. Leverett Saltonstall, now the Bay State's senior senator in Washington, was governor of Massachusetts at the time and, to help the Red Feather campaign, he and Mrs. Saltonstall gave a luncheon at their Chestnut Hill home for "the guest speaker" and a few of the fund drive officials, including a Harvard classmate of the host, Chairman Francis Gray who was orderly enough at the table but caused trouble later by suggesting that we all go skating at Hammond Pond in the vicinity.

I rather fancied myself as a skater — without the slightest justification — and expressed regret that my tubular hockey skates were back in New York. According to Governor Saltonstall, that was no difficulty at all. He reached into a hall closet and dug out an extra pair of his own for me. We adjourned to the pond and donned our skates. Leverett Saltonstall is six inches taller than I am and has feet to match. Neither under the Capitol dome on Beacon Hill, in the Senate chamber in Washington, nor on Hammond Pond could I fill his shoes. I couldn't even stand erect on his skates. They slopped over as though my ankles had well-oiled hinges. To move along the ice at all I had to be supported on one side by Governor Saltonstall and on the other by his chuckling classmate at Harvard, Mr. Francis C. Gray. It was a disgraceful exhibition. I must have looked like a drunk being escorted to the patrol wagon by a couple of Boston plainclothes men.

I demanded a return engagement when I had my own skates. I challenged my escorts to a race. F. C. Gray declined immediately but egged on his partner to accept, which he did quite modestly. How was I to know that Leverett Saltonstall had been a hockey star at Harvard and had scored the winning goal over a Princeton sextet led by the immortal "Hobey" Baker? Oxen and wainropes could never have haled me into a race with him had I known how fast he could skate! The great event took place on the rink of The Country Club in Brookline some weeks later. I made a special trip to Boston for the contest. Contest! What contest? With newspaper photographers and other witnesses on hand, Governor Saltonstall ran away from me on skates. I never was more humiliated in my life than when my "second," Red Sox Manager Joe Cronin who was holding my overcoat, jacket and street shoes at the finish line, threw them on the ice at my feet when I arrived there long after my rival and said: "Carry your own stuff. You can't skate worth a nickel!"

I reminded him sternly that I, as least, had finished second, whereas his Red Sox had to win a double-header on the last day of the season to finish fourth. I dismissed him forthwith from my service. But I held no grudge against Leverett Saltonstall and I even forgave Francis Gray who could have warned me that I was rushing to my doom when I made that rash challenge. We shook hands all around before we parted and ever since we have been on most friendly terms with regular reunions at which nobody ever mentions the subject of skating. Bostonians are civilized people.

Back to my books. About the time that Margaret and I were married, the flower portraits by Tabea Hofmann were completed and *An Introduction To Wild Flowers* appeared in 1948 in the same format as the earlier book on birds. It went reasonably well and the relentless Ferris Mack had another idea; a similar book on trees. I took my time with that one and so did the artist, Michael Bevan, who knew little about trees when he started and a good deal about them when he had completed one hundred watercolor paintings of tree trunks, branches, leaves, flowers and fruits of one kind or another. To my eye, *An Introduction To Trees*, which appeared in 1954, turned out to be the most attractive of the series. The artist did a wonderful job, especially with the leaves that he painted in autumn colors.

After 1947, of course, there were two professional authors — as distinguished from newspaper writers — in our house. During her years on the *Boston Herald* Margaret had turned out many magazine pieces, including half a dozen or more for *The New Yorker*, and the *Atlantic Monthly*. Random House had published her *David and the Magic Powder* for junior readers, which found favor with the moppets and sold out the entire printing. It also pleased Editor Bennett Cerf to the extent that he asked Margaret and me to team up and do a book together on John James Audubon for the Landmark Series that Random House was publishing and promoting vigorously. Margaret did most of the research and the writing while I kept order among the birds that were mentioned in the life story of the great artist-ornithologist. The book did moderately well and probably would have done better if I had kept out of it.

One book that I put together withered on the vine and I never could understand why. It was an anthology that I did for Doubleday under the title *Treasury Of Great Nature Stories* to which I contributed brief biographical sketches of the authors whose pieces I had selected. I also included a lot of nature poetry that I loved. Perhaps that did it. Charles Waterton's account of how he rode the alligator bareback was good stuff and so was George Borrow's tale of the King of the Vipers, but why did I have to weigh the book down with interpolated poetry? Because I loved every line of it; that's why. I am unrepentant. The anthology came out in 1957 and, for the most part, has been studiously ignored ever since. So depraved is my taste that I read it over regularly and take great delight in the selections, particularly the verse.

Even before that unwanted offering appeared in print I was slaving away at what was to become, after five years of writing based on fifty years of field work, my magnum opus, the 424-page volume entitled *A Natural History Of New York City* published by Houghton Mifflin in 1959. It was beautifully printed, delightfully illustrated by Henry Bugbee Kane, and well received by critics and book buyers when it first appeared on the market. I feel about the writing of that book as I feel about my soldiering in France in World War I; I'm glad I did it, but I certainly would hate to have to go through it again.

XVI

EARLY TELEVISION
WAS HOT STUFF

THE FIRST time my poor but honest features were scanned by a television camera was shortly before the outbreak of World War II when the now gigantic industry was in its sputtering infancy. Radio was all the rage and two stalwart brothers who were doing well in that medium were Tom and Bill Slater, Tom on the executive and advertising end and Bill as a broadcaster. Bill was a tall quiet chap, a graduate of West Point who had quit soldiering to teach school and then switched to radio broadcasting. Tom was a hustling and bustling graduate of Penn State with a lively sense of humor and an enormous amount of energy.

I remember Tom's college because he once had me as a guest at an alumni gathering in New York where the musical accompaniment was supplied by another Penn State alumnus, Fred Waring, who brought along with him a group from his famous band, The Pennsylvanians. Everybody knows about Fred's rapid rise in the entertainment world. Few know of his slower but perhaps more sensational rise in the educational field. In 1919 Fred Waring was water boy for a Penn State football team that knocked the much bigger University of Pennsylvania eleven for a totally unexpected loop. In the excitement Fred kicked over two buckets of water and had to rush out for refills. Thirty years later the former water boy for the Nittany Lions had risen to the exalted position of member of the Board of Trustees for his alma mater. I venture the opinion that no other former water boy rose to such heights in two quite distinct fields.

Back now to Tom Slater who knew a good thing when he saw it and rushed into television when it first began to rear its ugly antennas. He worked his way into some experimental studio in midtown Manhattan where he acted as producer. The studio equipment cost so much that there was no money to pay performers, so that Tom had to rely on cheap labor, meaning what acquaintances he had who would come around and work for nothing. This included his brother Bill who acted as staff announcer there. It also included me and my long-time friend Lou Little, then at the height of his fame as Columbia football coach.

On a sweltering evening in early September Tom lured Lou and me into his studio to do a fifteen-minute discussion before the cameras on the prospects for the intercollegiate football season just ahead. Getting our positions fixed, the lights set and the cameras at the proper angles took so long that we were in this inferno that Tom called a studio for nearly an hour. The lights they used in the TV studios of those early days were as hot as the open hearths in a steel mill. No amount of mopping could keep our faces dry. Perspiration kept bursting through the "pancake" that they put on us for make-up. Our clothes were soaked and our brains were baked. It was the closest call to cremation that I have had thus far. What they were trying to do was to telecast us the length of the studio. Whether we made it or not I never knew — and didn't care. We went through the torture to help Tom and Bill Slater, for whom we and all who knew them had an abiding affection.

My next dip into television came about a decade later and

was a much cooler venture. It paid better, too. By that time TV producers had money to spend and were paying the hired help enough to lure many of the top radio and stage stars into the newer field. Dan Golenpaul was approached with invitations to put Information Please on TV but we were still going strong in radio and he decided to wait until the infant industry, which was still afflicted with growing pains, came of age. In the end, I think he waited a bit too long, but in the interim he knew that we couldn't last forever on radio and he figured out another way of cashing in on the prestige of our program. He turned publisher and put out the *Information Please Almanac* that began with the 1947 issue and has been going well ever since. I bore the title of editor, but it was a hollow crown. The almanac and practically everything original in it came from the fertile convolutions of the Golenpaul brain and, after a few years, I persuaded him to turn me loose and own up that he was the editor as well as the publisher of the book.

However, I was still in the editor's chair in 1948 when a husky chap with prematurely gray hair came into the office and introduced himself as Paul Moss, a former fight manager who wanted to hire me for a television program he had in mind. He didn't look or act like a fight manager. I had known many of that breed and liked only a few. Most of them were "wheelers and dealers" and the truth was not in them. Indeed, they often boasted of outwitting one another in knavery. They smoked good cigars and used bad language. This chap in my office was well dressed and spoke quietly. He could see that he had me puzzled and he said with a smile:

"You don't know me but Grantland Rice and Frank Graham do. Ask them about me."

To clear up that part of the story, I did ask them and learned that Paul Moss was unique as a fight manager.

He was a college man and the only fighter he ever managed was his college roommate who had been on the same Penn State boxing team with him. And he only did that because his roommate, who had alluring offers to turn pro, wouldn't accept them unless Paul Moss managed him. Billy Soose was the name of the roommate. Paul managed him into the middleweight championship, which Billy won by a decision over Ken Overlin in Madison Square Garden in 1941. Soose outgrew the division within the year, had a few fights as a light heavyweight and then he and his manager joined the U.S. Navy together in 1942. The boxing game never saw either of them again. It must be a record of some kind in professional boxing.

How Paul drifted into the entertainment world I never knew. Possibly he married into it. In time I learned that his attractive wife was the actress Thelma Schnee whom I had seen on the Broadway stage. She played the part of the wild Welsh girl who upset Ethel Barrymore's school-teacherish dream in *The Corn Is Green* by trapping the hero into wedlock. I was there on opening night and it's my opinion that she did it deliberately.

All this came out much later. What I learned from Paul on our first meeting was that he had gathered a collection of remarkable movie shorts dealing with natural history and science and he proposed to adapt them for use as a television series on film. He showed me a list of titles and they were alluring. Astronomy — natural history — chemistry — physics — biology — even atomic energy with some official footage of one of our early experimental explosions in the Pacific. A few subjects had been filmed through a telescope but the most interesting ones had been filmed through microscopes. Originally these pictures had been made for showing in movie houses on a flat screen. Also, each one ran about twenty minutes and would have to be cut down to no more than twelve minutes of running time for a fifteen-minute TV program. New sound tracks would be needed, not only because of the cutting but because many of the original sound tracks were in some foreign language, mostly German. How would I like to do the narration for the new sound tracks?

First I had to see the films or at least some samples. I went to Paul's office the next day and he screened a dozen for me. I was amazed and enchanted. I thought they were wonderful, especially the rotifers and paramecia under the microscope, the insect larva rushing about under the surface of pond water, the rearing of young golden eagles in an eyrie on a cliff in Scotland, keeping canals clear in Europe, making steel in America, digging for oil all over the world!

I signed on immediately and Paul began to cut and hew the films to fit the new purpose to which he was going to put them. When they were trimmed to suit his taste, they were screened for me four or five times running until I was thoroughly familiar with the subject and the sequence of events. Often I had to study up on the subjects and I made repeated trips to the main public library at 42nd Street and Fifth Avenue. Now and then, where the films dealt with European birds or animals, I checked with my friends at the American Museum of Natural History to be sure that I had the right species. Common names in any language can be misleading. What I needed was the right Latin name for the bird, mammal, fish or flower before I could be sure of its identification.

When I was satisfied that I would know what I was talking about, we would take the film to the Reeves sound studio over near the East River on 44th Street where I would sit in the dark at a desk with a microphone and do the narration as the picture unrolled on the screen some twenty feet or so in front of me. I didn't need a light because I never used a script. We tried a script with the first film, which was on atomic energy. We agreed that my reading made the sound track too stilted. We threw away the script and we never had another. If I "fluffed" during the narration, we did it over again. One cursèd film had to be rolled five times before I had it right, but mostly I made it on the first or second try.

We made a total of 104 of these films, a two-year supply for a once-a-week series. It never made the big league, the New York stations, but it ran in many other big cities and often the whole series was re-run under the same sponsorship for another two-year term. We had some sales in Canada, England and Australia, too, but the fact that it never ran in New York caused me a moment of embarrassment one night at the annual dinner of the Thoroughbred Racing Association at the Plaza Hotel. Arthur Godfrey was the guest speaker and, having been on his program several times and having met him on other occasions, I walked up to the dais early in the evening to say hello to him. After we had exchanged greetings he raised his right hand in a characteristic Godfrey gesture and said: "Hey! I like that television show of yours — I do, I do, I do!"

I wasn't doing any television work at the time and I simply stared at him. Could he be confusing me with somebody else? He saw that I was puzzled and he added: "The one with the birds and the flowers and the wild animals — you know, I go for that stuff."

Now I recognized the series that he was talking about, the films that Paul Moss had produced and marketed as *John Kieran's Kaleidoscope*. But I was still puzzled and I asked him: "Where did you see that?"

"Up in Boston when I was lying on my back for weeks in the hospital after the operation on my hip."

He was one up on me. I never had seen any of the films on

the TV screen but once when I went to Detroit to be one of the speakers at a charity drive luncheon, I noticed that an undue number of persons seemed to recognize me as I walked along the street. I couldn't understand it until a Detroit friend told me that the local telephone company was sponsoring the *Kaleidoscope* and my picture adorned the advertisement for the program in all the pay station phone booths in town! That was almost indecent exposure.

Which reminds me that one day when Margaret and I were walking down Fifth Avenue Margaret stopped to look at a dress in a window and I went on ahead slowly. As she came along to rejoin me she heard one woman on the sidewalk say to another: "That was John Kieran — and he looks just like his picture."

Shucks, it's easy when you know how.

The only trouble with the *Kaleidoscope* was that Paul Moss tried to sell it as well as produce it and he didn't have time to do both jobs. The sales end lagged until he transferred the whole thing to the American Broadcasting Company's film syndication division whose able and amiable director, George Shupert, kept the film rolling hither and yon for almost a decade, by which time newer and better films were on the market.

I learned a lot doing those sound tracks and I liked working with Paul Moss, but I didn't dare tackle the next venture that he proposed. He had bought the motion picture rights to G. K. Chesterton's detective stories, the famous Father Brown series, and he wanted me to play the part of the deceptively innocent old priest on the screen. He said he planned to produce it in England and I would have loved to have spent those months over there with him but I knew that I was no actor and I turned down the Father Brown part with a laugh. So Paul flew to England and produced the motion

picture there with another man wearing the Roman collar of
Father Brown — a chap named Alec Guinness. Somehow I
thought that this was tremendously flattering to me in a
vague way.

I saw the picture when it ran in this country. I liked it and
it had fair success here and abroad, which delighted me because of my fondness for Paul who planned to go ahead with
more movie production in England. However, it was discovered that he was in need of comparatively minor surgery
and he flew to New York for the operation. What complications arose I never knew but, after the operation, he collapsed and died within a week. I never worked for a more
considerate employer and never met a nicer fellow. He died
much too young to suit me.

I had one other offer to play a star role and I have always
regretted that I didn't try it. It was one in which I would
have been heard but not seen. The Theatre Guild was plan-
ning a radio production of *Our Town* and Theresa Helburn
called me on the phone to ask me to be the narrator, the part
that Frank Craven played in the original Broadway production. But even the reading of an acting part frightened me
and I begged off. "O, what a rogue and peasant slave am I!"
Anybody who calls me coward and breaks my pate across
is unquestionably in the right — but give me credit for a
proper appreciation of my lack of talent in the realm of sock
and buskin.

In June of 1948, after a run of ten consecutive years as one
of the top shows on radio, Information Please vanished into
thin air. It was Dan Golenpaul's choice. The sponsor was
willing to go back on the air in the autumn at the same price
but, with a presidential election coming up and business conditions for the future uncertain, he didn't want to sign for a
long term. Dan wouldn't settle for anything short of a two-

year contract and, when he didn't get it, he withdrew the show. I was sorry because it was always a lot of fun but I didn't feel at all that "Othello's occupation's gone." I had plenty of other work to keep me busy. I was helping with the *Information Please Almanac* and I was pegging away in the field of natural history as usual.

I had a few odd jobs on radio now and then but nothing serious. The one I liked best was filling in for Lowell Thomas whose evening news spot at 6:45 had become an institution in radio. The reason that Lowell needed a replacement occasionally was that he kept rambling all over the surface of the globe and sometimes couldn't reach a broadcasting studio by sundown, New York daylight saving time. He had to call for help. Replacing him was an honor — and a cinch. The staff news gatherers, headed by the plump Prosper Buranelli, handed over the script. All I had to do was to read it in a clear voice.

Ordinarily this was just a one-night stand but once I filled in for him through a whole week. When he walked into Tibet and was carried out on a stretcher — he broke his hip in a fall out there — a battalion of his friends, one after another, filled in for him until he reached civilization again and could speak up for himself. Many of these substitutes were amateurs in broadcasting and a bit timid in front of a microphone, but they got away with it in good style. All but one. He decided to nerve himself for the ordeal with a few shots of bourbon. He overdid the treatment and the result was distinctly audible. However, no permanent harm was done. It merely provided a little mirth where none was intended, which is far better than providing none where much is expected.

During this period Dan Golenpaul had us working sporadically on a plan to put Information Please on television via film and we made a few "pilot films" for exhibition to the trade. To me, they seemed much like the old Information Please movie shorts that were lost to posterity by fire but, to my regret, we didn't have the original cast of characters. Most important of all, we had lost our incomparable master of ceremonies, Clifton Fadiman. After years of bickering over matters of which I knew nothing, he and Dan had parted without tears. Oscar Levant had settled down — if you could call it that — in Beverly Hills and was unavailable, even if Dan had wanted him, which I doubt. They, too, had enjoyed a falling out.

That left only F.P.A. and me of the original four. Half a loaf may be better than no bread but you can't cut everything as fine as that. Half a team can't function as well as a whole team and half a horse wouldn't get anywhere in racing. Some of our old friends showed up at the studios for these "pilot films" and we enjoyed the company of newer celebrities like Sarah Churchill and Alistair Cook but the problems of staging and filming the show for television never reached any happy solution and eventually the whole thing bogged down.

At the end — and it really was the end — Information Please went on "live television" as a summer replacement for the Fred Waring show in 1952. By that time Franklin P. Adams was in such poor shape physically that he had to retire after the first telecast. Thus I became the only survivor of the original quartet and I mightily missed the others. Furthermore, it was most difficult to get guest stars of note for the program in the sweltering summer in New York City. Those who could afford it stayed away in horror. Thus the shows that we put on lacked the zest and sparkle of the ancient days on radio. I was not surprised when there came no insistent demand for more of Information Please on television after Fred Waring and his Pennsylvanians came back to claim their own on Sunday nights.

I was, however, not only surprised but cruelly shocked by a letter I received in answer to a query that I put to the District Director of Internal Revenue at Albany, New York, that being the office to which I was then sending my annual tear-blotted individual federal income tax returns. Margaret and I were spending that summer on Nantucket and I "commuted" to New York each week for those Sunday night shows. Since the Nantucket airport is only too frequently "fogged in" when you want to come or go by plane, I couldn't take a chance on getting off Sunday afternoon for a night show in New York. To make sure of being at the studio on time, I had to take the 6 A.M. boat for the mainland each Sunday and follow that with a 6-hour train ride from Woods Hole to Manhattan. There was no late plane for Nantucket after the show, so I took the sleeper to Boston and flew back to Nantucket early Monday morning.

I didn't mind the early rising to catch the 6 A.M. boat. I have been up with the lark all my life, though not always to bed with the same. But that long train ride to New York in midsummer was a drill and a tiresome approach to a battle of wits on television that same night. The sleeper jump back to Boston was another chore, bearable but by no means festive. Somebody warned me that I might have trouble if I deducted my fare by boat, train and plane on these expeditions as business expenses on my income tax return.

"On what grounds?" I bellowed *ex imo pectore*.

"Don't ask me," said my friend. "Ask the Internal Revenue man."

I did ask and the result was shattering. The letter from the man in charge at the Albany office informed me that New York City was my residence, that nobody could deduct expenses for going from his residence to his place of business and that the Department of Internal Revenue was not to be bilked of a penny of its tax due because I and my wife elected to spend the summer on Nantucket for our personal pleasure. As the immortal James Yellowplush put it in his illustrious diary: "Phansy my feelinx!" Once again — to quote another great English authority — I agreed with the dictum of Mr. Bumble in *Oliver Twist:* "The law is a ass, a idiot."

A year or so before the death and burial of Information Please I did a short and successful series of television shows for NBC under my own steam. Somebody over there thought up the idea of showing on television some of the popular attractions of the city for residents and visitors — the parks, the museums, the great public library at Fifth Avenue and 42nd Street, the United Nations and so on. I was invited to do most of the talking on the program. My job was to visit each one of these places of interest and, with the aid of the custodians or other inmates, show what they had to offer in the way of wonders for public enjoyment.

The show, billed as Treasures of New York, was admirably staged by NBC and, beginning around the first of April, 1951, was an instant hit. The first recognition of it was a "rave notice" by Philip Hamburger in *The New Yorker*, and Phil wasn't too happy about a lot of things on TV at that time. The only error in *The New Yorker* review was that I received credit for thinking up the show. I wish I could remember the name of the man who did, because it turned out to be a bright idea. Also, it was a step forward in television at that time because all our shows were to be live "remotes" — done with mobile equipment in the field, not in the studio. NBC was proud of its big truck and the skilled electronic technicians who rolled with it through the streets of Brooklyn, Manhattan and the Bronx to telecast a series of thirteen live shows from the American Museum of Natural History, the Museum of Modern Art, the Hall of Fame on University Heights, the Botanical Garden in Bronx Park, the United Nations, the Museum of the City of New York, and other such places.

The show was skillfully set up and directed by Alan Handley and his assistant, Margaret Roberts. They made all the advance arrangements with the officials at the various institutions and set the stage for an orderly presentation of the "treasures" that were to be displayed. It was a half-hour show beginning on the stroke of noon each Saturday and my only part in the preliminaries was to show up on Thursday mornings for a rehearsal or "run-through" so that I would know the order of events and how I was expected to handle them. I worked with a hand microphone with long lengths of cord trailing behind as I wandered from gallery to gallery with either a rolling camera following me or one awaiting me as I came through an arch or a doorway. Often the distances through the galleries were so long that we had to have relays of fresh microphones along the way and I had to remember just where I was to put one down and scurry along — off camera — to pick up the next one in a hurry.

We ran into one bit of competition on the air that I found hard to fight my way through in the outdoor shows that we did from the uncompleted terrace of the United Nations building, the airy colonnade of the Hall of Fame on University Heights and the greensward of the Botanical Garden in Bronx Park. Just as we went on the air at noon each Saturday, the air raid warning sirens of those Korean War days sounded off for a fifteen-minute test. Indoors at the various museums I heard them only faintly but on that terrace of the United Nations building the wail of some nearby siren was almost deafening while I was interviewing a man who had a mighty big job at the lofty and shiny new building — he was a window washer. Luckily the racket had ended before Dr. Ralph Bunche came out to join me for a quieter talk on the terrace. The sirens weren't nearly as bad at the other outdoor sites, but they certainly were no help.

The series went along swimmingly. I was having fun and apparently the TV viewers and reviewers thought that it was entertaining. The NBC higher powers were so pleased that they proposed enlarging the scope and extending the series indefinitely as Treasures of the United States or some such title. Instead of stopping as planned with the thirteenth show in late June, they asked me whether or not I would continue through the summer and visit such places as the Grand Canyon, Yellowstone Park, the Yosemite, the Alamo, the Halls of Congress and so on. I vetoed this for several reasons. One was that Margaret had leased a place on Nantucket for the summer and we were counting on being there. Another and perhaps decisive reason was that Alan Handley was being called away to direct the Dinah Shore show that was to open on television in September. I felt that Alan's handling of our series was the most important element in its success and I didn't want to go on with it unless I had his expert guidance — especially through a hot summer of travel from town to town across the country.

However, I did agree to do an extra show beyond the New York area limits and we closed out the series with Alan Handley still on the job directing the action as I strolled through the galleries of the National Museum of Art in Washington, D.C., with John Walker (then assistant director, later director) at my side to point out to me — and the TV viewers — the priceless treasures of that imposing institution.

Perhaps the last was the best show of the series. Of that I can't be sure but I'm certain about which was the biggest mishmash. It was the one we were supposed to do from the deck of one of the Circle Line sightseeing steamers that take tourists for a watery jaunt around Manhattan Island starting from the foot of West 42nd Street. We didn't expect to make it all the way around Manhattan in a half-hour. We merely planned to sail south from 42nd Street on the Hudson toward the Bay, showing the famous skyscraper profile of the city en route and winding up at what was then called Bedloe's Island with the towering form of the Statue of Liberty on camera and my melodious (?) voice declaiming the deathless lines of Emma Lazarus:

> *. . . Give me your tired, your poor,*
> *Your huddled masses yearning to breathe free,*
> *The wretched refuse of your teeming shore.*
> *Send these, the homeless, tempest-tost to me,*
> *I lift my lamp beside the golden door!*

It was to be a picturesque voyage with a wonderful fade-out, but it didn't come out exactly as planned. It was really something of an adventure for those early days of television — a "remote" originating from a boat moving down the Hudson River. For previous shows on hard ground the big NBC truck that made the rounds with us served as our power house and control center but we couldn't run the truck aboard the sightseeing boat. Our engineer had to make other arrangements. He had a crew at the dockside at dawn and loaded a heavy dynamo aboard to furnish the power for our sea-going control center, the cameras, the lights, the inter-com telephone head sets and the transmitter that was to speed the picture and sound back to the receiving mast atop the RCA Building in Rockefeller Center, from which point the show would be relayed to home TV sets.

When I went aboard at 10 A.M. all this had been done ship-shape and Bristol fashion but nothing else went right the whole day, beginning with the weather, which was foul. Because it was to be a boat trip of a June day my wife came along just for the ride and we reached the pier in a thick fog and thin drizzle. From the upper deck of the boat I couldn't see more than two blocks in any direction. However, we had two hours to go before starting time and the Weather Man promised that things might change for the better. As our director, Alan Handley, began to outline what we were to do on the cruise I noticed that he was intermittently gulping aspirin. He was sick and shouldn't have been there at all. We finally persuaded him to lie down on a couch and he went off into a doze from which he didn't recover until the telecast was over. We had to work without a director but the engineer stepped into the breach and did well when the time came.

There were other complications. We had a new "floor man," one I never had seen before. The "floor man" is the one who works close to the cameras and actors, throwing cues and commands silently by waving his arms or pointing in some significant direction. He wears a telephone head set and gets his orders from the director offstage at the control center. At least, that's the way it was in those pioneer days. Perhaps the whole thing is done by digital computer now. This particular "floor man" showed up with a big thermos jug of what turned out to be dry martinis. Possibly to ward off any chance of catching cold from the fog and drizzle to which we were exposed in running through a sketchy rehearsal on the exposed upper deck of the boat, our hero began pouring himself libations from the jug as soon as we had descended to the protection of the main saloon. We still had about an hour to go before air time and our man did not neglect his martinis.

As noon approached the fog was still with us and we had word from NBC headquarters that they would put on a substitute program at noon and we were to start at twelve-thirty, weather permitting. As twelve-thirty neared, the drizzle had quit and the fog had thinned out but we still couldn't see the Empire State Building, so we had another reprieve to one o'clock. However, that meant that we lost our "barker," a cute blond young lady wearing a Circle Line uniform who knew all the ships on the river and all the Manhattan skyline and was to help me out at the microphone with her professional patter as we made the trip to the Statue of Liberty. She was scheduled to leave on her regular trip around the island on another boat — with paying passengers — at 2 P.M. and she couldn't make it if she shipped with us. She walked off and I felt as though I had been abandoned on a desert island.

By twelve-fifty the fog had thinned further and a wan sun was visible aloft. We had word to cast off and start telecasting at one P.M. and keep going for our regular half-hour. By this time the floor man had finished the jug and had one section of the main saloon floor to himself, face downward in slumber. I took stock of the situation. The weather was still a bit sticky for putting pictures on TV, our director was out sick, our floor man was out cold and I had lost the professional guide who was to help me carry the ball. At this juncture things took a turn for the worse.

A minute or two before 1 P.M. the engines began to throb and the crew made ready to cast off for the voyage down the river. I stood on the forward section of the upper deck flanked by two cameras that were to sweep the river traffic and the shore on both sides as we worked our way downstream. For the start of the telecast, one of the camera men had drawn a bead on me where I stood holding a hand mike with a long trailing cord to allow me leeway in moving about. The only other occupants of the upper deck were two attractive women with the same first name, Margaret — my wife and Margaret Roberts, Alan Handley's secretary and general assistant. They were wondering how I was going to deal with the situation. I knew most of New York's famous skyscrapers when I met them on the street but from the middle of the Hudson River I could easily be confused. My acquaintance with transatlantic liners was mediocre. Through the remnants of the fog that still lingered over the river I was taking a dim view of things when the red light appeared below the lens on the camera facing me, which meant that it was precisely 1 P.M. and we were on the air.

I had just begun my preliminary chatter — "Welcome once again to Treasures of New York — today we are taking you on a trip down the Hudson River" and so forth — when I looked toward the outer end of the dock and, to my horror, saw the nose of an incoming steamer edging upstream around the corner of our pier! It slowly revealed itself as an Italian freighter coming into our dock to tie up at the pier just across from the one at which we were still lying. We were trapped. We couldn't even cast off until that unspeakable ship came in and it was coming in by inches in my terrified opinion. We were on the air and had nothing to show the home viewers except a big freighter slowly nudging itself into the dock and blocking our way in the process. Our half-hour on the air would be over before we could get out into the stream. We were ruined before we started!

The quickest way out of my difficulty, of course, would have been to throw myself overboard but I knew my wife would resent that. She handles big problems nobly but often is upset by trifles. Then I had a better idea. A wife is supposed to be a helpmate. I was a husband in desperate trouble. I waved to Margaret to join me in front of the camera with the incoming freighter in the background and asked her to speculate on what far ports this ship might have touched and what curious cargo she might have in the hold — ivory, apes and peacocks, or cheap tin trays, all fit items for a freighter's manifest according to John Masefield, once a fore-mast hand himself. Margaret suggested olives, lemons and fine Italian wines. We worked harder getting that ship in than the tugs and the landing crew on the pier. We had to keep up the conversation until our half-hour on the air dragged itself to an exhausted end. Just before that happened, the final blow fell. Watching the show at NBC headquarters, the program manager noted that the freighter had been pushed and hauled out of our way and we were to be al-lowed — allowed, he said — to go on for another half-hour to carry on the program as originally planned!

We cast off, headed out, turned downstream and a half-hour later we were facing the Statue of Liberty where, in a hoarse voice and a partial stupor, I was muddling up the lovely closing line of the Emma Lazarus poem and bidding our TV viewers farewell with my dying breath. The trip down was a nightmare by daylight for me. All I know is that Margaret saved my life — and the show, what remained of it. I was hoping that no friends of ours had tuned in that day. Or that their sets were out of order. I hated to go out the next day, Sunday, or to the office on Monday morn-ing. I was afraid to face the music.

Incredibly, the music was pleasant when we heard it.

"I caught your TV show Saturday — the one on the boat."

I groaned and muttered an apology.

"No, it was fine. Very interesting."

One acquaintance after another voiced the same opinion. I thought the general verdict was enough to kill the jury system in this country. But at least Margaret received a re-markable tribute for her lifesaving part in the program from the mouth of my favorite elevator operator in our office building when I arrived there Monday morning.

"I saw your show Saturday," he said with a wide smile.

"Don't mention it!"

"Why not?"

"It was dreadful — all fouled up — I didn't know where I was or what I was talking about half the time."

"No, no," he insisted. "It was really good. I love to watch the boats going up and down the Hudson. What you said was very interesting — but who was that woman who kept interrupting you?"

There is no justice.

XVII

WE FOLLOW THE GLEAM

I N THE SUMMER of 1952 I passed my sixtieth birthday. All through the years of living and working in a great city I kept clinging to the hope or the vision of some day saying farewell to the topless towers of Manhattan, to the hurry and scurry of traffic in crowded streets, to the atmosphere laden with soot and poisoned with exhaust gases, to this vast area of concrete, steel and asphalt, to find a greener, cleaner, quieter home somewhere in the region of our land that I knew best and loved best — the New England countryside.

The older I grew the more determined I became to carry out the long thought that I had nourished since boyhood — a later life in a rustic setting where, before it was too late, I could enjoy roaming wooded ridges, hillside pastures and wet meadows not far from my own doorstep. If I lived in or near a little town, it would have to be one with a tiny park or village green dwarfed by towering elms above it.

> *How blest is he who crowns in shades like these*
> *A youth of labor with an age of ease.*

Such was my lifelong dream and, at sixty, I had reached the

age when it had to be made real if it was to be achieved at all. Ever since I had given up daily newspaper work in 1944 I had been spending more and more of my waking hours in the open, keeping track of the coming and going of birds, learning more about our native trees, shrubs and flowers, improving my acquaintance with nature in all its visible forms. Radio and television work was periodic and profitable, but writing about nature had become my principal and settled occupation. In the pursuit of that profession residence in a city was a handicap rather than an advantage. I was ready and ripe for the trek to my own Promised Land and so was Margaret who, Brookline bred and Boston fashioned, was appalled at the size of New York and the time it took to get from one section of the city to another, beginning with the trip from our home to the shopping center on Fifth Avenue.

We lived in what I always thought was the finest residential part of New York, the Riverdale region in the northwest corner of the city. Probably I was prejudiced because of being born in that section and living there through the succeeding sixty years. I loved it because of the lawns, shade trees, open fields and patches of woods that remained even up to the time of our departure. Man and boy, around the three houses in which I lived successively I pushed a lawn mower for half a century. (Somehow my two healthy sons never learned the knack, though they watched me often enough to see how simple it was.) We had oak trees around the house and a bird bath on the front lawn. At dinner on quiet summer evenings we were serenaded by a wood thrush singing in the shrubbery in the garden. Turning into the driveway late one night, I caught an opossum in the headlights of the car and watched it slowly shuffle off into the darkness. Every autumn we made a rite of gathering the last chrysanthemums from the garden to decorate the Thanksgiving Day table.

What we had — and enjoyed — was truly *rus in urbe*, suburban life within the city limits.

But we knew that it couldn't last. The city kept crowding in on us and we were losing ground steadily. Rows of new homes appeared where there had been open fields. The big blow came when apartment houses rose up in our neighborhood and our combined gorge rose with them. Our glorious sunsets over a wooded ridge were blotted out by great bastions of masonry. We felt as though we were living at the bottom of the Grand Canyon. We decided to run for it before we were crushed under the dreadful weight of so much steel and concrete.

I was all for taking to the hills because I was an uplander by birth and breeding. Though New York is one of the great seaports of the world, I saw little of the ocean as a boy. From our home in the northwest Bronx it was twenty-five miles or more to Rockaway or Coney Island and nobody had automobiles in those days. It was a long tiresome trip by railroad, elevated train and trolley to the ocean front and I made it just twice in all my boyhood. Once with a school picnic group I was taken to Midland Beach on Staten Island and once my mother and father took me bathing with them at Manhattan Beach hard by Coney Island. As for Coney Island and its famous attractions, I never set foot on that hallowed ground until I was of voting age and on that occasion I was taken there by my brother-in-law, Paul Reilly, who had just come to New York from his native Pittsburgh and was eager to see all the sights of the great city.

To explain my unfamiliarity with one of the famous sights of the city, I digress. It's just possible that Theodore Dreiser delivered coal at our house when I was a toddler. At least he was driving a truck for our local coal dealer at the time. A score of years later, by which time Dreiser was famous, I met his first wife through the fact that her niece was married to my college classmate and fellow staff member on the *Times,* Frank Hughes. The ex-Mrs. Dreiser lived with a sister or a cousin in a little apartment in Greenwich Village and we younger folk often visited them. They were charming ladies and we all loved them. Through the niece we learned to call them Aunt Jug and Aunt Handy. Aunt Jug was Mrs. Dreiser, who retained the name after her divorce.

One evening Aunt Jug learned from our casual conversation that I never had visited the Statue of Liberty, a landmark of the city, a national shrine and a mecca for sightseers from all over the country. She was astonished and perhaps a little bit shocked. She challenged me immediately. Why in the world hadn't I made the little trip by water to visit the Statue of Liberty and go up the inside of the towering figure to look out over the harbor?

I gave an honest answer. It was probably because I was born in New York. A native doesn't have the curiosity of newcomers or tourists.

"But why," said Aunt Jug, "didn't your father take you there when you were a boy?"

"Because he was born in New York, too."

I make one further confession. I never went up to the observation platform at the top of the Empire State Building until two grandchildren on a visit from California demanded that I take them there.

Revenons à nos moutons. I was further conditioned to upland life by my summer vacations on the family farm in Dutchess County. It was fruit and dairy country in a small way and, even after I learned by experience that I couldn't make a living there, I still loved the area so much that, as a young dreamer, I planned to make it my haven of ultimate retreat when I had enough money to retire. I even had the tract of land picked out on which I would build my dream house. It was another abandoned farm of about 50 acres of rolling land with a nice stream running through it. No buildings. They had all fallen into ruins. Only the cellar holes remained as testimony of former habitation.

For more than twenty years I kept my eye on the place. My father had sold our old farm while I was overseas in World War I. It had served its purpose of providing a summer playground for a brood of seven children who, with one exception, had all outgrown its charms. I was the one exception. When my own children came along, I "put them out to pasture" each summer on a large neighboring farm owned by the Wing family that had provided four of the six pupils I had during the year I held forth as teacher at the little wooden schoolhouse at Anson's Crossing. I drove up there as often as I could get away from work in the city. The children loved it as much as I did and soon became part and parcel of the Wing family. They knew the names of each of the horses, cows and dogs on the place and even gave names of their own choice to all the pigs in the orchard and the more important chickens in the barnyard.

The active head of the farm was Charley Wing who was a chubby, towheaded six-year-old when he came trudging into my one-room schoolhouse. He had grown into a successful farmer and was building up a fine herd of milch cows. I discovered that Charley had leased the land on which I had fixed my fancy. He used it as a pasture for his "dry cows" and young stock. With a brook running through it and plenty of grass all around, he could turn cattle in there and have no worries about them through the growing months of the year.

The property was owned by a woman doctor who lived in New York. When I told Charley that I would like to buy the place, he volunteered to write the owner and ask her to put a price on it for him. It was natural that he might be interested in buying it. He had never seen the lady in his life until, in response to his letter, she appeared at the Wing farm, asked him some questions about boundary lines and took off again for New York without putting a price on the place. Our plan was to have Charley buy it for me and I would let him pasture his stock there free of charge. The plan vanished into thin air when the lady notified Charley that she had sold the place to somebody else and he was to remove his cattle at the end of his current lease. A little later came a lethal blow. I was driving up to visit the children on the Wing farm one day when I saw on the crest of a lovely open ridge near the farm a big sign reading: Building Lots For Sale.

Farewell to Dutchess County. I would have to retreat deeper into the woods, far beyond the confines of "building lots." I brooded over the matter for years during which I adhered to my habit of taking long walks every morning in the Riverdale–Van Cortlandt Park region with my customary companion, Fred Nagler, who loved the outdoors as much as I did. Fred was originally from West Springfield, Massachusetts. He came to New York to study at the Art Students League. Another student in the same class was a girl from Spuyten Duyvil whom I had known since school days, Edith Kroeger. Indeed, our families were friends and we often met at neighborhood parties.

My first meeting with Fred came after the Giants had defeated the Yankees in the world series of 1922. Later in the autumn I was walking along the river road with the noted third baseman of the losing team, "Jumping Joe" Dugan. He lived in a downtown apartment and complained that he wasn't getting any exercise. I invited him to take a long walk with me any time he felt ambitious. This was the first time that he had accepted the invitation. He was wearing his Yankee

baseball cap and his uniform sweater with the Yankee mono-
gram on it and we were walking along briskly when we encountered a couple walking in the opposite direction. Joe
and I concentrated on the man for the simple reason that
he was wearing a dark pointed beard that gave him the appearance of something out of a Rembrandt gallery. Just as the
couple came abreast of us my eye shifted to the lady. It was
Edith Kroeger, whom I hadn't seen since I went off to France
in 1917.

We exchanged greetings and introductions.

"My husband, Fred Nagler."

"My friend, Joe Dugan."

I was glad to see Edith again and meet her husband. In no
time after that introduction Fred and I were cronies and
regular companions on walks around our home territory.
That is, during the colder half of the year. The Naglers spent
the warmer half in their home on a hillside in the Berkshires
four miles out of the little town of Huntington, Massachusetts.
They returned to the city in October or November largely
because Edith's parents were growing old and wanted the
company of the younger couple in their big house that overlooked the Hudson at Spuyten Duyvil.

Over the years Fred kept telling me how attractive the
country was around Huntington and often invited me to go
up with him and see for myself but I put it off until late in
1941 when Fred discovered that the property across the road
from his home was on the market. We drove up together to
look at it and within a matter of months I was the owner of
record of two hundred acres of steep hillside territory completely covered with second-growth hardwoods about fifty
feet tall.

My son Jim and I — he was a medical student at the time
— cleared a camp site and hewed down enough timber on the
hillside below to give us a full view of the valley and the op-

posite slope beyond the river that we could hear all summer but see only in winter when the trees were bare. We put up a simple five-room camp and ultimately had all the conveniences of civilized living and no major annoyance. I mean that we had electricity, a gravity water system fed from a well higher up on the hill, modern plumbing — and no telephone! The last item was a guarantee of peace and quiet when we were in camp.

As a retreat from the rush of New York it was utterly delightful. That is, in the warmer months. It was habitable from May to October but for warmth in cold weather we had only the open fireplace and electric heaters. The water had to be drained off from the end of October until early May lest the pipes freeze and burst. Margaret and I loved our visits there. The damp woods were filled with ferns and orchids and wildlife of all kinds. There were ruffed grouse along the lane to the gate and pileated woodpeckers often clamored hoarsely and chopped loudly away at the trunks of big sugar maples on the ridge above the camp. Hermit thrushes sang all around us in the twilight and in the darkness we would go out and exchange hoots with barred owls. The vibrant calls of whippoorwills floated up faintly through the night from somewhere in the valley.

We thought seriously of building an all-year home there and making it our place of retirement from New York but, when the time for decision arrived, we agreed that it was a little too deep in the woods for — let's face it — persons of our age.

"Let me show you Cape Ann," said Margaret. "You'll love Folly Cove."

Some time later we were visiting her mother in Brookline and, on an overcast day, we took the train from the North Station in Boston to Rockport. When we arrived there it was drizzling and a fog was rolling in from the sea. We had lunch in a tiny tearoom in Dock Square and, except for the girl who served us, we were alone in the place. After lunch we went outside, waited for a big gray bus to come along, rode about four miles over a very winding road in the thick fog and debarked. Margaret led me down to the water's edge, waved an arm in an outward gesture and said: "This is Folly Cove."

All I could see was the water at my feet and the thick fog all around.

"Never mind," said Margaret, who doesn't give up easily. "I know the path along the cliff. Follow me."

I followed as she turned left and began a climb along the shore line up a hillside covered with drenched shrubbery that shed a good deal of its watery content on our clothes. We walked along the edge of the little cliff and saw absolutely nothing on the seaward side. The water below was invisible in the fog. Ultimately I was led back to the main highway through a rustic graveyard and we sat on the cemetery wall to wait for a bus to rescue us.

"Which side of the road should we wait on?" I asked. "Which way is Gloucester, — right or left?"

"Both," said Margaret, "take the first bus in either direction."

The fog, I decided, had seeped into her brain. But what had me baffled is the simple truth on Cape Ann. The only through road is a circle that starts in Gloucester and can be traveled in either direction. Now that we know our way around, when returning home from "the mainland" by car I always ask Margaret: "Shall we take the short road or the grand tour?"

The "grand tour" is the longer way around through Annisquam, Folly Cove and Pigeon Cove and is by far the more picturesque approach to Rockport.

At the time of the foggy expedition to Folly Cove I was

still tied to New York by radio and television commitments and could get away only for a summer vacation. We sampled Nantucket for several summers and found it alluring — lovely moors, endless beaches for wonderful ocean bathing, and a geographical location that made it an ideal stopover for southbound upland and shore birds during the fall migration. We began to think of making the island our home but the jury was still out when Margaret suggested another trial trip to Folly Cove. This time we saw it on a clear day and one glance was enough for us both. We finally knew where we wanted to settle down; somewhere on Cape Ann within sight and sound of the sea.

Four years and four houses later we were living in the little town of Rockport and beginning to cut the ties that bound us to the big city. First we leased this house for three months in the summer. Next we leased it for six months. By that time we had sold our home in Riverdale and were living in an apartment in Bronxville with most of our furniture and books in storage. This we called "biding our time" while the radio and television programs with which I was affiliated were dying of natural causes. I let them expire peacefully. Beyond that I was writing books about birds, trees and flowers and I could do that anywhere — certainly better in Rockport than Bronxville.

The last hurdle was cleared when I turned down the best television contract that ever was offered to me. It was a newscasting program to be sponsored by a famous manufacturing corporation offering a prestige product — a status symbol, if you wish — and it would have had me speaking from a television studio in midtown Manhattan at 11 P.M. five nights a week. I remembered my age. I decided that I didn't care to work that late at night largely for the benefit of the income tax collector. I wanted time to read a great many books and perhaps write a few before I died. I felt that great days afield were awaiting me in Massachusetts. Margaret wanted to get back to her outdoor painting. Together we made the decision; we would be poor but happy. So we bought this house, remolded it a little nearer to our hearts' desire, waved farewell to metropolitan New York and settled down in this little town.

Rockport was well named. Before steel, reinforced concrete, aluminum and glass put granite out of the building business, the local quarries were the most famous and busiest in the country. The great pits, now filled with water and maintained as private ponds or swimming pools, furnished the granite blocks used in the construction of banks, libraries, churches, museums and halls of ivy all across the United States in the old days. The rock from Rockport went into the solidity of the huge locks of the Panama Canal.

Silent they lie now, those pits large and small that once were loud with the din of steam drills, creaking derricks, puffing locomotives and exploding dynamite. Concrete crushed the quarryman just as ruthlessly as the automobile ran over the village blacksmith. Except for one lone quarry that turns out — cut by flame now — curbstones for streets and headstones for burial plots, the Stone Age of Rockport is over. A few houses of native granite and occasional bits of fine stonework in the form of doorsteps or garden walls are all the visible relics of a lost art and a vanished industry.

Even so, arts and letters flourish here as they did a century ago when William Cullen Bryant, Henry Wadsworth Longfellow, Ralph Waldo Emerson and their literary cronies walked the region and wrote of the beauty they found here. Winslow Homer came here to sketch and paint before he retired to the Maine coast where he ended his days. Rudyard Kipling lived in neighboring Gloucester for a brief period and the long result was *Captains Courageous*, that stirring story of Gloucestermen on the high seas. Gloucester has many resident painters, sculptors and writers of note but the city is best known for its fishing fleet and its seafaring history. With Rockport it is otherwise. The artists hold the foreground here. The sculptors and writers go about their work in comparative privacy but painters are out in the open all over the town. They set up their easels on the sidewalks and lawns. They perch on rocky headlands. You find them, often surrounded by coveys of pupils, far out in the field and far down the beaches.

James Abbott McNeill Whistler, the acid expatriate, lamented in London that Art was upon the town. He was out for Philistine blood and critical scalps and his remark was cutting. Here the words would be taken in a different sense. Art is all over the town and everybody loves it that way. It seeps in everywhere and touches every town activity. One striking example is that for many years the player-manager of the Rockport town baseball team was a man legally entitled to sign his wintry landscape "A. T. Hibbard, N.A." No other town in the United States has had that distinction since Woodstock, New York, lost it nearly forty years ago when George Bellows died.

Aside from arts and letters, our town is a seaport in miniature, and our seagoing citizens are lobstermen, cabin cruiser owners, outboard addicts and small boat sailors of all ages and both sexes. T-Wharf is the hub of activity through most of the year and our little harbor is a stippled Seurat picture in summer with its innumerable class boats of a dozen types and different colors tied up at their moorings. Beyond the curving breakwater with its flashing light at the narrow harbor entrance lies the open Atlantic.

XVIII

HAPPINESS BECOMES A HABIT

WHAT we have found here is happiness in habit-forming quantities. Margaret reads, writes, keeps her Journal, paints — mostly watercolors — practises the piano and busies herself with household chores, which I share. When the sun is high and the wind is low, or perhaps even in a gentle rain, we walk together in the woods or along the shore. She is a spur of the moment walker. With no previous warning she suddenly decides that the weather is too wonderful to stay indoors. Close up that typewriter; put down that book. To Margaret, nothing is more important than to catch this hour's color on the autumn hillside or this minute's sparkle on the wide blue sea.

She's right, but I'm more routine. I stick to a schedule of walking for my own purposes, the enjoyment of nature and an ever-increasing interest in its constantly changing beauties and its everlasting wonders. Except during December and January, when the sun is a late riser, I put in at least an hour's walk in the woods or fields before I sit down to my 7 A.M. breakfast of fruit and tea. About nine o'clock I take to the road again with some cronies who are as fond of walking as I am. You must meet them.

The first is a character whom Molière might have labeled "L'avocat malgré lui." He is a retired lawyer who never did like the profession of law in the first place and looked upon it with increasing distaste as he grew older. His name is Elliott C. Rogers, lifetime resident of Cape Ann and a good long life at that. His mother was an ardent amateur botanist and Elliott followed in her footsteps. He knows all the native shrubs and flowers of Cape Ann by their first names in English and their first and second names in Latin. He is short, stocky, carries a cane and has his pockets filled with dog biscuits that he doles out to canines who come out to greet us — or assault us — on our regular walks.

The other regular member of the team is a retired educator, Dr. Melvin T. Copeland, Bowdoin alumnus and former dean of the Harvard Business School. Like Elliott, Mel is short, stocky, carries a cane and has passed his three-quarter century milestone but he doesn't pack dog biscuit in his pocket and he doesn't give a hoot about botany. He loves flowers, wild or cultivated, and has them growing in multitudes all around his house but he categorically refuses to keep in mind the names of obscure shrubs or lowly weeds that Elliott keeps thrusting upon him. He walks for the fun of walking and he's a good man for cross-country work over rough terrain. He also is an ardent fisherman and has a 32-foot power boat on which we occasionally take to the sea in search of oceanic birds — petrels, shearwaters, gannets, kittiwakes, phalaropes and such.

A part-time or summer resident member of the team is Dr. Samuel F. Haines, a medical man from the Mayo Clinic where he spent most of his professional life doing research on thyroid deficiency in the human system and what can be done about it. Officially he is retired but he still spends the colder half of the year at Rochester, Minnesota, carrying out experi-

ments at the clinic and writing papers that he didn't have time
to finish during his regular tour of duty. Sam is a good
walker, an eager birder and, with the help of his wife, Emily,
an increasingly knowing botanist. Sam can look down on the
rest of us. He's the tall member of the quartet when we
walk down the road.

Almost every weekday morning we go roaming about
Cape Ann, often over the uninhabited center of the outer part
of the cape called "Dogtown," one of the deserted villages of
New England. This is an upland area of beech forest and
overgrown fields turning back to the wild state. It is dotted
with swamps and bogs and littered with monstrous arrays of
closely packed boulders left there when the last glacier melted
away to the northward. The most flourishing growth of the
region is the finest grade of catbriar whose thorny entangle-
ments keep much of the territory free from human invasion.
They are havens of refuge for yellowthroats, catbirds, brown
thrashers, rabbits and field mice.

For summer residents and tourists the notable attractions
of Dogtown are the occasional huge boulders — geologists
call these "erratics" — that loom high above their surroundings, the marked cellar holes of the long-vanished inhabitants, and the bumper blueberry crop that the region usually
produces. To me the place is a wild and wonderful garden.
It was in a Dogtown swamp that Elliott showed me my first
rhodora in bloom. There also we find those lovely wild orchids, the arethusa, the calopogon and the rose pogonia.
To see these at close hand we don boots and trudge into the
sphagnum bogs that they prefer as living quarters. There also
we find sundew and horned bladderwort and an abundance
of poison sumac that we take great care to avoid. Later in the
season in another bog higher up we find the white fringed
orchis, the curious pitcher plant and sturdy fronds of Wood-
wardia or Virginia Chain-fern. The bunchberry flourishes in

little clumps in the shade and, standing in one spot under the beeches on the hillside above the swamp one day in early June, I counted seventeen pink lady's-slippers in view above the dead leaves of the forest floor.

We adjust our morning journeys to the calendar. We make an annual pilgrimage to a mosquito-infested wooded region in neighboring Essex in early June to pay homage to a goodly patch of the dainty twinflower, the *Linnea borealis*, in tiny pink-and-white bell-shaped bloom. In July we go to one spot for a sight of round-leaved pyrola in flower and to another place far removed to look for the shrub called mountain-holly (*Ilex mucronata*) hoping to find it laden with fruit in the form of thin-stemmed red berries. In August we must inspect a certain section of the woods in West Gloucester because that's the time and place to find the rattlesnake plantain displaying its stalked little alabaster flowers that look nothing like orchids to the ordinary eye but are true members of that cherished (and often expensive) tribe.

These are just scattered samples of the objects of our botanical searches in season. We have caches that we do not reveal to the multitude lest our tender treasures — a small bed of trailing arbutus, a single frond of cut-leaved grape-fern — be torn up or trodden underfoot. We enjoy the wealth of common flowers along the way, the white daisies, the yarrow, the wild carrot, the maligned goldenrod, the fragile bloodroot and the innumerable asters of the autumn fields and woods. In August this whole region is fragrant with the odor of the clethra or sweet pepperbush. If there is an offshore breeze you can smell it a mile at sea.

We have our favorite trees that we take delight in visiting from time to time — a great elm here, a noble red oak there, a cluster of tupelos along an old wall, tall white birches standing out in the gloom of the woods, the Adams pines on Dogtown and close to them a magnificent row of larches whose "rosy plumelets" — the pistillate flowers — never fail to draw exclamations of wonder and praise from us "when spring brings back blue days and fair."

Of course, in the leafless winter our morning walks are mostly for the exercise and the fun of being outdoors. We explore odd nooks and corners of the woods that were curtained off by greenery in midsummer. You come to know your home territory much better in late autumn when the leaves have fallen and the strong bones of the countryside can be seen through the naked trees. And on the coldest and windiest walk in winter there is always the warming thought:

Can spring be far behind?

Thus much of our mornings afoot and I am ashamed that I have given such a spiritless report of such wonderful walks. I am as bad as Borachio in *Much Ado About Nothing* and should confess with him: "I tell this tale vilely." When my companions come to read it I probably will be drummed out of their honorable ranks, and deservedly so.

Of course, I always carry my field glasses with me on these walks and keep looking and listening for birds along the way, but the real hunt for birds is staged at other hours and on other days. The crack of dawn is my alarm clock through most of the year. In the depths of winter I become impatient at the tardiness of the sun, get up in the dark and push out in the predawn half-light to walk, look and listen in the neighboring lanes and fields. Sometimes these winter walks are graced with morning moonlight on the snow. But dark or light, the early hours of the day are the most precious and the most fruitful for my purposes and I would feel deeply deprived — robbed is a better word — if I were kept from enjoying them to the full.

I am ready to believe that sleep is a necessity but I view it esthetically as a complete waste of time. We'll sleep soon enough and long enough. Daybreak is a magic word to me. The whole idea of it is moving, exciting, thrilling. I cherish those lovely lines of Tennyson in "The Princess":

> *Morn in the white wake of the morning star*
> *Came furrowing all the orient into gold.*

Sunrise is as beautiful as sunset and has extra advantages. You have the streets, lanes, fields and woods to yourself at that hour. Not even farmers get up early any more; only conspirators, poets, birds and bird watchers. From March into June I spend these prebreakfast walks welcoming the birds back from the south. At that time of day they are most active and vocal, hungry after sleep or travel, engaged in lyrical challenge or busy with housekeeping chores. In March the robins appear on the lawn, the grackle in the village streets, the rusty blackbirds and the redwings in the swamp, the kill-deers in the pastures and the woodcock and snipe in the wet meadows. The sparrows follow in April and the warblers, vireos, and fifty more songsters in the fullness of the May.

Keeping track of all of these, particularly the warblers in the third week of May, is heady work, exhilarating and also exhausting. After that the ornithological tumult and shouting die down and there is little to do on these early walks except keep good watch on regular summer residents and look for any distinguished visitors that might wander into our region. But in August business picks up again in a reverse direction. The southward hegira is on, particularly on the part of the shore birds and that brings up the most striking feature of the year-long bird watch on almost any coastal stretch, the wonder and delight of the shore bird migration in autumn.

For the pursuit of shore birds in early autumn and offshore

birds all through the winter and on into early spring I am
joined with two men and a boy for all-day excursions on Saturdays and holidays. Compared to me the men are so young
that Margaret, making up my sandwiches of cream cheese
and olives for noon sustenance on these trips, always refers to
my three companions as "the boys." Her usual question is:
"Where are you and the boys headed for today?" A good
wifely question, but my usual answer is that I leave it up
to "the boys." It's the oldest of the trio — and he's still a
youngish man — who usually is the navigator. More often
than not it's his car we go in and he does the driving. Let me
call him "our gallant leader" because he organized our little
group, makes the big decisions on the trips in search of shore
and sea birds and — the clincher — was in the United States
Coast Guard on the Greenland patrol during World War II.

He is H. Lawrence Jodrey of Rockport, native and to the
manner born, lawyer by profession and, by choice, specializ-
ing in real estate law and probate court proceedings five
days a week and bird-watching Saturdays, Sundays and legal
holidays. He is tall, broad-shouldered, clean shaven and unmarried. The second-in-command (I'm the supercargo) is
Gerald Soucy of nearby Beverly, a few years younger than
Counselor Jodrey but just as tall and broad-shouldered — and
as clean shaven and unmarried. Jerry, as we call him, is in the
office of the Register of Deeds at Salem. The junior member
of our group is Tommy Martin, Beverly resident and high
school student who, at six feet three and a quarter inches, is
the tallest by a little and the thinnest by far. We often encounter high winds on our birding trips along the ocean front
and we keep urging Tommy to put on more weight lest some
day he be blown out to sea before we can grab him.

For shore birds we have to travel. The outer edge of Cape
Ann is a rocky coast hung with seaweed between the tides

and, of all the shore birds, only the purple sandpiper that comes down to us from the Arctic in winter actually prefers such feeding grounds. We do have a few small beaches, mostly pebble-strewn, and along these we get a scattering of other species — sanderlings, semipalmated and spotted sandpipers and an occasional ruddy turnstone — but for the massed battalions, the regiments, the brigades and the army corps of mixed flocks of shore birds that cover mud flats at feeding time and gather on higher sandy, grassy or plowed areas to rest at high tide, we head for Newburyport and adjacent territory.

Down the long years old Newburyport has turned out four famous products: silverware, rum, Lord Timothy Dexter and John P. Marquand. Lord Timothy Dexter and John P. Marquand (Alas, poor John, I knew him, Horatio; not a fellow of infinite jest but a most excellent writer) have passed from the scene but the great silverware plant and the noted rum distillery continue in operation. I don't know whether it is the artistic appeal of the silverware or the wide reputation of the rum that draws so many rare birds to the region. Whatever the local attraction, there we find them year after year, somewhere along this last reach of the Merrimac where it broadens into Newburyport Harbor before funneling into the Atlantic through a turbulent channel between two breakwaters of tumbled blocks of granite. On the eastern side of the mouth of the river lies Salisbury State Park, a public bathing and recreation area. On the western side is the northeastern tip of Plum Island with a Coast Guard station overlooking the tide rips of the narrow channels and the dangerous shoals piled up by the river silt offshore.

Many of our Saturday sorties in winter take us over this territory — Newburyport, Amesbury, Salisbury and the eight-mile length of Plum Island. It's a poor day that doesn't

turn up at least one thrilling or heart-warming sight in the way
of a notable bird. On a frigid January day a good bird is a
hand-warming and foot-warming sight, too. It's remarkable
how quickly cold hands and feet are forgotten in the excitement of spotting a prize bird in the air, on the water or
perched on a post far out on a marsh. But no added warmth
is needed in August, which is when the shore birds appear on
the mud flats and upper parts of beaches by the thousand.
On a still bright day in summer Plum Island can be — or
seem — as hot as the Sahara. This favorite haunt of birders
is just a long narrow strip of sand with dunes above a wonderful beach on the ocean side and a wide salt marsh on the
landward side. It is well-named, since a large part of the
sparse shrubbery growing in the dunes consists of beach plum
bushes that ordinarily yield a fine harvest in September. The
major section of the island has been set apart as the Parker
River National Wildlife Refuge and has impoundments for
breeding waterfowl as well as feeding grounds for migrants.

For shore bird or waterfowl viewing we are armed with
telescopes as well as field glasses. At best sandpipers are a
tricky lot to identify with certainty and when they are feeding far out on mud flats a telescope is a necessity. It also en-
ables a birder to look over resting flocks without going close
enough to disturb them. I well remember when word went
up and down Plum Island that a buff-breasted sandpiper was
on the marsh just off the causeway. When we reached the
spot we saw a wide semicircle of birders with telescopes fo-
cused on a single spot — the location of the bird on the
grass. A stranger might have mistaken the array of telescopes
for a field class in the science of surveying. It was my first
sight of this never common but fairly regular distinguished
visitor in late summer or autumn and, like all the others, I kept
at a respectful distance lest the bird be disturbed. When I

came to see more of it and know it better, I discovered that it is one of the tamest of wild birds and actually can be driven along slowly like a barnyard duck.

We have, however, a dozen other sandpipers, seasonal residents or migrants, that are not so approachable or easy to identify. Some of them have to be well seen in a good light in order to note the shape or size of the bill, the markings on the back or the color of the legs to make sure of the species. I suspect that the problem is worse in Europe where they have more different species of sandpiper to deal with than we do here in North America. Donald Culross Peattie quotes the baffled Buffon as writing in reference to a group of "water birds" that he was trying to fit into his *Histoire Naturelle:* "Ces tristes oiseaux d'eau, dont on ne sait quoi dire, et dont le nombre est accablant!"

It's ten to one (in francs) that he meant the sandpipers and I think I know what his trouble was. He was born too soon. In those eighteenth century days they didn't have the binoculars and telescopes with which the modern birders go afield. Field glasses for the masses are twentieth century products. With a telescope and a typewriter a competent modern birder could write a book about the sandpipers that Buffon viewed with dumb despair and whose numbers he found overwhelming.

Of course, sandpipers do not travel alone. Along with them in the great flocks of August and September we find dowitchers, whimbrel, yellowlegs, godwits and that famous long distance migrant, the golden plover, a prize bird among the much more numerous black-bellied plover and other smaller and less distinguished members of the plover family. In one respect, I think sandpipers and most of their traveling companions are a silly lot; they leave just when the weather and the scenery are combining to make the region a paradise.

The sun is warm, the breeze is cool, the dune grass on Plum Island has turned a golden hue and the salt marsh is brilliant with long patches of red samphire.

What glorious days these are! Never mind the birds; just to be alive and on Plum Island in October is pure joy. As if that weren't enough, there is more to come. As the sun and the shore birds go southward, the ducks and the geese begin to come in from the north and the west. They are everywhere, on the ponds and lakes, on the Merrimac River, on the marsh by the hundreds and on Newburyport Harbor by the thousand. The Plum Island impoundments are loud with the quacking of ducks and the sky overhead is resonant with the honking of arriving Canada geese. There are dabblers and diving duck of two dozen species. There are grebes and loons on the bays and along the ocean front.

We "log them" as they come and look for rare ones among the common species in this region — the occasional gadwalls and shovelers on the ponds, the spectacular harlequins and Barrow's goldeneyes on the bays or the ocean, the snow geese that wander in with the Canada geese or occasionally pass through in great flocks of their own kind. These we watch for and see regularly in our Saturday expeditions to Plum Island and the Newburyport area. There also we find the white-winged gulls from the Arctic that come down in winter and such stragglers from Europe as the little gull, the black-headed gull and the tufted duck. It's an embarrassment of riches and I wouldn't blame any reader from my former bailiwick in New York who came up here and choked me to death out of pure envy.

Eagles we see occasionally up the Merrimac, over the bay or perched on the marsh. Snowy owls keep watch for prey from the tops of duck blinds and short-eared owls sweep the impoundments on Plum Island. As the car rolls slowly down the island road we are often escorted by flocks of Lapland longspurs and snow buntings chattering cheerfully while they swirl along around and ahead of us. From the headlands, the bay fronts and the breakwaters of our own Cape Ann we look for — and find — dovekies, murres, guillemots and razor-billed auks. All I saw of such birds before I came here were stuffed specimens under glass. I could rave on vaingloriously about our great days afield but I desist out of pure pity for the non-bird-watcher reader who, by this time, must feel as stuffed as those guillemots under glass I mentioned a minute ago.

XIX

MUSICAL INTERLUDE

O N SATURDAY afternoons in winter our road trips in
search of birds have the added attraction of a musical accompaniment. We tune the car radio to the Metropolitan Opera
being broadcast from New York and discuss the performance
and the singers. For many years my father and mother had
subscription seats at the Metropolitan and when they couldn't
use them, they offered me the tickets and thus I heard most
of the popular French, German and Italian operas that are repeated each season. I even sat through the Ring Cycle and
enjoyed it immensely. Larry and Jerry are great music lov-
ers. They attend concerts in Boston, have hi-fi sets at home
on which they play classical records, know the scores of
many operas by heart and, when they were in Italy a few
years ago, they made a pious pilgrimage to that shrine of
opera, La Scala in Milan.

As a young fellow I heard — and saw — Caruso, Scotti,
Madame Schumann-Heink, Marcella Sembrich and other stars
of that long-lost day. In later years I came to know a fair
number of Metropolitan bassos, baritones and tenors as
fellow-members of the Dutch Treat Club. At the Tuesday
luncheons of the club at the Park Lane they had the loudest

and merriest table — they all had strong voices — under the informal leadership of the late and beloved Edward Johnson, then general manager of the Metropolitan, and his equally cheerful and energetic assistant, Francis Robinson. I loved to stop by the table to chat with "Eddie" and "Francis" and the other members who qualified as "Dutch Treat choir boys" such as James Melton, Robert Merrill, Jan Peerce, Frederick Jagel, Richard Tucker, Felix Knight and John Charles Thomas before he took up residence in Beverly Hills.

Not only that, but through the good offices of Edward Johnson and Francis Robinson, the great divas of the Metropolitan were persuaded to appear at the luncheons and give free samples of their "pear-shaped tones" to enchanted audiences. Come to think of it, those Dutch Treat luncheons are the things that I miss most since I left New York. Just as Eddie Johnson "headed up" the opera table each week, another group of us gathered around Grantland Rice at a table in the back row. The regulars there included Arthur Train, Ted Roosevelt, Will Beebe, Roy Chapman Andrews, Trubee Davison, Rex Beach when in town and assorted sports celebrities who came as guests of Grant Rice. Indeed, we stuck so closely and regularly to our last row table that a member who looked sourly at our clannishness each week leaned over one day to say: "When are you fellows going to join the club?" I called it envy.

But we were talking of the opera and its cast of characters. One discovery of an opera singer among the club members came to me as a shock. I was invited to lunch at the Canadian Club of New York that is housed high up in the Waldorf-Astoria. My host was a former Olympic 1500-metre champion and World War I hero in a British uniform. He was Lieutenant Colonel Arnold Nugent Strode Strode-Jackson, D.S.O., of the Guards and he looked the part. Tall, lean, hawk-featured and wearing a dark mustache, he was an amazing athlete and soldier. At the Olympic Games of 1912 at Stockholm he outran the greatest group of milers this country ever sent to Olympic competition. As a British officer in France in World War I he was wounded severely several times and won a hatful of medals. Later he married an American girl, engaged in business here and became a citizen of the United States.

We struck up a friendship through the fact that he read my sports column when, more than thirty years ago, I set down the prophecy that somebody was certain to run a mile in less than four minutes and received only one letter agreeing with me. It was signed "A. N. S. Strode-Jackson." Everybody else who wrote in insisted that I was off my rocker and some of my best friends tearfully begged me to recant lest I be judged mentally incompetent and lodged in a padded cell. Strode-Jackson's letter not only assured me that a four-minute mile was certain to come but that it would be done in a jiffy if somebody would put up a prize of $25,000 for the feat. This comforting message, standing out among a lot of epistolary brickbats, led to a long and beautiful friendship. That was how I came to be invited to this luncheon at the Canadian Club of New York in the Waldorf-Astoria.

There were four couples at the table and one of the men was a chap I saw regularly at the Dutch Treat luncheons and with whom I had often exchanged greetings and passing pleasantries without knowing who he was, where he worked or what he did. To me he was just a friendly Dutch Treater who called me "John" and whom I called "Charley" at the club gatherings. "Jacker" — short for Arnold Nugent Strode Strode-Jackson — is a wonderful host and an accomplished raconteur and the lunch was a lively affair. While things were being cleared up I wandered into a reception room, saw a piano and sat down to test the tone. It could do no harm. Nobody else was in sight. I had just started a few bars of "La donna è mobile" from *Rigoletto* when my friend Charley appeared in the doorway and picked up the air with a clear and powerful voice that astonished me. As he sauntered toward me, caroling out the Italian words with exuberance and nonchalance, the effect was almost shattering. With a little added effort I think he could have blown out the windows of the comparatively small room.

Of course, this performance called for an explanation and it was only then that I learned what my friend "Charley" of the Dutch Treat Club did for a living. He was currently and for many happy years thereafter one of the top tenors of the Metropolitan Opera, Charles Kullman. Apropos, I recall one Dutch Treat luncheon at which the expected musical talent failed to appear for one reason or another and Clarence Budington Kelland, club president and presiding officer for years, called for volunteers from the club members present. In two minutes he had the organist of the Fifth Avenue Presbyterian Church, our own Harry Gilbert, at the piano and a volunteer quartet of club members harmonizing some such touching number as "Sweet Adeline" or other similar barbershop classic. What distinguished the quartet we heard free of charge was that each singer was a paid performer at the Metropolitan Opera that season. It isn't every luncheon club that can come up with a volunteer group of songsters of such caliber.

As a bird watcher on Plum Island and a long distance opera lover I had one other link with the Saturday afternoon broadcasts from the Metropolitan stage in New York. The network announcer for the opera was the same Milton Cross who had been network announcer for our Information Please program for a number of years. I told my fellow birders

how Milton was caught in the crossfire when our Mr. Golenpaul engaged in battle with the great George B. Hill, head of
the American Tobacco Company, when we were being sponsored by its Lucky Strike Division. It was during the war
years and the commercials on our program began notifying
the radio audience that "Lucky Strike green has gone to war."

Dan Golenpaul thought that this was an attempt to make a
profit out of phoney patriotism and he demanded that the
statement be withdrawn from the commercials. George B.
Hill was magnificently disdainful of the request. He took no
notice of it whatsoever. In the process of warming up for
battle, Mr. Golenpaul's attorneys began handing out sub-
poenas to every person connected with the sponsorship of the
program and a process server gave one to Milton Cross who
immediately pulled back as though he had been bitten on the
hand by a rattlesnake. One of the mildest of gentlemen, I
doubt that Milton ever had been implicated in a legal brawl
up to that time. Getting caught between such born and bred
battlers as Messrs. Golenpaul and Hill was a harrowing situation for a man of peace. Milton was the picture of outraged
innocence when he came into the studio to do his chore on
our program a few hours after the process server had served
the subpoena.

Tut, tut! Milton needn't have worried. I don't recall
whether the commercial was modified or not (having once
had the chilly experience of meeting Mr. Hill, I doubt it)
but I do know that nobody was haled into court or dragged
off to jail. Our contract with Lucky Strike ran out and we
were taken on at once at a higher fee by the Standard Oil
Company of New York whose commercials never mentioned the war but merely asked motorists to fill their tanks
"at the sign of the Flying Red Horse" whose approach
through the air was heralded by a loud cloppity-clop of hoof-

beats. They were nice sponsors, but they never made clear to me how their "Flying Red Horse" produced those noisy hoofbeats while prancing on nothing firmer than air. Even after all these years it still remains — like so many other things I encountered in radio and television — a deep mystery to me.

XX

A MATTER OF LIFE AND DEATH

During much of the year my early morning walks take me through lovely Beech Grove Cemetery, our ancient and now our only local burying ground. It is well named. There are some elms, maples, lindens and evergreens within its quiet confines but for the most part the summer shade over the green graves and the gray headstones is provided by the beeches that are the dominant species of deciduous tree on Cape Ann. I suppose you would call the terrain a knoll. The lower part is a gentle hillside rising to an uneven and slightly tilted plateau. Except for the recent addition of a flat open section on the southwest side, I doubt that there is enough level ground in the cemetery for the laying out of an ordinary tennis court. The place is well ordered and well kept.

I am not one who loves to sit upon the ground and tell sad stories of the death of kings but I must confess a fondness for strolling through this little cemetery in the early morning before anybody else is about. The workmen who cut the grass, trim the shrubbery, rake the paths and dig the graves when needed do not report for work until seven o'clock. By that time I am back home sitting down to breakfast. What started me on these sepulchral rounds was a simple fondness

for going lightly shod on walks when the day's at the morn
and the hillside's dew-pearled. City dwellers may not know
that, through more than half the year, if the night has been
still and clear there will be dew or frost on the grass and
the shrubbery in the early morning. That means wet feet for
a walker unless he wears some kind of waterproof boots or
sticks to sidewalks, paths and roadways. It's astonishing
how quickly you can get soaking wet to the knees simply
by walking through a clover patch or a hayfield before the
morning sun has had a chance to dry off the dew or the hoar
frost.

I wear boots deliberately on some early sorties, particularly
in March and April when I splash my way through flooded
meadows and alder swamps looking for snipe, rail, woodcock, dabbling ducks and stray members of the heron tribe.
Boots are "de rigueur" for invading bogs in search of orchids
in June. But rubber boots are heavy and clumsy. They are
hot in summer and cold in winter. I go without them gladly.
Light shoes with rubber soles are much more comfortable.
Even in the wake of a heavy rain, while grass and shrubbery
are still heavy with droplets, rubber soles are sufficient protection against wet pavements and damp paths.

That's why, on so many early morning walks, I stick to
paved streets, wood roads, trodden lanes and what few sidewalks we have in town. At the hour that I saunter forth the
sidewalks are empty, the streets are empty, the wood roads
are empty and the cemetery is empty except for its permanent residents. The cemetery entrance, guarded by native
granite pillars, is only about ten minutes by foot from my
doorstep. I ramble its outermost driveways, go out the rear
on a footpath leading into a pine grove, follow a wood road
back toward town and paved streets and return home by way
of Old Garden Beach just a few blocks from our house. It

takes me about three-quarters of an hour, which means that the circuit is some two miles in extent. I do about three miles an hour at a fairly easy pace if I don't stop too often or too long interviewing birds or flowers along the way.

I long ago noticed that birds have a fondness for cemeteries. Chipping sparrows dote on well-kept lawns and the grass of gently-mounded graves is short and smooth, cut just to their taste. I always hear wood peewees and their melancholy notes seem particularly appropriate in the surroundings. The Baltimore oriole, on the other hand, flits lightly through the upper branches of the trees singing boldly and cheerfully. The wood thrush in the undergrowth over the wall takes a singing position halfway between the mournful peewee and the rollicking oriole. The notes of the wood thrush are strong and clear. No dying fall there; no weeping or wailing; but also no chuckling or bold whistling over consecrated ground such as the swaggering oriole indulges in. Just music, pure music; that's the wise thrush who beats Browning's bird by singing his two phrases over and over again. Then there are the downy and hairy woodpeckers that hammer away at the cemetery trees, keeping things in order as the workmen tend the graves below. There also are the white-breasted and red-breasted nuthatches announcing their gleanings on the trunks and branches of trees with repeated nasal notes.

Occasionally in the singing season I am favored with the rich rolling aria of the purple finch or the baritone warbling of the rose-breasted grosbeak. There are always song sparrows in the vicinity urging somebody to "quick, quick, quick, put on the tea kettle, kettle." Flickers flash by, displaying in flight the bright feathering that earned them the descriptive name of "golden-winged woodpecker" to which some farmer folk still cling. Robins build nests in the trees and shrubs of the cemetery and raise two or three broods with considerable clamor. Goldfinches pass by, matching a bounding flight with a bounding song. Towhees call from the underbrush and then peer out to see who goes by. Catbirds mew in the open and then retire to a tangle to toss off some brilliant passages of brittle music. A little thin and squeaky at times, but talented. Other songsters — the scarlet tanager, the brown thrasher — put in irregular appearances with a musical accompaniment, and always there is the red-eyed vireo with its running comment on the rival singing acts: "Fair — just fair — oh, very good, that bit — do it again —no, no — too loud — not that, please — who said so? — pure flattery — softer, softer — well, have it your own way — you want my opinion — phew!"

It is quite natural that cemeteries should be well stocked with birds. Like golf courses, they are bird refuges without being designed for that purpose. They are isolated areas of lawns, shrubs, and trees with few persons to be seen and only occasional motor traffic at a funereal pace. Mount Auburn Cemetery in Cambridge, Massachusetts, is famous as a birding spot during the spring migration. So is Sleepy Hollow Cemetery in Concord where I paused beside the grave of Henry David Thoreau one sunny morning in mid-May, hearing and seeing in the trees and shrubbery around me the warblers that perhaps he heard and saw there a century earlier. It brought to mind those lines about the immortality of bird songs in William Johnson Cory's lament for Heraclitus:

And now that thou art lying, my dear old Carian guest,
A handful of gray ashes, long, long ago at rest,
Still are thy pleasant voices, thy nightingales, awake;
For Death, he taketh all away, but them he cannot take.

The truth is that I like cemeteries. They are restful regions in a world seething with unrest. I ramble through our little monumented burying ground with a placid stride and pleasant thoughts. I am not a whit disturbed that I am surrounded by the cold "hic jacets" of the dead. As I pass between the stone pillars at the entrance I often think of the lines of the old Scottish song: "Ye living men come view the ground where ye shall shortly lie." This "memento mori" troubles me not at all. Why should it? Any sensible person accepts the fact that he was sentenced to death at birth but he doesn't dwell on the thought too often or too long. Indeed, that would be selfish. There are more important things to keep in mind.

Thus on I saunter, reading the names and dates on the headstones of more recent vintage. Most of the older carvings have been weathered away by more than a century of rain and wind. I recognize family names that go back generations in local history. There were men in this town who marched off to fight at Bunker Hill. I often pass the headstone on which is graven "Elliot H. Paul, 1891-1958" and I think: Here "in this neglected spot" in this little New England town sleeps the gay boulevardier of Paris, once a dashing figure among the international literary set, an amusing writer of merry tales. Who now holds down his old chair on the sidewalk at the Deux Magots or sits at his favorite table at the sign of the Nègre de Toulouse? His grave is at the highest point in the cemetery, the geographical Montmartre of the terrain. He lived through the time of F. Scott Fitzgerald, Gertrude Stein, James Joyce and Ernest Hemingway in Paris — through scandals in the French Cabinet, through riots in the Rue Royale, and now he lies silent under a stone in this little country cemetery a thousand leagues from his beloved Champs-Elysées and Boule Miche. Thinking of him I recall a line from *Les Misérables* that perhaps he might have chosen for his tomb:

La mort, c'est la nuit de ce jour inquiet qu'on appele la vie.

I thank him for the hours of pleasant reading he gave me and I move along. Since this is Rockport, famous for its granite and its stone masons, there are handsome monuments over some of the mounds. I survey the sepulchral architecture with a critical eye. Some of it seems a bit too imposing, almost boastful, swollen with the self-importance of the deceased. I note one huge oblong block about ten feet by five by four over a grave with a man's name carved on the side. Rockport granite weighs 165 pounds per cubic foot. I make a quick calculation — 200 cubic feet — 33,000 pounds — more than sixteen tons — oh! oh! (I say to myself), come Resurrection Day he'll *never* get out from under that!

But most of the monuments are models of modesty and sincerity. I am well pleased with them. And I am well pleased with the familiar but none the less wise and thoughtful lines of Bryant:

> So shalt thou rest, and what if thou withdraw
> In silence from the living, and no friend
> Take note of thy departure? All that breathe
> Will share thy destiny. The gay will laugh
> When thou art gone, the solemn brood of care
> Plod on, and each one, as before, will chase
> His favorite phantom . . .

So they will and I rejoice that this is so. I would not willingly blight a moment of any friend's life with a grim thought or a sad recollection. As I live and breathe, I nourish no black sorrow or wild regret "in looking on the happy autumn fields and thinking of the days that are no more." The most I confess to is an occasional touch of mild nostalgia or poetic melancholy when I look back across the years to my childhood in Kingsbridge and the lively and happy household of father, mother and seven children, of whom my brother Laurence and I are now the only survivors. But even if tinged with melancholy, these are fond and beautiful memories. I cherish them. My earliest clear recollection is of watching the lamplighter with his magic long wand coming up the snowy street as I stood by my mother's knee when she was having tea in an upstairs room in the early twilight of a winter afternoon.

I not only remember lamplighters, I rode in horse cars and elevated trains pulled by steam locomotives down Ninth and Sixth Avenues — and Second and Third Avenues, too — in New York City. And yet in one single day of my later life I was ten thousand feet above our Pensacola naval base in a Navy jet fighter-trainer plane in the morning and down under the surface of the Gulf of Mexico in a Navy submarine in the afternoon. (This was when I was a member of a civilian orientation tour of Army, Navy, Marine and Air Force installations sponsored by the Department of Defense.) Until I was eighteen I never set foot outside the boundaries of New York State, but later wanderings took me to the streets of London and Paris, to the spruce-covered slopes of the Austrian Alps and the palm-studded splendor of the French Riviera. I humbly admit that I have been lucky. Life owes me nothing. I have lived long and happily and of the days that remain to me I promise that none will hang heavy on my hands because every step that I take outdoors leads me to exciting adventure, every shelf of my bookcase lures me with books that I long to read and deep within me is a craving that will last my lifetime, the desire

> *To follow knowledge like a sinking star,*
> *Beyond the utmost bound of human thought.*

Therefor I walk the quiet ways of Beech Grove Cemetery with calm contentment but eager eye in the early morning,

always on the lookout for fresh flowers or familiar birds —
or glorious cloud effects above the rising sun. If the headstones stir any thought of death or immortality as I read the
names and dates in passing, I am inclined to respond with the
words that one of my favorite poets, Jean-Paul Béranger, put
in the mouth of his legendary Roger Bontemps:

> Dire au ciel: Je me fie,
> Mon père, à ta bonté;
> De ma philosophie
> Pardon la gaieté;
> Que ma saison dernière
> Soit encore un printemps;
> Eh gai! c'est la prière
> Du gros Roger Bontemps.

EPILOGUE

THIS and all the previous pages were typed out in the little upstairs room in our home that I use as a study. On the right of this desk is a window through which I look out over the Atlantic Ocean whose edge is less than two hundred yards from our door. The nearest land beyond the watery horizon is Spain.

Under a summer sun and a light breeze the sea is a sparkling blue but now the sky is overcast and a winter wind is whipping up whitecaps on a dark gray ocean. Half a mile out a long white line of tumbling spray marks the reef that, at low tide, emerges as a sinister row of jagged black rocks. The wind is onshore and if I stepped outside now I would hear the hoarse clang of the swaying bell buoy anchored off the south end of the reef. Gulls are wheeling and crying above the shoreline, white figures against a dark sky. The ground is covered with snow and the rocks at the water's edge are fringed with ice. The scenery is wild, wintry and wonderful!

But the tide of the young year has turned. The dark mornings are getting lighter each day. The sun lingers a little longer each afternoon. The buds are beginning to swell on the poplar and the alder catkins are lengthening in the frozen swamp. Soon in the hush of dusk over the inland meadows we will hear the first shrill quavering notes of the peepers — the dauntless invisible heralds of ever-returning spring. And cheerfully I echo Browning:

> *Grow old along with me!*
> *The best is yet to be,*
> *The last of life, for which the first was made* . . .

Reader, farewell. May your life and loves be as happy as mine have been.

JOHN KIERAN

Rockport, Massachusetts, 1964

INDEX

INDEX

DATE DUE

JAN 5			
MAY 3 1 '76			
GAYLORD			PRINTED IN U.S.A.